NORTHERN IRELAND

THE BACKGROUND
TO THE CONFLICT

Edited by
John Darby

APPLETREE PRESS

SYRACUSE
UNIVERSITY PRESS

First published and printed in 1983 by
The Appletree Press Ltd
7 James Street South
Belfast BT2 8DL
Northern Ireland

First published in the U.S.A. in 1983 by
Syracuse University Press
Syracuse
New York 13210

1   2   3   4   5   6   7   8   9   10

British Library Cataloguing in Publication Data

Northern Ireland: the background to the
conflict—(Modern Irish Society, ISSN
0263-595X)
1. Northern Ireland—Social conditions
I. Darby, John   II. Series
941.60824   HN398.N6

ISBN 0-904651-90-8
ISBN 0-904651-89-4 Pbk

Library of Congress Cataloging in Publication Data

Northern Ireland.

Bibliography: p.
1. Northern Ireland—Politics and government—1969-
2. Northern Ireland—Social conditions—1969-
I. Darby, John (John P.)
DA990.U46N675   1983   941.60824   83-4114

ISBN 0-8156-2298-8

Contents

Contributors

John Darby is a lecturer in Social Administration at the New University of Ulster. Publications include *Conflict in Northern Ireland* (Gill and Macmillan, 1976) and *Violence and the Social Services in Northern Ireland* (with Arthur Williamson, Heinemann, 1978).

Hastings S. C. Donnan is a lecturer in Social Anthropology at Queen's University, and his research interests are in North Pakistan and Northern Ireland.

Paddy Hillyard is lecturer in Social Policy at the University of Bristol. Co-author of *Law and State: The Case of Northern Ireland* (Martin Robertson, 1975) and *Ten Years On in Northern Ireland: The Legal Control of Political Violence* (Cobden Trust, 1980).

Ian McAllister is researching electoral behaviour at the Australian National University, Canberra. Published work includes *The Northern Ireland Social Democratic and Labour Party* (Macmillan, 1977) and *United Kingdom Facts* (with Richard Rose, Macmillan, 1982).

W. Graham McFarlane is a lecturer in Social Anthropology at Queen's University, Belfast. He has carried out research in Northern Ireland and Shetland.

Dominic Murray is a lecturer in Education at University College, Cork, and has written widely on the ramifications of segregated educational structures in Northern Ireland.

Michael Poole is a lecturer in Geography at the New University of Ulster, and his interests are in social and quantitive geography, especially segregation measurement.

Bill Rolston lectures in Sociology at the Ulster Polytechnic. His publications include *Northern Ireland: Between Civil Rights and Civil War* (with Liam O'Dowd and Mike Tomlinson, CSE Books, 1980).

John Simpson is a Senior Lecturer at Queen's University, Belfast. He worked with Professor T. Wilson in the drafting of the Northern Ireland Economic Development Programme in 1963–64, and is the author of many papers on the Northern Ireland economy.

Barry White has been commenting on Northern Ireland politics since the early 1960s as political correspondent, columnist and chief leader writer of the *Belfast Telegraph*. He won the prize for Northern Ireland feature writer of the year in 1980.

Introduction

The most recent bibliography on the Northern Irish conflict contains
more than 3,000 references, almost all published since the eruption of
community violence in the late 1960s. Their variety is intriguing and
bewildering: political scientists, psychologists, historians, demo-
graphers and social scientists of all descriptions suspiciously rub
shoulders, and occasionally commit the cardinal academic sin of
invading each other's territory; polemicists and propagandists of every
shade in the Irish political spectrum—orange, green, red and, since the
arrival of the British army in 1969, khaki—vie with each other in
broadsheets, pamphlets, newspapers and manifestos; to add spice to
the stew, more than one hundred novels have been located in the back
streets, bogs and beds of Northern Ireland, as if there were not enough
fantasy already. The first problem for any new book, therefore, is to
justify an addition to the list.

To start by clearing the ground, this book is not an attempt to
present another definitive analysis of the Northern Irish conflict. On
the contrary, the aim is to provide a more realistic understanding of
the variety and complexities of the issues and relationships within the
province, avoiding a single diagnosis and solution. For writers outside
Northern Ireland in particular, the main interest in the conflict is the
apparent starkness and intransigence of its divisions. On closer
examination it might be argued more convincingly that the real contribution of the Northern Irish conflict to a better appreciation of
community violence lies in the understandings and accomodations
which add subtlety to the relationships between Catholics and
Protestants in Northern Ireland.

This, of course, is not enough. Every book is based on certain pre-
sumptions, sometimes explicit, sometimes disguised and sometimes
unknown even to the author. They are important because they exclude
certain concerns from the book, and impose limits on its intentions.
Why is the issue defined as Northern Irish, rather than Irish, problem?
Why are the chapters organised as they are? What are the political and
ideological assumptions which underpin it? In the case of a book
which contains nine papers by different authors, similar types of
questions might be posed for each chapter and can only be answered

within that context. However, even before any of the nine pens touched paper, the conception of the book, and the invitations to contribute papers to it, reflected explicit premises. Two were particularly important in directing the aims of the book and shaping its form, and require a brief justification. One is the decision to confine the papers to an internal study of Northern Ireland, and the other concerns the effects of the current violence.

One hundred years ago the issues which provoked political dissension in Ireland were the questions of Irish self-determination and Anglo–Irish relations; Ulster was an irritating subplot to more historic developments. In 1921, however, the island was partitioned. Since then, sixty years of separate institutions have formalised the differences between the two parts of Ireland, and concentrated the constitutional issue within the six counties of Northern Ireland.

For Protestants the reluctant acceptance of the new constitutional arrangements in 1921 had hardened by the 1980s into a fierce loyalty to Northern Ireland. Catholics were more ambivalent; while most aspired towards some association with the rest of the island, many saw an accomodation with Protestants within Northern Ireland as a greater priority. Even the most nationally-minded were affected by sixty years of living within the institutions and rivalries of the province, and even the form of their opposition accorded a level of *de facto* acceptance to the unit, and ambivalence towards the south. The Irish question of 1883 had become the Northern Ireland problem of 1983. For many in Northern Ireland, the issue of Anglo–Irish conflict had been overtaken by the question of Protestant–Catholic relations within Northern Ireland.

The theme of this book is an examination of these relations. The omission of papers on the external dimensions of the conflict arises from this, and is deliberate. To consider properly the roles of Britain, the Irish Republic and the United States would have required a different type of book, and distracted from the primary emphasis of this one. This is not to suggest that the broader setting is unimportant. On the contrary, the presence of the British army since 1969, and the operation of Direct Rule from Westminster since 1974, are only two of the more obvious illustrations of how central are external elements in the origins and nature of the issue. They are clearly essential subjects for study. Indeed the conflict is often discussed exclusively at this level, as if the only important parties in effectively reducing violence are outside the province, despite the fact that their initiatives have been frustrated so often by their failure to find internal acceptance. Local factors are likely to be primary determinants of the duration and violence of the conflict, and they provide the deliberately limited subject of this book.

The second premise is that the violence since 1969—Northern Ireland's longest sustained period of civil disorder—has affected the nature of the conflict and of group relationships. In some respects this is a truism; the abolition of Stormont and the subsequent introduction of Direct Rule from Westminster, and the coincidence of an economic depression and a terrorist campaign aimed at the collapse of the province's economic structure, inevitably altered some of the issues in dispute. Most of all, it seems likely that more than 2,000 deaths, including a number directly resulting from violence between Catholics and Protestants, could not but have affected relationships between the two communities.

A picture of polarised violence, however, while seductive, is very misleading. In fact the level varies greatly from time to time, and between different parts of the province, so that visitors are often confused by the apparent co-existence of violence and normality. One of the themes which recurs in a number of the papers in this book is the constraints and limitations to which both the conflict and violence are subject. These help to maintain a level of accomodation and adjustment in social relationships, which contrasts with the intransigence at political level. They also suggest that the search for non-existent stroke-of-the-pen solutions might fruitfully be abandoned in favour of more modest, and more realistic, strategies, such as those suggested by Arthur Koestler:

> What we need is an active fraternity of pessimists. They will not aim at immediate radical solutions, because they know that these cannot be achieved in the hollow of the historical wave; they will not brandish the surgeon's knife at the social body, because they know that their own instruments are polluted. They will watch with open eyes and without sectarian blinkers for the first sign of the new horizontal movement; when it comes they will assist its birth; but if it does not come in their lifetime, they will not despair. And meantime their chief aim will be to create oases in the interregnum desert.

No attempt has been made to establish a single ideological or theoretical basis for the papers in the book and the views expressed in them reflect a broad range of opinions. They do, however, have two important characteristics in common: all the authors have spent a substantial part of their working lives in Northern Ireland, and most were born and grew up in the province. More important, each has made an important recent contribution, through research or writing, and is well equipped to set his own research and analysis within the broader context of knowledge in his own field. The marriage of general surveys and individual expertise was one of the central objectives in the book.

The chapters themselves are designed to introduce readers to an appreciation of the major themes in the conflict. While the book deals with the origins of the grievances in the years before 1969, there is a progression through the chapters towards an emphasis on subsequent developments.

Chapter 1 sets out to provide an historical backcloth to the main themes developed in the book; in a sense it is a history of community relations in the province before 1969.

The next five chapters examine specific aspects of Northern Ireland's social structure which have particular relevance to the conflict. As already indicated, this decision to concentrate on formal and informal relationships within the context of Northern Ireland did not result from ignorance of broader contexts—particularly the Irish and British dimensions—but rather from a desire to emphasise elements of the conflict which are sometimes neglected. One of the most basic of these elements is law and order, the subject of Chapter 2 by Paddy Hillyard; the issues of policing, extraordinary legislation and internment all underlined fundamentally different views about the legitimacy of the state within the community. The reasons for the failure to construct a workable political system is the subject of Chapter 3 by Ian McAllister. John Simpson's survey of the complex relationship between community conflict and the economy in Chapter 4 is the first analysis of the issue by an economist. Chapter 5 by Hastings Donnan and Graham McFarlane provides the most comprehensive examination of informal social organisation within the province. Finally the relationship between Northern Ireland's segregated education system and the broader community conflict, often regarded by observers as the aspect of the conflict most amenable to change, is assessed by Dominic Murray in Chapter 6.

The fundamental importance of demography in determining the nature and forms of conflict has taken on an added dimension as violence spread during the 1970s. Chapter 7 by Michael Poole, on violence and demography, carries on the examination of aspects of the conflict in chapters 2 to 5, and also leads on to the two chapters dealing specifically with the violence itself. These are Chapters 8 and 9, which examine more closely the influence of the violence during the 1970s and 1980s on the underlying conflict. In chapter 8 Barry White describes the patterns of violence in the province since the late 1960s. The political changes which took place during the same period are evaluated by Bill Rolston in Chapter 9.

For those who intend to carry out research themselves, whether for undergraduate dissertations or major projects, Chapter 10 provides a preliminary guide to the more important sources of primary data, statistics and centres of study.

In content and style the book sets out to introduce readers who are unfamiliar with the conflict to some understanding of its origins and development, and the issues which characterise it. Readers wishing to pursue more detailed study on particular aspects of the conflict will find references in each chapter to the most useful secondary publications and more substantial research in the field. There is, also, an extensive, but selective, bibliography. The intention, therefore, is to provide the opportunity for further study at a number of different levels.

My principal thanks are due to the contributors who, without exception, responded to the irksome editorial need for internal consistency; to Tom Hadden and Bill Rolston, my colleagues on the Appletree Social Studies editorial group; and to Douglas Marshall of Appletree Press for his support and encouragement. Grateful acknowledgment is made to Gill and Macmillan, Ltd., for permission to use material from *Conflict in Northern Ireland* (1976), which forms the basis for Chapter 1 of this book.

John Darby
New University of Ulster
1983

1

The Historical Background

John Darby

W. C. Sellar and R. J. Yeatman in their comic history of Britain, *1066 and all that*, decided to include only two dates in the book, because all others were 'not memorable'. They would have had much greater difficulty writing an equivalent volume on Irish history. 1170, 1641, 1690, 1798, 1912, 1916, 1921, 1969—all these dates are fixed like beacons in the folklore and mythology of Irishmen. They trip off the tongue during ordinary conversation like the latest football scores in other environments, and are recorded for posterity on gable walls all over Northern Ireland.

To some extent this chapter is a history of the above, and other, dates. It is not intended as a pocket history of Northern Ireland, and anyone who wishes a more comprehensive account of the history of Ulster or Ireland will have no difficulty in finding suitable books (see for example Beckett 1966, Lyons 1971 and Hepburn 1980). The intention here is to construct a short introduction for readers unfamiliar with the general sweep of Irish history before 1969, when the latest period of serious violence started. Since the book is concerned mainly with the interactions between the inhabitants of the state of Northern Ireland and their relations with their immediate neighbours, this chapter attempts to isolate some of the historical events and developments which illumine or at least are germane to this theme. In a sense, it is a history of community relations in the province.

Nevertheless Ulster* has a history of separateness which is not explainable in purely regional terms. Before the plantation of the early

* The term 'Ulster' is popularly used in Ireland to describe two different areas. The first is the nine counties of the traditional province—Antrim, Down, Armagh, Derry, Tyrone, Fermanagh, Donegal, Monaghan and Cavan. The other area is the administrative and political unit which since 1921 has formed the state of Northern Ireland: it comprises the first six counties in the list above. In this book the term 'Northern Ireland' will be preferred when describing the latter area.

seventeenth century it was, apart from a few precarious coastal fortresses, the most Gaelic part of the country, and had successfully resisted Engligh colonial ambitions. Nor were the relationships between its chiefs and those in the rest of Ireland particularly close, except when they faced each other across interminable battlefields. Links with Scotland, however, were close; western Scotland and eastern Ulster exchanged immigrants long before the middle ages.

It would be a mistake to regard pre-Plantation Ulster as a cohesive unit. Like the rest of Ireland it was dominated by a number of territorially jealous chiefs, and internal wars and vendettas were not uncommon. But the dominance of the O'Donnells in Donegal, the MacDonnells in Antrim and particularly the O'Neills in the centre of the province did produce some stability; it also produced military cohesion against Elizabeth I's armies and, for a time, success. It took nine years and a blockade of the province to bring the Ulster chiefs to their knees.

It was this very intransigence that accounted for the comprehensive nature of the Plantation of Ulster in 1609. There had been earlier attempts at colonising parts of Ireland during the sixteenth century, but they had usually consisted of little more than the confiscation of land and the grafting on of a new aristocracy. This also happened in Ulster. The leaders of the Ulster families were forced to flee to Europe and their lands were confiscated. By 1703, less than a century later, only 14 per cent of the land in Ireland remained in the hands of the Catholic Irish, and in Ulster the figure was 5 per cent. But these figures are not a real measure of the changes introduced within the Plantation of Ulster. What made it unique in Irish plantations was the comprehensive attempt made to attract, not only British gentry, but colonists of all classes, and the fact that the colonists were Protestant and represented a culture alien to Ulster. This policy of comprehensive colonisation was a result of the advice of the Solicitor General to James I, and was an attempt to replace one entire community with another. The Catholic Irish remained, of course, but in conditions which emphasised their suppression. They were relegated to a state below servility, because the Planters were not allowed to employ the native Irish as servants in the new towns which they built. The towns themselves were unashamedly fortresses against the armed resentment of the Irish. Outside the town they were banished from the land they had owned and worked, and were confined to the boggy and mountainous regions. The reality differed from the intention, however.

There were simply not enough settlers to achieve comprehensive control, and Irish servants were quietly admitted to the towns.

The sum of the Plantation then was the introduction of a foreign community, which spoke differently, worshipped apart, and represented an alien culture and way of life. It had close commercial, cultural and political ties with Britain. The more efficient methods of the new farmers, and the greater availability of capital which allowed the start of cottage industries, served to create further economic differences between Ulster and the rest of Ireland, and between Catholic and Protestant within Ulster. The deep resentment of the native Irish towards the planters, and the distrustful siege mentality of the planters towards the Irish, is the root of the Ulster problem.

The next two centuries supplied a lot of the dates and other trappings essential to the conflict. The Rising of 1641 against the Planters provided a Protestant massacre, and the Cromwellian conquest in the 1650s a Catholic one. Most important of all was the battle of the Boyne in 1690, sanctified on a hundred gable walls and Orange banners as the victory of the 'Prods' over the 'Mikes'. Historians keep trying to debunk these myths, but historical scholarship has never had much effect on a folklore socialised into generations of Ulster people.

The aftermath of William of Orange's victory at the Boyne was much more important than the campaign itself. It was a mark of the sustained hostility between Planter and Gael that the Penal laws, often included in the catalogue of England's evils in Ireland, were enacted by Irishmen through the Irish parliament in Dublin. The laws were of vital importance in broadening the differences between the Irish establishment and its opponents. Having established an exclusively Protestant legislature in 1692, a comprehensive series of coercive acts against Catholics were implemented during the 1690s and after: they were excluded from the armed forces, the judiciary and the legal profession as well as from parliament; they were forbidden to carry arms or to own a horse worth more than £5; all their bishops and regular clergy were banished in 1697, although secular clergy could remain under licence; Catholics were forbidden to hold long leases on land or to buy land from a Protestant, and were forced to divide their property equally among their children in their wills, unless the eldest conformed to the Anglican faith; they were prohibited from conducting schools, or from sending their children to be educated abroad. Some of these laws, and notably those affecting property, were rigidly enforced, while others were unenforceable. Their main effects were to entrench the divide between Catholics and Protestants, to strengthen Irish Catholicism by adding a political component to it, and to drive underground some aspects of the Catholic Gaelic culture, notably education and public worship.

During the second half of the eighteenth century relations between the religious communities in Ireland were in a situation of considerable flux. Acting as a counterbalance to tendencies dividing Catholics and Protestants, the coerced and the coercors, was the rivalry between Presbyterians and members of the Church of Ireland. The fact that there were also penal laws against the Presbyterians which excluded them from a share of political power—although certainly not as severe or comprehensive as those against Catholics—created a Catholic-Presbyterian relationship which was in some ways closer than that between the Protestant sects. This was particularly true in Ulster, and some of its fruits have persuaded some historians that this was an age of tolerance. Most of the Penal laws were repealed by the 1790s; a convention of the Irish Volunteers—an exclusively Protestant body aimed at creating greater Irish independence from Britain—met at Dungannon in 1782 and passed a resolution 'that as men and as Irishmen, as Christians and as Protestants, we rejoice in the relaxation of the Penal laws against our Roman Catholic fellow-subjects' (Beckett 1966, 222). Belfast Volunteers, Protestant to a man, formed a guard of honour for Father Hugh O'Donnell as the first Catholic Church in Belfast, St Mary's in Chapel Lane, was opened, and Protestants contributed £84 towards the cost of its building. The early success of the Society of United Irishmen in attracting both Presbyterians and Catholics into a revolutionary republican movement during the 1790s appeared to indicate a new Irish cohesion which disregarded religious denominationalism and was determined to establish an independent republic of Ireland. The abortive 1798 rebellion, best known for the Catholic rising in Wexford, also included risings in Antrim and Down; in the resulting judicial investigations thirty Presbyterian clergymen were accused of participation, three of them were hanged, seven imprisoned, four exiled or transported and at least five fled the country (Boyd 1969, 2).

Such a benign interpretation of the late eighteenth century ignores equally powerful evidence pointing towards the existence of strong community divisions. Secret organisations like the Defenders, the Peep o' Day Boys and the Steelboys, strongly sectarian and determined to ensure that tenancies were prevented from passing into the hands of the other religion, waged persistent and occasionally bloody skirmishes with each other in the country areas. Indeed it was one of these skirmishes in Armagh which led to the formation of the Orange Order, an organisation which stressed the common interests of all Protestants and effectively challenged the Presbyterian-Catholic alliance in the United Irishmen. Inside Belfast the tolerance towards Catholics was not unrelated to their numbers in the city. In 1707 George McCartney, the Sovereign of Belfast, reported to his superiors that 'thank God we are not under any great fears here, for... we have not among us above seven papists' (Beckett and Glasscock 1967, 47). The industrial expansion of the city towards the beginning of the nineteenth century attracted very large numbers of Catholics to the city. Between 1800 and 1830 the proportion of Catholics in Belfast rose from 10 per cent to 30 per cent and the first signs of serious urban conflict occurred as a result of competition for jobs and for houses. The same period saw considerable changes within the Presbyterian church. The liberals within the church came under increasing challenge from hardline opinion which was represented by Henry Cooke and closely linked with the Orange Order. The dispute was along both theological and political lines, and resulted in a complete victory for Cooke and his supporters. The liberals under Henry Montgomery broke away and formed the Non-subscribing Presbyterian Church. The community divisions in Ulster began to assume a form similar to that well-known today.

The first serious communal riots in Belfast took place on July 12, 1835, and a woman was killed. An English witness to the riot, John Barrow, contrasted Belfast with the industrial cities in Britain where such disturbances were frequent. 'In Belfast, where everyone is too much engaged in his own business, and where neither religion nor politics have interfered to disturb the harmony of society, it could not fail to create a great and uneasy sensation.' (Barrow 1836, 36). It was a sensation which Belfast citizens were to experience frequently ever since. Andrew Boyd mentioned eight other years 'of the most serious rioting' during the rest of the nineteenth century, and indeed few years passed without some disturbances (see Boyd 1969). The main effect of these riots was to ensure that the expanding population of the city was separated into sectarian areas, and to fortify the communal differences between Catholics and Protestants.

The nineteenth century also witnessed the growth of conscious separatism between Ulster and the rest of Ireland. The effects of the industrial revolution in Ireland were confined almost entirely to the northern part of the country, strapping even closer its industrial and commercial dependency on Britain. The greater prosperity of the north, its economic structure, even its physical appearance, increased its alienation from the rest of Ireland. The potato famine of the 1840s, undoubtedly the most far-reaching event in nineteenth-century Ireland, had much more severe consequences in the south than in the north and had profound effects on political, economic and social developments there which were less dramatic in Ulster. Economic differences found a political voice when the campaign for the repeal of the act of Union with Britain caused a petition to be organised as early as 1834 against repeal or, if a Dublin parliament was restored, in favour of a separate legislature in Ulster. In 1841 Daniel O'Connell, the champion of repeal, visited Belfast. His coach had to avoid an ambush, the meeting hall was stoned, and his entourage was protected by a strong police force on its way southwards.

It was the Home Rule campaign in the 1880s which was to give Protestant Ulster its organised basis and its tradition. As late as the general election of 1885, 17 out of 33 Ulster seats were carried by the Home Rule party. The next two decades transformed this picture and stiffened Ulster's resistance to Home Rule. The resistance was strengthened by the growing identification between Ulster unionism and the Conservative party in Britain. The basis of the new Conservative policy was an identification with Protestant fears, and particularly with the province of Ulster. If the motive was frank political opportunism from the Conservatives, the Ulster Unionists were glad of such powerful support. Nevertheless, although this support was important, it was events inside Ulster which gave the anti-Home Rule campaign its real power. Amidst the outbursts against Home Rule by churchmen, Unionists, MPs and Conservative politicians, it was the Orange Order which emerged to provide the leadership and organisation to maintain the union. The Order's fortunes during the eighteenth century had been chequered; outlawed and abused on many occasions, it had nevertheless survived. The anti-Home Rule campaign served to transform the Order from a disreputable to a respectable body. For its part the Order supplied the ready-made framework of an effective organisation for growing Protestant dissatisfaction, especially in Ulster. By 1905 it had played a major role in uniting disparate unionist voices within the Ulster Unionist Council—the coalition from which the Unionist party was to emerge.

The Home Rule campaign against which this unionist reorganisation was aimed was not confined to parliamentary strategies. The Irish parliamentary party which attempted to achieve Home Rule by legislative action, was at times complemented and at times rivalled by revolutionaries of both the physical force and the cultural variety. The Irish revolutionary tradition, represented by the Fenians from the 1850s, and later by the Irish Republican Brotherhood, the IRA and others, loomed over the parliamentary campaign. It was strategically useful to Charles Stewart Parnell, the Irish Nationalist leader, as evidence of what would happen if Home Rule were rejected—but it became a serious and in the end a more powerful rival to the parliamentary party as public impatience grew. The formation of the Gaelic Athletic Association to encourage Irish sports, and the Gaelic League to encourage interest in Irish language and literature, reflected a growing nationalism which was more closely tuned to the revolutionary than the parliamentary tradition. These developments were adopted with enthusiasm by nationalists in the north of Ireland, just as the organisation of the anti-Home Rule campaign included branches all over the country. But as the crisis came to a head between 1906 and 1914, the quarrel was regarded in increasingly general geographical terms as one between the northern and southern parts of the country. Lip-service was paid to the existence of minorities within the enemy camps, but their causes did not receive really serious attention until the 1920s when their minority conditions had been confirmed within separate states.

The decade between 1912 and 1922 was a momentous one for Ireland. Civil conflict between north and south, where private armies were openly drilling, was averted by the outbreak of the First World War; the Easter 1916 rising in Dublin and the subsequent guerrilla campaign shifted the spotlight southward; the signing in 1921 of a treaty between the British government and Sinn Fein, the political wing of the Irish Republican Army, established a state from which Northern Ireland opted out. These events and the first years of both new states were accompanied by civil disorder. Belfast experienced a guerrilla campaign and sectarian conflicts. The new state was created in the midst of the troubles and divisions which were to characterise its history.

As J. C. Beckett has pointed out, it is not correct to regard the establishment of Northern Ireland as a response to the current European demand for self-expression. 'The six north–eastern counties of Ireland were grouped together and given a parliament and government of their own, not because anyone in the area wanted (let alone demanded) such an arrangement, but because the British government thought that this was the only possible way of reconciling the rival aspirations of the two Irish parties.' (Beckett 1972, 11). Indeed it was intended as part of a wider settlement which never materialised. The Government of Ireland act (1920) proposed two states in Ireland, one for the six counties and the other for the remainder of Ireland. Each was to have its own parliament to deal with domestic matters; each was to have representatives at Westminster; and a Council of Ireland was to deal with matters of common interest. In fact the terms only came into operation in Northern Ireland, and the Council of Ireland never met. Having fought against Home Rule for almost a century Unionists were, in the words of Rev. J. B. Armour, 'compelled to take a form of Home Rule that the devil himself could never have imagined'. (Lyons 1972, 682).

The size of the new state was a case in point. The county boundaries had never been intended as anything more than local administrative limits, and fairly arbitrary ones at that. Now some of them became international frontiers. As to why six counties had been selected rather than four or nine or any other number, the reasons were unashamedly straightforward. The traditional nine counties of Ulster held 900,000 Protestants, most of whom supported the British connection, and 700,000 Catholics, most of whom wanted to end it. However, in the six counties which were later to become Northern Ireland, the religious breakdown was 820,000 Protestants and 430,000 Catholics. In 1920 C. C. Craig, brother of James Craig, the first Prime Minister of Northern Ireland, expressed the case frankly in the House of Commons: 'If we had a nine-county parliament, with sixty-four members, the Unionist majority would be about three or four: but in a six-county parliament, with fifty-two members, the Unionist majority would be about ten.' (Shearman 1971, 16). It was this more than any other consideration which persuaded the Unionists to accept the six-county area.

The two most pervasive problems of the new state of Northern Ireland were the continuing polarisation of the nationalist and unionist communities which occasionally flared into violence, and relations with its two closest neighbours, Great Britain and the southern part of Ireland. Both of these problems were closely related to economic circumstances. The troubles of the 1930s were triggered off by the depression and, indeed, accusations of economic discrimination were among the most bitter reasons for discontent by the Northern minority. And the relationships with southern Ireland and Britain became increasingly dependent on economic ties and divisions.

Northern Ireland: Internal Matters

The new state was born amid bloodshed and communal disorder. In 1922, 232 people were killed in the violence in Northern Ireland, and almost 1,000 wounded. The nationalist minority refused to recognise the new state; the twelve anti-partitionist MPs refused to attend parliament; Catholic teachers shunned the educational system, submitting pupils for examinations in Dublin and even refusing salaries. At the very time when the institutions of the new state were being established, a considerable minority of its citizens were refusing to participate on committees or to perform any action which might lend support to its authority.

As time passed, and the state remained, most nationalists decided on a reluctant acceptance of the need to come to some accommodation, at least in the short term. In some cases they found that the institutions which had been established and those which were still being set up were so arranged as to effectively exclude them from positions of power. Partly as a result of Catholic unwillingness to participate in a state whose existence they opposed, and partly as a result of bias by the establishment against a section of the community which it considered as traitorous, many of the institutions were heavily biased in favour of Unionists. The local government franchise, for example, which remained unreformed until 1969, reflected property rather than population, excluding non-ratepayers and awarding many people with more than one property extra votes. Housing allocation and the gerrymandering of constituency boundaries were actively used in some cases, notably Derry city, to maintain Unionist majorities. In the membership of the police force and the Ulster Special Constabulary, formed to help combat the IRA threat in 1921, a combination of nationalist unwillingness and Unionist distrust created forces which were to become largely Protestant. As late as 1961 only 12 per cent of the Royal Ulster Constabulary was Catholic, and the 'B' Specials were exclusively Protestant. Education too was an area where Catholics felt bitterly that the system established by the Education Act (NI) of 1930 was one which had been tailored by Protestant pressure, producing a state education system which was in fact Protestant, and forcing Catholic schools to find 50 per cent of the cost of education. In the administration of justice Catholics have long alleged that the Special Powers Act, which placed considerable powers in the hands of the Minister of Home Affairs and which, although emergency legislation, operated permanently within Northern Ireland, was designed exclusively against the nationalist minority. Further allegations have been made, and vindicated by the Cameron Report in 1969, about discrimination against Catholics in public employment. The most serious general allegation in this field was that the government operated a policy of deliberate discrimination against part of the province—counties Derry and Fermanagh in particular—creating conditions which encouraged emigration to counter the higher Catholic birth rate in these areas. Disputes about the extent of institutional discrimination, and about the reasons for it, have always been particularly bitter, but one point is clear. Far from resolving intercommunal suspicion and fear, the establishment of the state actually served to render them more precise.

Beckett's judgement that 'between the early 1920s and the late 1960s Ireland enjoyed a longer period of freedom from major internal disturbance than it had known since the first half of the eighteenth century' (Beckett 1972, 14) holds less validity if confined to the Northern state. The years which followed immediately upon the establishment of the state were among the most violent in the history of Ulster, although they were clearly related to political opposition to the new state. The familiar relationship between economic recession and inter-communal strife was bloodily revived in the depression of the 1930s. The dependency of Northern Ireland on exports made her particularly vulnerable to world trends. The linen industry was severely restricted; in 1933 no ships were launched from Belfast shipyards for the first time in over 100 years. Between 1930 and 1939 the unemployment rates in the province never fell below 25 per cent. The bitter competition for too few jobs inevitably took a sectarian turn, which was exacerbated by worsening relations between the United Kingdom and the Irish Free State. The Ulster Protestant League was formed in 1931 and encouraged Protestants to employ other Protestants exclusively, a sentiment endorsed by Basil Brooke, the Minister of Agriculture and future Prime Minister. Whether this was a concerted policy or, as Hugh Shearman claims, merely caused by 'the nervous and vituperative atmosphere of the early 1930s' (Shearman 1971, 174) made little difference to those who were jobless.

Certainly the early 1930s were nervous and vituperative years. Widespread riots in 1931, some of which involved the IRA, resulted in between 60 and 70 people being injured. 1932 saw riots in Belfast, Larne, Portadown and Ballymena. In 1935 the troubles reached their peak. Twelve people were killed and six hundred wounded. Incidents like the 1932 Shankill riots in support of the Falls hunger marchers who had been baton charged by the police disturbed the pattern but did not alter it. The frequency of sectarian violence gradually faded as the employment situation improved, but few believed that it had retreated far below the surface.

The comparative peacefulness, by Northern Ireland standards, of the next twenty years set the scene for the important changes which appeared to be taking place in the 1950s and 1960s. This period of communal peace, or rather of absence of overt conflict, coincided with a growing and deliberate emphasis on economic expansion for the province. In the first place, the war years brought unprecedented prosperity to Northern Ireland. Her shipbuilding, engineering and aircraft production boomed; agricultural production shot up; and the economic expectations of the people rose accordingly. The post-war years consequently saw determined attempts on the part of the Northern Ireland government to attract foreign capital and industry, and its success was considerable. As a result of various incentive schemes 150 new factories, supplying 55,000 new jobs, were established. The new industries, many of which were branches of international combines, offered hopes to Catholics, especially from the middle and lower managerial classes who had formerly found promotion prospects restricted, although recent research suggests that the newcomers often came to adopt local practices (O'Dowd 1980, 66).

An improvement in the prospects and conditions of the minority was also evident in other spheres. The post-war legislation which greatly broadened the social benefits of the welfare state particulary benefited the poorer classes in society, and in Northern Ireland this included a disproportionate number of Catholics. The 1947 Education act opened doors of educational opportunity by introducing free secondary education, and the remarkable rise in the number of Catholics attending university was one measure of its effectiveness. Although the extent of these changes is often debated, there is no doubt that the 1950s saw a growing tendency for Catholics to see their future in terms of a Northern Ireland context rather than in an all-Ireland state. The most dramatic pointer to this change was the failure of the IRA offensive of 1956–62. Its defeat owed more to apathy than to the efficiency of law enforcement machinery, and this was recognised by the IRA in its statement formally ending the campaign. The decision taken by the IRA shortly afterwards to abandon military methods and concentrate on socialist objectives by political means seemed to promise that the 1960s would be free of republican violence. This coincided with a Social Studies conference at Garron Tower in 1958, where G. B. Newe called for greater participation by Catholics in Northern Ireland affairs and Terence O'Neill, the future Prime Minister, appeared to indicate that they would be welcomed. In 1959 there were other signs of a possible erosion of traditional attitudes. The republican party, Sinn Fein, lost its two seats at Westminister, their percentage of the votes plummeting from 26 to 14. Just as dramatic was the attempt by some leading Unionists to suggest that Catholics might be permitted to join the party. The attempt was thwarted by the obduracy of the Orange Order, but that it had been made at all was seen as a sign of changing times.

So the 1960s started as the decade of hope. The retirement in 1963 of the Prime Minister, Lord Brookeborough, who was to many Catholics the personification of right-wing Unionist opinion, and his replacement by Terence O'Neill, appeared to be another victory for moderation. The policies of the new premier encouraged this view. In 1964 he declared, 'my principal aims are to make Northern Ireland prosperous and to build bridges between the two traditions.' (O'Neill 1969, 23). The same year saw an important step in facilitating both aims. The southern connections of the Irish Congress of Trade Unions, to which most Northern workers were affiliated, had ensured its non-recognition by the Brookeborough administration. In 1964 a compromise was reached whereby the Congress was recognised by Stormont in return for greater independence being granted to its Northern Ireland Committee. But the most dramatic gestures towards reconciliation were the exchange visits between Captain O'Neill and the southern premier, Mr Lemass, in 1965. As a direct result of this visit the Nationalist party in Northern Ireland agreed to become the official opposition party in Stormont.

Such developments persuaded many contemporaries and not a few later observers to regard the 1960s as an age of tolerance reminiscent of the 1780s and 1790s. Like the earlier epoch, however, there were many warning signals, remembered in retrospect but underrated in the exuberant optimism of the 1960s, that basic attitudes had not altered significantly. Moderate values in Ulster have their mythology, just as extremist values; and, like all mythologies, they ignore those pointers which challenged the popular view of the tolerant sixties. The traditional Ulster values, which would have been threatened by reconciliation, may have been in temporary hiding, but they soon emerged with banners flying. Indeed the flying of a banner and an attempt to remove it—in this case a tricolour in the Divis Street headquarters of Liam McMillan, the Republican candidate for West Belfast—provoked a riot in 1964, when liberal mythology had republicanism at its lowest ebb.

A man who played a leading role in demanding the removal of the flag was to provide leadership to those Unionists and Protestants who opposed the current doctrines of political reconciliation and religious ecumenism. The attitudes expressed by Ian Paisley, head of the Free Presbyterian Church and the Protestant Unionist Party, had roots which stretched far into history. But the classic duel between liberal and right-wing Presbyterianism fought between Cooke and Montgomery in the 1820s was repeated when the Presbyterian General Assembly was picketed and attacked by Paisley in 1966. In the same year the murder of a Catholic in the Malvern Arms public house, and the apprehension of the murderers, revealed the existence of the UVF (Ulster Volunteer Force) which saw itself as the loyalist equivalent of the IRA. The presures for change in Northern Ireland society had produced defenders of the status quo.

The changes which they were resisting seemed less substantial to some Catholics. Indeed the failure of the O'Neill administration to translate its intentions into practice caused considerable frustration and resentment. A series of measures—notably the closure of the main rail link to Derry, the decision to establish a new university at Coleraine instead of in Derry where a University college was already operating, and the establishment of a new growth centre at Craigavon— were seen by both Catholics and Protestants in the west of the province, and especially in Derry city, as blatant discrimination against the disadvantaged west. In March 1967 the Republican Clubs, which represented an attempt by Republicans to find a legitimate method of political expression, were declared illegal by the government, a move which seemed narrow and repressive to many people who did not share republican views. As late as 1969, the failure of a Catholic to secure the Unionist nomination as a parliamentary candidate led to his resignation from the party. Louis Boyle, in his resignation statement, declared:

> One of my main hopes and guiding aims as a member of the party, has been to work towards a newly structured Unionist Party in which Protestants and Catholics could play a part as equal partners in pursuing a common political end. Now I know this is not possible... The Unionist Party arose out of, and is still essentially based on a sectarian foundation, and only a reconstitution of the party away from its sectarian foundation could make Catholic membership a real possibility. (Boyle 1969).

Other Catholics too had decided that reform would not come without pressure, believing that, whether Captain O'Neill wanted reform or not, the conservatism of his party would sabotage any changes. Housing allocation provided the issue for this pressure, and the success of the Civil Rights campaign in America suggested non-violent protest as the means. The Campaign for Social Justice in Northern Ireland, formed in Dungannon in 1964, developed through Housing Action committees in many parts of the province. In 1967 the broader-based Northern Ireland Civil Rights Association (NICRA) was formed. Its campaign, followed with increasing interest by international news media, was to make the Northern Ireland problem an international issue, and ushered in the most dynamic years in the history of Northern Ireland.

One of the most remarkable aspects of the Civil Rights campaigns of 1968 was their success in forcing through some reforms. After two marches, to Dungannon in August and to Derry in October, the O'Neill administration agreed to replace Derry City Council with a Development Commission, to establish an Ombudsman and to abolish the unfair company vote. Certainly complaints remained, notably about the Special Powers act and remaining inequalities in the franchise (one man, one vote), but promises were given that the schemes for allocating publicly-owned houses would be clarified and the Special Powers act reviewed. These successes ultimately split the Civil Rights movement. Those, like the members of the People's Democracy (PD) who were moving towards a more radical position, believed that it would be foolish to abandon a successful campaign before it had achieved all its objects. Others felt that both the reforms and the dismissal from office in December of William Craig, the Minister of Home Affairs, demonstrated the government's good intentions, and that a suspension on marches should be agreed to enable the passing of further reforms. The decision by the People's

Democracy unilaterally to march from Belfast to Derry in January 1969, and the violent opposition to the marchers at Burntollet Bridge, destroyed any hopes of non-violent protest. Many Protestants and liberal Catholics who had participated in the early campaigns now drifted out. The campaign became more radical. Nineteen sixty-nine was one of the seminal years in Irish history.

It was the events during the summer of that year which set the province on a new and violent course. Community tensions had been increased by the events of 1968, and the months leading up to the traditional celebrations were marked by riots in Strabane, Derry and Belfast. On 12 August the Protestant Apprentice Boys of Derry held their march and were attacked. The violence of the police reaction in the Catholic Bogside produced two important responses. The Prime Minister of the Irish Republic, Jack Lynch, made his famous 'we will not stand by' speech, the strong language of which it is now clear was intended to compensate for his inability to do anything else; and the violence spread to Belfast. In August the Catholic Lower Falls area was invaded by a hostile mob, seven people were killed, more than 3,000 lost their homes. On August 14 the British government sent the army into Derry, and on the next day to Belfast. Ironically its initial function was the protection of Catholic families. More important, however, it restored the ultimate republican symbol of oppression— British troops on Irish soil. By January 1970 the Provisional IRA had been formed, and the stage was set for the violence of the 1970s.

Any attempt to assess the internal performance of the Northern Ireland state between the early 1920s and the late 1960s must consider its record in economic matters. After an abysmal inter-war record in housing and employment, considerable advances were made after the Second World War—changes which altered the economic and social structure of the province. When it comes to measuring attitudes, the most significant development had been on the Unionist side. The downright opposition to or reluctant acceptance of the new state in 1920 had been converted to a pride and loyalty towards its institutions. The steadfast prime loyalty to Great Britain was both fortified and challenged by this more local pride. But no significant improvement had been made in the age-old community problem within Northern Ireland. The very processes and institutions which had created fierce loyalties among Protestants had deterred Catholics from accepting the state as their own. The apparent willingness of Catholics to accept the status quo in the post-war years was always conditional. For a genuine transition towards full participation in the new state Catholics demanded a number of institutional and social changes. The failure of the government to produce these changes made pressure inevitable. The pressure was applied seriously from 1969.

Northern Ireland: External Relations

Her relationships with the southern part of the country and with Britain provide Northern Ireland with the issue which determined prime political loyalties. In simple terms this issue has been whether the Northern Ireland area should be included within the United Kingdom or within an all-Ireland state. The state of diplomatic relations between southern Ireland and Britain to some extent was reflected in the relationship between the two communities inside Northern Ireland, as were the interactions between the two parts of Ireland.

The relationship between the Northern Ireland and British legislatures was not defined in any great detail by the Government of Ireland act (1920). Nevertheless some indisputable guidelines were laid down. One of these was the superiority of the Westminster parliament to which Northern Ireland sent twelve representatives. The subservience of the Northern Ireland parliament precluded it from some areas of government, notably foreign affairs and defence, which remained the responsibility of Westminster. This meant that all dealings between the northern and southern parts of Ireland were outside the jurisdiction of Northern Ireland's legislature.

During the first decade after the treaty, both Irish governments were more preoccupied with internal affairs to court conflict between each other; Britain was determined to remain, as far as was possible, outside Irish affairs. The attitude of the Cosgrave administration, which remained in power in Dublin from 1922 until 1932, was relatively benign. In 1925 an agreement was signed by Great Britain and both Irish administrations which formally acknowledged the existing partition of the island.

Governments are transitory things, and the history of Ireland from the 1920s was to demonstrate that fluctuations in North–South relations depended more on governmental changes south of the border than on those in Northern Ireland. The coming to power of de Valera and the Fianna Fail party in 1932 had an immediate effect on these relations. Their aggressive policy of separatist nationalism immediately affected the Irish Free State's relations with Britain. De

Valera's decision in 1932 to end the annuities which had been repaid to the British government since it had financed land purchase schemes for Irish tenants, produced retaliatory British tariffs on Irish cattle and finally led to the raising of general tariff walls between the two countries. The new Irish constitution of 1937 introduced a distinctly Catholic and Irish flavour, recognising the 'special position of the Holy Catholic Apostolic and Roman Church as the guardian of the faith professed by the great majority of the citizens.' Northern Ireland was directly affected by these new policies. In 1933 de Valera marked the new Northern policy by standing as an abstentionist for a seat in South Down. More important, Article 2 of the 1937 constitution stated unequivocally, 'The national territory consists of the whole island of Ireland, its islands and its territorial seas.' The trade war between Eire and Great Britain ended with the trade agreement of 1938. But the challenge against partition was not so readily dropped.

Paralleling the deterioration of relations between Northern Ireland and the Irish Free State during the 1930s was a less spectacular but critical tightening of the bonds between Northern Ireland and the rest of the United Kingdom. This development particularly applied to the economic lnks between the two areas. Originally it was thought that taxes levied in Northern Ireland would adequately cover its expenditure, and even leave a surplus for an imperial contribution which was determined at £6.7 million for 1922–23. With the rise of United Kingdom social expenditure and a decline in Northern Ireland's industrial expansion, it soon became clear that such hopes were illusory. Although a token Imperial contribution was maintained—descending to £10,000 p.a. during some of the depression years—a situation was rapidly reached where the rest of the United Kingdom was subsidising Northern Ireland's social benefits. The British Chancellor of the Exchequer recognised and supported this situation in 1938. The Simon declaration of that year not only acknowledged Northern Ireland's entitlement to similar social standards as Great Britain, but that the Westminster exchequer must supply the necessary funds for this if a deficit occurred in Northern Ireland. This principle of parity was naturally welcomed in Northern Ireland. Its short-term effect was to further widen the standards of social services north and south of the border; it was some time before it became clear that such financial concessions might imply conditions and obligations from Westminster which had been avoided in the early years of the new state. The increase in Britain's financial involvement in Northern

Ireland following the Second World War—the establishment of the welfare state—led to the first British insistence that Stormont was obliged to adopt British standards in legislation. The Education Act (NI) in 1947 and the increase in family allowances in 1956 were two examples of British intervention to prevent the possibility of social services funds being distributed in a discriminatory fashion.

The immediate post-war years also saw statements in both Southern Ireland and Great Britain about the position of Northern Ireland. Ironically enough, the declaration of an Irish Republic and its withdrawal from the British Commonwealth was carried, not by Fianna Fail which had lost office in 1948, but by a coalition government under John Costello. Sheehy may exaggerate when he claimed that these actions 'set the seal on Irish disunity' (Sheehy 1955, 66) but they certainly aroused fervour among Northern Ireland unionists. The 1949 general election there, known as the Union Jack election, was fought largely on the issue of the union, thought by some to be in danger from a Labour government in Britain. In 1949 the Ireland act was designed to dispel such fears:

> It is hereby declared that Northern Ireland remains part of His Majesty's dominions and of the United Kingdom, and it is hereby affirmed that in no event will Northern Ireland or any part thereof cease to be part of His Majesty's dominions and of the United Kingdom without the consent of the parliament of Northern Ireland.

This strong British guarantee, and the severing of the Commonwealth relationship between Southern Ireland and Great Britain, might have been expected to inflame passions between the two parts of Ireland and within Northern Ireland itself. There were indeed communal stresses in the North following the election, and the Republic launched an international anti-partition campaign. But by the early fifties matters returned to normal, and a period of comparative stability returned for almost two decades. Britain had Conservative governments between 1951 and 1964. Never keen to enter the murky waters of Irish politics and diplomacy unless dragged in, they confined their interest to the economic field. Today Britain takes almost 70 per cent of the Republic's exports, and supplies more than half her imports; and this relationship is reflected in emigration patterns from the Republic. Before 1936 well over half of Ireland's emigrants went to the United States; after that date, Great Britain became the main destination. The economic dependency on Britain was conspicuous enough for Boserup to claim that, in economic terms, the union between the Republic of Ireland and the United Kingdom was being restored. Nor was this all. The Republic of Ireland, quite apart from her relations with Britain, developed a much more outward-looking foreign policy from the 1950s, becoming actively involved in the United Nations movement, and eventually joining the European Economic Community in 1973.

It was in this new context of internationalism that the first few cautious steps of North–South co-operation began. Significantly, they were largely confined to economic interests which affected both areas. Thus in 1952 agreement was reached that both governments should take over the Foyle fisheries. This was followed by joint involvement in draining the Erne basin and in a hydro-electric development there. Between 1953 and 1958 the Great Northern Railway, which included the Belfast–Dublin line, was operated jointly by the two governments and has since been operated jointly.

The meeting which took place in 1965 between the Northern and Southern premiers, Terence O'Neill and Sean Lemass, was a logical extension of these developments, but its symbolism was not lost in both parts of the island. They seemed to many to represent the new Ireland which had at last shaken off the past, men interested in prosperity rather than politics, in opportunities for co-operation instead of excuses for conflict. The effect inside Northern Ireland was considerable. The Nationalist party agreed to become the official opposition at Stormont and the Catholic hierarchy appointed a chaplain to parliament. 'Twin towns' were established across the border, their citizens exchanging visits and experiences. Relations between north and south, and between both of them and Britain, had never been closer, and the prospects of a period of community harmony seemed good. They were to be destroyed by a mixture of majority tardiness and minority impatience. The events following from the Civil Rights campaign were to alter radically both internal relations inside Northern Ireland, and Northern Ireland's relations with her immediate neighbours.

2

Law and Order

Paddy Hillyard

The principal aim of this chapter is to describe the different strategies which the authorities have used to deal with political violence in Northern Ireland over the last twelve years. The analysis will attempt to draw out some of the more important features which have tended to be overlooked in those accounts which have been more concerned to highlight the sectarian aspects of the strategies. The principal conclusion of the analysis is that the form of the repressive strategy adopted during the last six years, far from being exceptional and a product of the unique circumstances of the political violence in Northern Ireland is, on the contrary, the form which many modern capitalist states are evolving.

No understanding of the various strategies adopted over the last twelve years is possible without a discussion of law and order in the period from the setting up of the regional government and parliament in the six counties by the Government of Ireland Act (1920).

1920–1969: Special Powers Extraordinary

By mid-summer 1920 the British government had to contend with two law and order problems in the six counties. Both were to remain a feature until the present day. On the one hand, it had to deal with attacks by the IRA and on the other it had to cope with the sectarian attacks, which were mainly carried out on Catholics. It had two forces at its disposal: the Royal Irish Constabulary (RIC), which was controlled by a divisional commissioner outside Belfast and a city commissioner within the city; and various military units stationed in the North. (see Buckland 1979, 179–205). At the time the British government was hard-pressed in the south and west and no more troops could be sent north. Indeed, there was in fact pressure for troops from the north to be sent south (Farrell 1980, 126). In October 1920, the

British government announced the establishment of the Ulster Special Constabulary (USC). (For full details of the creation of the USC see Farrell 1980, 125–137). It was based upon the UVF—a totally Protestant paramilitary force—which had been reorganised a few months earlier with the tacit approval of the British government. Hence, the USC was from the outset exclusively Protestant. It was divided into three classes. Class 'A' was for those willing to do full-time duty and be posted anywhere within Northern Ireland; Class 'B' was for those willing to do part-time duty in their own locality; and Class 'C' was for those willing to go on reserve and who could be called upon in an emergency. This last class was vaguely defined and became little more than a device to give gun licences to loyalists and refuse them to Catholics. (Farrell 1979, 127). By August 1922 there were 7,000 'A' Specials, 20,000 'B' Specials and 17,000 in a re-constituted 'C' Class. There were also 1,200 full-time members of the newly formed Royal Ulster Constabulary (RUC) which had replaced the RIC in May of the same year.

The Specials played the central role in the establishment of the authority of the new government in Northern Ireland. From the outset their activities were controversial. They were undisciplined and partisan and were regarded by Catholics with a bitterness exceeding that which the Black and Tans inspired in the South.

Their sectarian conduct, as Farrell (1979, 184) points out, contributed to the peculiarly intense hatred with which the RUC has been regarded ever since by the Catholic population in the North. Not only were the two forces linked together in the public mind, but also half the initial recruits for the RUC came from the 'A' Specials.

While Farrell emphasises the role of the British government in the creation of the USC, Bew, Gibbon and Patterson (1979, 57–74) draw attention to the changes which were taking place within the Protestant class bloc. They argue that, in order to challenge republicanism independently of the British, the Unionist leadership had to give up some of its power to the Orange section of the Protestant working class. The form of the Unionist state apparatus can therefore be seen as a product of the class relations within the Unionist bloc coupled with British approval and support. In other words, they argue that the form of the Unionist state apparatus was not exclusively a product of external politics.

Another central element of the Unionist repressive state apparatus was the Civil Authorities (Special Powers) Act. This was passed in

1922 and gave the Minister of Home Affairs power 'to take all such steps... as may be necessary for preserving peace and maintaining order'. It conferred wide powers of arrest, questioning, search, detention and internment on the police and other agents of the Ministry of Home Affairs. It constituted an effective abrogation of the rule of law in the sense that the forces of law and order had the power to arrest and detain anyone they pleased without having to give any justification and without fear of being called to account in respect of any decisions later shown to be unjustified. Northern Ireland from the outset was therefore a state with extraordinary powers.

The Civil Authorities (Special Powers) Act was renewed annually until 1928 when it was extended for five years. At the end of 1933 it was made permanent. It was extensively criticised in the late thirties by NCCL (1935).

The law and order strategy of successive Unionist governments was unequivocal. A constant watch was maintained on Catholic communities and, whenever the state appeared to be under threat—for example, during the IRA campaigns of 1921–22, 1938–39 and 1956–62—the government introduced internment under the Civil Authorities (Special Powers) Act. It was also used on other occasions, as for instance when Republican politicians were interned for a week during a Royal visit in 1951. The main point to emphasise about internment was its wholly executive nature. The formal power provided for in the Civil Authorities (Special Powers) Act permitted the arrest and detention of anyone who was acting, had acted or was about to act 'in a manner prejudicial to the preservation of the peace and maintenance of order'. The responsibility for making the internment order after arrest lay with the Minister who was also personally responsible for ordering the release of internees. While there was provision for the appointment of an advisory committee to review the cases, the Minister was not bound to accept the recommendations. Internment was therefore a wholly executive measure. Its use highlighted the executive's direct involvement in suppressing political opposition. It was not surprising that the Cameron Commission found that its presence on the Statute book, and the continuance in force of regulations made under it, had caused widespread resentment among Catholics (Cameron 1969, 62–63). It had after all been used almost exclusively against them to suppress all political opposition to the Northern Ireland regime.

As well as the lack of confidence in the forces of law and order and the festering grievance of the Civil Authorities (Special Powers) Act, Catholics also had little confidence in the courts in Northern Ireland. This stemmed principally from the composition of both the judiciary and juries. The Northern Ireland judiciary throughout its history had been mainly composed of people who had been openly associated with the Unionist party. Of the twenty high court judges appointed since 1922, fifteen had been openly associated with the Unionist party and fourteen of the county court appointments had similar associations. Residents magistrates had also been drawn from the same source. While it does not follow that the decisions of judges and magistrates would be partisan, the composition of both the magistracy and the judiciary did little to inspire the confidence of Catholics in the administration of justice.

The composition of juries further exacerbated the problem of confidence in the administration of justice. Partly as a result of property qualification and partly as a result of the rules concerning the right to stand by or challenge jurors, the composition of juries was mainly Protestant. The qualification for jury service was based upon the ownership of property and as Catholics owned less property, this ensured that the majority on the jury list were Protestants. At this stage, the prosecution was entitled to stand by any number of jurors and the defence might challenge up to twelve without giving any reason, and might object to others for good cause. The end result was that most juries, particularly in Belfast, were Protestant. The risk of bias against Catholics was therefore always present.

It can be seen from this brief analysis of the law and order strategy adopted by successive Unionist governments that it was highly repressive, sectarian and centralised. Moreover, throughout the period, no attempt was made to disguise the political nature of the struggle nor of the response. It was successful in so far as it maintained the regime in power for fifty years. But from the outset it continually alienated the minority community from both the law and the state.

1969–1971: Reform and Repression

The response of the British government, after deploying troops in Northern Ireland in August 1969, was to pressurize the government at Stormont to introduce a series of reforms which, in essence, were aimed to establish a series of institutions to guarantee equality of treatment and freedom from discrimination for the Catholic community.

The principal reforms in the area of policing followed closely the recommendations of the Hunt Committee (1969). The object of the reform was to neutralise the political control of the police and to establish a wholly civilian and non-armed police force. Consequently, the 'B' Specials were disbanded and a new force, the Ulster Defence Regiment, was established under the control of the British Army. In addition, the RUC was disarmed and made accountable to a Police Authority. The continuing violence, however, soon led to the rearming of the police.

The Hunt Committee also recommended the introduction of an independent prosecutor on the Scottish model. But the Unionist government delayed in the implementation of this reform by establishing a committee to consider the proposals (MacDermott Working Party 1971). It was not until after Direct Rule in 1972 that a new office of a Director of Public Prosecutions was set up with full responsibility for the selection and prosecution of all serious criminal charges.

At the same time as the police was being reformed the Unionist government brought in tougher legislation under the Criminal Justice (Temporary Provision) Act (1970) to deal with rioters (Boyle 1970). The Act provided a six months minimum mandatory gaol sentence for anyone convicted of 'riotous behaviour', 'disorderly behaviour' or 'behaviour likely to cause a breach of the peace'. The new law immediately gave rise to numerous allegations of the partisan way in which the legislation was being enforced.

Outside the area of the administration of justice, other reforms were taking place. The discriminatory practices of local government were dealt with by extending local government franchise but at the same time denuding local authorities of considerable powers. A new centralised housing authority was established and administrative units were set up to manage education, planning and health and social services. (For full details see O'Dowd, Rolston and Tomlinson 1980; and Birrell and Murie 1980.)

While all these legislative changes were taking place, the situation on the streets was deteriorating. The relations between the army and the Catholic community were rapidly declining as the army took a tougher line against rioters. In 1970, a routine house search precipitated a large scale riot and the army introduced a curfew (O'Fearghael 1970). The conflict was slowly escalating into a guerrilla war between the army and the IRA.

In summary, in this period the strategy of the British government was not to define the problem in terms of law and order but to deal with it at a number of different levels. On the one hand, there was a very real attempt to correct the arbitrary and inequitable administration of criminal laws and to establish institutions which would deal with the widespread problem of discrimination. Liberal notions such as the separation of powers, the rule of law, the impartiality and objectivity of judges, and democratic institutions to check the exercise of power were mobilised in support of the reforms but no attempt was made to ensure that the notions were realised in practice. The creation of new institutions and the dispersal of power has meant that the various bodies, which are relatively autonomous, have established their own modus operandi; they have structured their own targets and objectives. The dominant feature has been their tendency to reconstitute practical and legal problems as technical matters. On the other hand, the increasing violence on the streets, coupled with the demands of the Protestant community for tougher measures, led to the development of a more coercive strategy to deal with the problem of violence.

1971–1975: Internment and Military Security

The strategy in this period was dominated by the use of internment and the development by the army either through encouragement or by default of its own military security policy. This involved the introduction of a series of techniques which have been used in colonial emergencies in the past and developed by Brigadier Kitson (1971). The combined aim of these techniques was to collect as much information on the IRA in particular and the Catholic community in general. I will deal with each component in turn.

Internment and Detention

Internment was introduced with the agreement of the British government on the 9th August, 1971. The army and police arrested 342 men on the initial sweep. Within six months 2,357 persons had been arrested and 1,600 released after interrogation. The introduction, impact and subsequent use of internment has been extensively documented and the details need not concern us here (see, for example, McGuffin 1973; Faul and Murray 1974). The main point to emphasise is that its use provided an example of unfettered ministerial discretion and highlighted the political nature of the struggle. The state's involvement in suppressing political opposition was clear and unequivocal.

After internment, the level of violence increased rapidly. Many Catholics holding public appointments withdrew from these offices and a rent and rates strike was begun. In January 1972 the army killed 13 civilians during a Civil Rights march in Derry. An official inquiry by the Lord Chief Justice only inflamed the situation as his report exonerated those responsible. (Widgery Tribunal 1972; for critical commentaries see Dash 1972; McMahon 1974).

After Direct Rule was imposed in March 1972, a slight shift took place in the internment strategy. Following the breakdown of discussions between the IRA and the government, a new system of detention without trial was introduced. The principal development was to replace the executive authority of the Minister under the Special Powers Act by a new system of judicial determination. All cases now came before an independent judicial Commissioner (see Boyle, Hadden and Hillyard 1975, 58–77). The aim was to distance the executive from the day-to-day administration of the emergency powers in an attempt to depoliticise the nature of the response in order to gain the confidence of the minority community in the system. It represented the beginning of a strategy which was to find its ultimate and most sustained and strongest expression in the criminalisation policies which were introduced in 1975. The operation of these new procedures received widespread criticisms (see, for example, Faul & Murray 1973). The whole system of detention appeared to be dominated by the policies of the security forces and the quasi-judicial hearings were farcical. The new scheme did little to gain the confidence of Catholics. When the government began detaining Protestants in February 1973 the opposition to detention became more widespread.

The last point to note about detention is that those who were detained were not treated like other convicted persons. They were placed in compounds and accommodated in huts rather than cells and were permitted considerable autonomy within the compounds. They were also granted the same rights as prisoners on remand. This meant that they could wear their own clothes and have more visits, letters and parcels than convicted persons. Similar rights were also extended in June 1972 to those who had been convicted in the courts and who claimed to have been politically motivated. These concessions amounted to what was called 'Special Status Category'.

Further changes were made to the detention procedures after the review of measures to deal with terrorism by a committee chaired by Lord Gardiner (1975). These changes were incorporated in the

Northern Ireland (Emergency Provisions) Act of 1975 and involved a slight move back towards a system of executive detention. But they were of little importance as the use of detention without trial was suspended in February 1975 and a totally new strategy for dealing with those involved in political violence was introduced. During the period in which internment and detention had been in operation a total of 2,158 orders were issued.

Diplock Commission

At this point it is useful to consider the Diplock Commission (1972) because it strongly influenced the way in which the police and army operated in this period. It was also responsible for the form of the strategy adopted in the period 1975 onwards, which will be dealt with later.

The first point concerns the composition of the Commission. The members of the Commission were Lord Diplock, Lord Rupert Cross, Sir Kenneth Younger, a former Intelligence Corps Major, and George Woodcock, a former General Secretary of the TUC. The late Lord Cross was a Professor of Criminal Law and had been a member of the Criminal Law Revision Committee which recommended the abolition of the right to silence (1972).

The second point concerns the type of evidence the Commission collected. The Commission did not go to Northern Ireland. Only Lord Diplock visited the Province and then only on two occasions. The bulk of the evidence was oral and was taken from people with responsibility for the administration of justice in Northern Ireland, and from representatives of the Civil and Armed Services.

The third and most important point is that the report was produced for the authorities responsible for law and order and not for the people of Northern Ireland as a whole. The underlying problem of the political struggle between opposing groups of very different aspirations was totally ignored and the sole focus was upon the maintenance of public order. In this context, civil rights in general and the rights of suspects in particular, appear as exceptional, anachronistic and even subversive. Long-established common law principles were reconstituted as 'technical rules'. For example, the principle concerning the admissability of statements, which is fundamental in an adversary system of criminal justice, was described in a number of places as a 'technical rule'. Burton and Carlin (1979, 83–84) appear to make a similar point, regrettably in jargon-ladened and absurdly complex language, when they describe the Diplock report in the following way:

> Its intra-discursive logic is as incoherent as its epistemological justi-
> fication. Though argued in terms of essentialised justice, relocated
> within legal evolution, the changes in the technical guarantees of
> objectivity remain but a part of the syntagmatic strategy which
> orders the paradigms of the common law mode towards a unity of
> its discursive object: the discursive appropriation of an official word
> whose otherness is beyond recognition.

Most of the Commission's recommendations were included in the
Northern Ireland (Emergency Provisions) Act which came into force
in August 1973. The army was provided with the power to stop and
detain a suspect for up to four hours, and both the army and police
were also given the further power to stop and question any person as
to his or her identity and knowledge of terrorist incidents. In addition,
the police were given the power to arrest any one they suspected of
being a terrorist and detain them for up to 72 hours. No grounds of
reasonableness were required. This particular provision, it should be
noted, was introduced to enable the administrative procedures
required by the Detention of Terrorist Order to be carried out. The
Act also provided extensive powers of search. Finally, the Act
abolished juries and introduced far-reaching changes in the rules of
evidence.

The Northern Ireland (Emergency Provisions) Act, like the Special
Powers Act, constituted an effective abrogation of the rule of law.

Military Security

The Act provided ample opportunities for the army to extend its
military security policy, which it had been developing throughout 1970.
This involved among other things the creation and maintenance of as
complete a dossier as was practicable on all inhabitants in Republican
areas. The military strategists referred to this as 'contact information'
(Kitson 1971, 96). The principal methods involved interrogation in
depth, frequent arrest for screening, regular house searches and head
counts.

Internment provided the first opportunity for interrogation in depth
to be used by the army. A group of internees were selected and
interrogated in depth using a selection of techniques based upon the
psychology of sensory deprivation. (see for details McGuffin 1974;
Amnesty International 1973; Faul and Murray 1972). The impact and

effect of these techniques were considerable (Shallice 1973). While subsequently there was a committee of enquiry set up under the chairpersonship of Sir Edmund Compton to consider the allegations of torture and brutality during interrogation, the principal issue as to whom authorised the techniques was never investigated (Compton 1971). As it was, the Compton Committee produced a most unsatisfactory conclusion that while the techniques used did constitute physical ill-treatment they did not amount to brutality. A further enquiry was later established under the chairpersonship of Lord Parker to consider whether interrogation in depth should be permitted to be continued (Parker 1972).

In the meantime, the Irish Republic filed an application before the European Commission of Human Rights (1976). The case eventually went to the European Court where it was held that the techniques, contrary to the findings of the Commission, did not constitute a practice of torture but of inhuman and degrading treatment. The British government undertook that the techniques would never be reintroduced. The government subsequently paid out £188,250 in damages to the persons involved.

The other methods of army intelligence gathering included the use of foot patrols to build up a detailed picture of the area and its inhabitants, house searches, and frequent arrests for questioning. While these methods were used extensively under the Special Powers Act, their use was increased after the introduction of the recommendations of the Diplock Commission in the Northern Ireland (Emergency Provisions) Act.

No figures are available on the number of people stopped and questioned on the street. Nor are any figures available on the number of persons arrested and detained up to four hours. But it is known that these methods were used very widely. On occasions large scale arrest operations were initiated and people arrested at random for apparently no other reason other than to collect more information on the local community (Boyle, Hadden and Hillyard 1975, 41–53).

Figures are, however, available for the number of house searches and these provide some indication of the extent of the army's intelligence gathering operations and how they expanded over the period after the introduction of the Northern Ireland (Emergency Provisions) Act. In 1971, there were 17,262 house searches. By 1973, this had risen to 75,000, one fifth of all houses in Northern Ireland.

Many of the intelligence gathering activities carried out by the army were of dubious legality. It is very doubtful whether large scale house searches or the extensive screening was justified under the Act.

In 1974, the powers of arrest and detention were extended still further under the Prevention of Terrorism Act. This was introduced for the whole of the United Kingdom in the wake of the Birmingham bombings. It provided the power of arrest upon reasonable suspicion and forty-eight hours detention in the first instance, which could be extended by up to a further five days by the Secretary of State. In practice, this was another form of executive detention, admittedly for only a three day period. (For a detailed analysis of its operation see Scorer and Hewitt 1981.)

As the conflict between the army and the IRA intensified the army resorted to a variety of other techniques in order to attempt to defeat the IRA. There is considerable evidence to suggest that the army used agents provocateurs, a variety of undercover techniques and assassination squads (Lindsay 1980; Brady et al. 1977; Geraghty 1977). In addition, it developed new technologies. These included new methods of crowd control, new surveillance apparatus and the computerisation of all its intelligence information (see Ackroyd et al. 1977; Wright 1977; Wright 1978).

The RUC during this period took a subordinate role. It was largely excluded from policing the main Catholic areas. There was thus a very clear difference in the deployment patterns of the security forces with the police mainly controlling Protestant areas where they used an approach closer to traditional police approach and the army operating principally in Republican areas where it used the methods described above. This differential deployment served only to alienate further the Catholic community.

One response of the RUC to the crisis of confidence within the Catholic community was to concentrate on developing community relations work. A community relations branch was established in October 1970 and the Chief Inspector in charge of the branch was despatched to London to study the methods used by the Metropolitan Police in both youth and community relations. The branch worked mainly with young people organising discos, rambles, adventure holidays and football matches. In addition, the RUC has made strenuous efforts to establish working relationships with all the local politicians.

From a broader perspective, it can be seen that the strategy in this period had three dominant features. In the first place, the strategy openly acknowledged the political dimensions of the struggle. Detainees were treated like 'prisoners of war' and the politics of those convicted in the courts was recognised in the granting of 'special status category'. Secondly, the strategy gave the army considerable autonomy. There was little attempt to control its operations and practices, many of which were of dubious legality. The third feature of the strategy was the extensive use which was made of judges. They were not only used to provide a veneer of detention, but were also used to chair enquiries. Up to the end of 1975 seven enquiries had been chaired by judges. These were of two types. On the one hand, there were those which investigated some controversial incident or event, such as a Bloody Sunday. On the other, there were those which reviewed the appropriateness of particular policies, for example the Diplock Commission's review of the 'legal procedures to deal with terrorist activities'. The role of judges in part stemmed from the nature of the investigations, but it also reflected the extent to which the authorities hoped to diffuse a difficult political situation or to distance themselves from recommendations which were likely to be controversial. As Harvey (1981, 6) has pointed out:

> The fiction of the doctrine of the constitutional separation of power has never been more clearly exposed than by these attempts to assure the public that British judges can provide solutions to the political problems of Northern Ireland.

1975–1982: Reconstituting the Problem of Political Violence

Following the Labour Government's victory in 1974, it began to reconsider the strategy of dealing with violence in Northern Ireland. It subsequently initiated a totally different strategy. The central aim was to deny totally the political dimensions of the conflict and to reconstitute the problem in terms of law and order. To this end, the Government initiated three related policies. First, it began to restore full responsibility for law and order to the RUC. This policy has since been described as Ulsterisation. Second, it stopped the use of internment in February 1975 and began to rely upon the courts as the sole method of dealing with those suspected of violence. Third, it announced that special status category would be withdrawn for any prisoner sentenced for crimes commited after March 1st, 1976. The latter two policies have been widely referred to as a policy of criminalisation.

Ulsterisation

The first indication of the Ulsterisation policy came in April 1974 when the new Secretary of State for Northern Ireland, Merlyn Rees, announced that he intended to restore 'the full responsibility of law and order to the police'. Later in the year he announced a five-point plan for the further extension of policing. The plan consisted of setting up a series of new local police centres in selected communities to act as focal points for policing. They were to be mainly staffed by RUC reserves working in their own areas.

The impact of the policy of Ulsterisation can be best illustrated by considering the numbers in the security forces. In 1973, there were 31,000 security personnel of whom 14,500 were in the UDR, RUC and RUC Reserve. In 1980, the total numbers were roughly similar, but the numbers in the UDR, RUC and RUC Reserve had expanded to 19,500. As the vast majority of personnel in these forces are Protestant, one effect of the policy of Ulsterisation has been to replace British security personnel by Ulster Protestants. The policy of Ulsterisation has also been characterised by an expansion in the weaponry for the force. The RUC is now armed with pistols and sterling sub-machine guns, M1 carbines and SLRs. In this respect, the RUC has therefore returned to being a military force rather than a civilian force which the Hunt Committee had recommended.

Perhaps the most important development since the start of the Ulsterisation policy has been the strengthening of the intelligence capacity of the RUC. This has taken a number of different forms: an expansion in the number of confidential telephones, the use of police informers and various surveillance techniques and the use of arrest and detention powers to interrogate at length all those whom the police consider may provide them with information. The use of these powers for interrogation has been a major feature of the strategy and it appears that the widespread screening and trawling which the army carried out in the previous period is now being carried out by the RUC.

The police, as has been noted, have very extensive powers of arrest and detention under the Northern Ireland (Emergency Provisions) Act and the Prevention of Terrorism Act. In addition, they have ordinary powers of arrest under the criminal law. The most frequently used power is Section 11 of the Northern Ireland (Emergency Provisions) Act which allows the police to arrest anyone they suspect of being a terrorist. The use of this power is not surprising as this power is broadest in scope in terms of the degree of suspicion required and allows detention for a longer period than all the other provisions except the seven day power under the Prevention of Terrorism Act. The almost exclusive use of Section 11 rather than ordinary powers of arrest illustrates very clearly the way in which emergency powers become the norm. More importantly, the effect of mainly using this particular power has been to shift the basis of arrest from suspicion of a particular act to suspicion of the status of the individual (Hillyard and Boyle 1982, 8).

No figures are regulary published for the number of arrests and pro-secutions under the Northern Ireland (Emergency Provisions) Act in contrast to the practice for arrests under the Prevention of Terrorism Act. However, two sets of arrest figures have been published which illustrate not only the extent to which arrest and detention powers are used only for intelligence gathering, but also how the practice is on the increase.

The Bennett Committee (1979, 141) noted that 2,970 persons were arrested under the Northern Ireland (Emergency Provisions) Act and Prevention of Terrorism Act and detained for more than four hours between the 1st September and 31st August, 1978. But only 35 per cent were subsequently charged with an offence. In other words, over 1,900 people were arrested, interrogated and subsequently released.

The other set of arrest figures was published in reply to a parlia-mentary question in Hansard on the 7th December. These figures show that between 1st January and 30th October 1980, 3,868 persons were arrested under the Northern Ireland (Emergency Provisions) Act and Prevention of Terrorism Act and detained for more than four hours. Yet only 11 per cent were charged. When the actual number of persons arrested, interrogated and released are compared and adjusted so that the figures refer to periods of the same length, they show that the number of persons involved has more than doubled from 1,900 in 1978 to 4,131 in 1980.

Even those who were subsequently charged are often extensively questioned about 'other matters' not associated with the offence in question. In the most recent survey of the Diplock Courts it was found that in over 80 per cent of all cases the suspect made a confession within the first six hours of detention. Yet the vast majority of these people were interrogated for substantial periods after the confession (Walsh 1982, 7).

The evidence is therefore unequivocal. The powers of arrest and interrogation are being primarily used by the police to collect information on individuals and communities rather than to charge and prosecute. Policing in Northern Ireland has therefore moved from a retro-active form, where those suspected of illegal activities are arrested and processed through the courts on evidence obtained after the event, to a pre-emptive form, where large sections of those communities which are perceived as being a distinct threat to the existing *status quo* are regularly and systematically monitored and surveilled.

Monitoring and surveillance of problem groups is being extended in other directions. In January 1979, a committee was set up under the chairpersonship of Sir Harold Black to review legislation and services relating to the care and treatment of children and young persons. It recommended a comprehensive and integrated approach to provide help for children emphasising the important roles of the family, school and community (Black Review 1976). More specifically, it proposed a dual system of coordinating teams in schools and at district level. The school-based care teams are to be made up of the appropriate counsellor, the education welfare officer, the educational psychologist, the social worker familiar with the catchment area, as well as representatives from the police and probation service. At the district level, it was suggested that representatives of statutory agencies concerned with the interests of children should meet together to discuss the best policies to deal with identified problems. In December 1979, the government endorsed the strategy proposed by the report and accepted its recommendations in principle. The government is at present consulting the various interests concerned.

The report appears to be remarkably progressive. It begins with an analysis of the social and economic problems of Northern Ireland. Throughout, it emphasises that the needs of children are paramount. Furthermore, it argues that it is imperative to avoid as far as possible segregating children from their families, schools and communities or labelling them as deviant, abnormal, troublesome or delinquent. The Report, however, is totally uncritical of its own assumptions. In particular, it assumes that the task of identifying children in need is unproblematic and that professionals and parents will agree. But how many working-class parents in West or East Belfast, would view 'the lack of attainment at school, apathy, persistent behaviour, truancy, or involvement in delinquent or criminal activity' as 'the outward manifestation of complex, personal or family problems' (Black Review 1979, 6) rather than the result of their children's position in the broader cultural and political environment in which they are brought up?

If the strategy of a coordinated approach through school-based and district care teams is implemented in full, it will extend the monitoring and surveillance of particular populations. It is clear from the Report that this is the principal aim of the approach. It states (Black Review 1979, 9):

> There should be a free exchange of information among the agencies involved in the multi-disciplinary team. Problems manifesting themselves in the school, in the home or in the community, whether they first come to the attention of the education authorities, the social services or the police should be referred to the School-based Care Team for discussion and consideration of what help, if any, each of the agencies might provide for the child and his family to help solve the problem.

The more efficient control of particular populations has been attempted at other levels. There is now some evidence to suggest that both the RUC and the Army are playing a significant role in the physical planning of Belfast. An article in the *Guardian* of the 13th March, 1982 claimed that the Belfast Development Office, to which the Housing Executive forwards all its proposed building plans for clearance, has representatives from the security forces. It was also suggested that the security forces has interfered with a number of planning decisions: they had insisted that a group of houses were removed from a planned development in the Ardoyne; asked for reinforced pavements in the new Poleglass estate to bear the weight of armoured vehicles; and recommended high 'security walls' in new developments in the Lower Falls and at Roden Street in West Belfast (see also Alcorn 1982).

Other sources have argued that the involvement of the security forces has been more extensive. It is claimed that new housing estates have been built with only two entrances and that factories, warehousing and motorways have been deliberately constructed to form barriers. The aim of these developments, it is suggested, is to prevent residents in Catholic areas from moving from one part of the city to another through safe areas and to force people out on to the main roads, which are more easily policed. If all these developments have occurred then the authorities would appear to be making strenuous attempts to confine the problem of violence within particular areas. In other words, they seem to be deliberately creating ghettos in which dissident populations may be easily contained.

The role of the army in the period from 1975 has changed considerably. Its method of intelligence gathering has altered substantially with the rise of the RUC's work in this respect. There has been a very sharp decline in the number of houses searched by the army and the large-scale screening operations have been curtailed. However, there is evidence to suggest that the army still carries out undercover and substantial surveillance operations. In addition, they are responsible for all the bomb disposal work.

The strategy of Ulsterisation has not been without its problems. The army has resented the curtailment of its operations and has developed its own strategies on occasions to deal with those involved in political violence. In a series of incidents, a number of alleged terrorists have been shot dead. While the strains between the RUC and the army have been in existence for a long time, they appear to have deteriorated since the RUC took the dominant role. In August 1979 following the assassination of Lord Mountbatten and the killing of eighteen soldiers at Warrenpoint, the Prime Minister visited Ulster and was told that the strategy of Ulsterisation had failed and that the army should once again take the dominant role. A few weeks later Sir Morris Oldfield was appointed as Security Coordinator. The appointment clearly was an attempt to deal with the differences of approach between the two forces.

The Diplock Court Process

The strategy of relying upon the courts was made possible by the radical modifications in the ordinary criminal process which the Diplock Commission recommended in 1972 and which were enacted in the Emergency Provisions (Northern Ireland) Act 1973. These changes, however, did not become significant until the courts were relied upon as a sole method of dealing with those involved in political violence from the end 1975 onwards.

It was abundantly clear from the Diplock Commission's report that interrogation was considered to be an essential element for the successful prosecution and conviction of those involved. The Commission was critical of what it described as 'technical rules and practice' concerning the admissibility of statements. It drew attention to the 'considerable rigidity' with which the judges rules had been interpreted in Northern Ireland. It noted a decision of the Court of Appeal in which it had been ruled that the mere creation by the authorities of any 'set-up which makes it more likely that those who did not wish to speak will eventually do so' renders any confession involuntary and inadmissible. It clearly disagreed with judgments such as these and it pointed out (Diplock Commission 1972, 30):

> The whole technique of skilled interrogation is to build up an atmosphere in which the initial desire to remain silent is replaced by an urge to confide in the questioner.

It recommended that all statements in breach of the common law should be admitted provided that they could not be shown to have been produced by subjecting the accused to torture or to inhuman or degrading treatment. The recommendation was enacted in the Emergency Provisions (Northern Ireland) Act 1973. The provision not only eliminated any retrospective control over the way interrogation was conducted but also legalised, in combination with the power to detain a person up to 72 hours under the Emergency Provisions Act or seven days under the Prevention of Terrorism Act, prolonged interrogation.

The Commission however was not only responsible for legalising prolonged interrogation. In not supporting the Court of Appeal position concerning 'set-ups' which were designed to make it 'more likely that those who did not wish to speak will eventually do so', it gave the green light to the authorities to create special interrogation centres. Two were built, one at Castlereagh and the other at Gough Barracks and were designed to create the most conducive environment for the interrogation process. Castlereagh was opened in early 1977 and Gough later in the same year.

The subsequent history of these centres is now well-known (Taylor 1980). From early 1977 the number of complaints against the police in respect of ill-treatment during interrogation began to increase. The Association of Forensic Medical Officers made representations to the Police Authority as early as April 1977. In November 1977 Amnesty International carried out an investigation and called for a public enquiry into the allegations (Amnesty 1978). The Government, shortly after receiving Amnesty International's report, established the Bennett Committee not however to investigate the allegations themselves but to consider police interrogation procedures. Notwithstanding their restrictive terms of reference the Committee (1979, 136) however did conclude that:

> Our own examination of medical evidence reveals cases in which injuries, whatever their precise cause, were not self-inflicted and were sustained in police custody.

Apart from the evidence of ill-treatment, the other aspect of the interrogation process which gave rise to concern during this period, and subsequently, has been the extent to which the outcome of the trial was in fact determined in the police interrogation centres. In an analysis of all cases dealt with in the Diplock Courts between January and April 1979, it was found that 86 per cent of all defendants had made a confession (Boyle, Hadden and Hillyard 1980, 44). Of these, 56 per cent of prosecutions relied solely upon evidence of admission, and in another 30 per cent this was supplemented by additional forensic or identification evidence which pointed to the guilt of the accused, although this additional evidence would often not have been sufficient to justify a conviction on its own. In a more recent study, a very similar pattern has been found (Walsh 1982). What these figures show is the extent to which the forum for determining guilt or innocence is only very occasionally the courtroom.

The Bennett Committee made a large number of recommendations to prevent abuse of the suspect during interrogation. The most important of which was perhaps the recommendation that all interviews should be monitored by members of the uniformed branch on close-circuit televisions. Most of the Bennett Committee's proposals have now been implemented. It should be emphasised, however, that all the recommendations were designed to prevent physical abuse during interrogation. The safeguards do little to curtail the extreme psychological pressures which are at the heart of the interrogation process.

Since the introduction of the Bennett Committee's suggestions there have been far fewer complaints against the police in respect of ill-treatment during interrogation. It is however hard to ascertain whether this is simply due to Bennett. The underlying assumption was that the pressure to break rules and physically assault suspects stems from the individual policemen themselves. It was assumed that they are either over-zealous or in some circumstances deviant. A similar assumption can be found in the deliberations of the Royal Commission on Criminal Procedure (Hillyard 1981, 86–87). It is a highly questionable assumption, however. There is a considerable body of evidence which suggests that the pressure on the police to break the rules does not stem from the personality characteristics of the policeman but is located within the organisation of policing. The pressures generating physical assaults during questioning tend to be developed in response to the perceived seriousness of the problem and often decisions concerning particular responses are taken at a very high level. Taylor's analysis provides some support for this view. In a chart noting the number of complaints it is clear that there was a tendency for complaints to increase when political pressure was exerted on the police to produce results, such as when there was some public outrage, for example, at the La Mon bombings. When there was public concern about police behaviour, complaints tended to decrease (Taylor 1980, 323).

It is more likely that the introduction of new policies following the appointment of Jack Hermon as the new Chief Constable from the 1st January, 1980 may have been more influential in changing the practices at Castlereagh and Gough than any of the Bennett recommendations. It is certainly known that Hermon was opposed to a policy which relied on confessions to defeat the IRA.

Apart from the centrality of confessions to the effectiveness of the Diplock Courts, there are a number of other important features of the whole process. To begin with, the Diplock system is now handling a large proportion of offences which do not appear to be connected with Loyalist or Republican paramilitary activity or with sectarianism. It is estimated that 40 per cent of all cases processed through the Diplock Courts have nothing to do with the troubles (Walsh 1982, 2). In other words, a system which was widely regarded as a temporary measure to deal with the particular problems of political violence is now becoming the normal process for all offences.

A second feature of the Diplock Court system is the extent to which judges appear to have become case-hardened (Boyle, Hadden and Hillyard 1980, 60–62). Since the introduction of juryless trials, the acquittal rate has been declining. There are a number of possible explanations for this. One widely stated explanation is that the prosecuting authorities are now taking greater care in the selection and preparation of cases. But when the trends for jury trials, for which the same prosecuting authorities have responsibility, are considered, no similar decline in the acquittal rate is observable. On the contrary, jury acquittals have been increasing. These very different trends provide strong support that the declining acquittal rate is principally a result of judges becoming case-hardened.

A third feature of the Diplock Court system is the extent of bargaining. This may occur in connection with either the charges, where the defence enters into negotiations to secure the withdrawal of the more serious charge or charges, or the plea, where the defendant pleads guilty to lesser charges in the expectation of a lower sentence in return for the subsequent saving of time and costs. No research has been carried out to ascertain the extent of plea bargaining, but two separate groups of researchers (Boyle, Hadden and Hillyard 1980, 71–74 and Harvey 1981, 32–33) both note that those involved in the trial process have confirmed that it takes place. Boyle, Hadden and Hillyard (1980, 72) in their study of the cases which were dealt with in the Diplock Courts between January and April 1979 found specific evidence of charge bargaining. In about 20 per cent of all cases the prosecution withdrew or substituted a number of charges which were already on the indictment sheet and in which the defence pleaded to the remaining or substituted charge.

Charge and plea bargaining are, of course, features of other criminal justice systems. What is important about the phenomenon of bargaining in Northern Ireland is that the pressure to bargain is likely to be much more intensive than in other systems. The number and seriousness of cases in Northern Ireland are of a different magnitude and this will tend to place certain organisational demands upon the prosecuting and court authorities to encourage bargaining. In addition, the Bar in Northern Ireland is very small. The importance of this has been well expressed by Harvey (1981, 32):

> Defence lawyers, both solicitors and barristers, are under their own professional, institutional and financial pressures to co-operate with the prosecuting authorities and avoid judicial disapproval. The smaller the bar the greater the presure on its members to avoid a reputation for contesting cases with little likely chance of success.

The study of the Diplock courts in 1979 could not establish that any specific sentence had been reduced as a result of bargaining (Boyle, Hadden and Hillyard 1980, 73). But what did emerge from the data was that the severity of sentences were imposed on defendants refusing to recognise the court while the lowest sentences were imposed on those who pleaded guilty at the very start. In between were sentences on those who pleaded not guilty and seriously contested the case against them. The evidence suggests that the differential in terms of length and severity of sentences as between Loyalist and Republican defendants is not to be explained, as is often suggested (Workers Research Unit 1982) in terms of simple religious or political bias, but rather in terms of the defendant's choice whether to co-operate or not to co-operate with the system. This important point emphasises the need to consider decision making in this or any other criminal process not as a series of sequential phases which can be dealt with in isolation but rather a process involving a complex series of interacting stages in which decisions taken cumulatively contribute to outcomes. Thus, the much discussed argument of whether judge or jury is superior for normal offences should not be conducted without emphasising that decisions as to guilt or innocence are in fact an outcome of this complex bureaucratic process where the principles of criminal law and its procedures interact with the demands of the administration. The context in which judge or jury operates is much more important than whether the final decisions are left to judge or jury or solely to a judge.

The fourth feature of the Diplock Court system which needs to be mentioned is that a higher standard of proof appears to be required in the case of charges laid against the security forces than against civilians. The Bennett Committee (1979, 82) notes that, between 1972 and the end of 1978, 19 officers were prosecuted for alleged offences against prisoners in custody or during the course of interrogation. Of these, only two were convicted but the convictions were set aside on appeal. Another case was *nolle prosequi* and the rest were acquitted. The 1979 study of cases dealt with in the Diplock Courts between January and April 1979 found an acquittal rate of 100 per cent for members of the security forces (Boyle, Hadden and Hillyard, 1980, 79).

Special Category Status

The other strand in the Labour Government's criminalisation policy was to phase out special category status. This, as has been noted above, was granted in 1972 to members of paramilitary organisations who had been convicted in the courts and who had claimed to have been politically motivated. The Gardiner Committee had considered that its introduction had been 'a serious mistake' and argued that it should be abolished (1975, 34). One argument was that the compound system in which the special category prisoners were held made it more likely that prisoners would emerge with an increased commitment to terrorism. The other argument was that it could see no justification in granting privleges 'to a large number of criminals convicted of very serious crimes, in many cases, murder, merely because they claimed political motivation' (Gardiner 1975, 34). The Government concurred with these arguments and announced that no prisoner sentenced for crimes committed after 1st March 1976 could be granted special status category. In March 1980 it announced that this would apply to any prisoner charged after 1st April, 1980 for crimes wherever committed. In practice, this meant that all those convicted would be put into a conventional cellular prison and denied the special privileges which had been granted in 1972. To accommodate the prisoners the government built 800 cells in the form of an H, hence the H-Block protest, at the cost of £19,000 per cell.

There have been many previous struggles in British prisons over special or political status (see Radzinowicz and Hood 1979). But the decision to phase out special category status in Northern Ireland was to lead to the longest ever collective struggle over this issue. (For a detailed account see Coogan 1980). The protest started in September 1976, when Kieran Nugent was sentenced to the new cellular prison at the Maze. He refused to wear the prison clothes issued to him. The authorities reacted with considerable severity. He was kept in solitary confinement, denied exercise and all 'privileges', visits, letters, parcels. In addition, he lost a day's remission for every day of his protest. He was soon joined by other prisoners. The Blanket Protest, as it became known, as the prisoners had only blankets to wear, had begun. The protest soon escalated. In early 1978, after what appeared to be considerable intransigence by the authorities combined with a desire to make life as uncomfortable as possible for the prisoners, the prisoners extended the protest by smearing their cells with their own excreta. In 1980 the women in Armagh prison joined the dirty protest (see McCafferty 1981). On October 10th, 1980 it was announced that prisoners were starting a hunger strike on October 27th, four and a half years after the initial protest had begun.

Hunger strikes have a long tradition in Irish history. They had been used in previous prison struggles and under early Irish Brehon law of the sixth and eighth centuries an offended person fasted on the doorstep of an offender to embarrass them into resolving the dispute. On October 27th, seven men went on hunger strike. This strike was called off on December 18th mainly because one of the seven was about to die and there was, at that time, a widely held view in the prison that the British Government would make a number of important concessions. When the concessions were revealed, they failed to meet the prisoners' expectations. It was their understanding that they were to receive their own clothes and then be issued with civilian prison clothing. The British Government statement, however, issued on the 19th December announcing the concessions, reversed the sequence. Civilian prison clothing had to be accepted before the prisoners could be moved to clean cells (For full details see Browne 1981).

Inevitably, another hunger strike was organised but on this occasion it was decided that volunteers should begin their fasts at intervals. Sands was the first volunteer and began his hunger strike on 1st March, 1981. He died on the 5th May. Nine others died before the hunger strike was ended on the 5th October, 1981, after the Government made a number of concessions. Prisoners were granted the right to wear their own clothes, and new facilities to improve association between prisoners were promised. In addition, a proportion of the loss of remission arising out of the protest was to be restored. In terms of penal reform, these concessions were trivial, but in the face of the Government's intransigence over the five and a half years of prison protest, they were considerable.

Throughout the length of the protest numerous attempts were made by various individuals and organisations to seek a solution to the problems. In 1978, a number of protesting prisoners initiated procedures before the European Commission of Human Rights. They claimed that the regime under which they lived amounted to inhuman and degrading treatment and punishment in breach of Article 3 of the Convention. They also claimed that their right to freedom of conscience and belief under Article 9 of the Convention was denied to them because the prison authorities sought to apply to them the normal prison regimes. The British Government's case was that the conditions were essentially self-inflicted and that the Convention afforded no preferential status for certain categories of prisoners.

In June 1980, the European Commission declared that the major part of the case was inadmissible. It concurred with the British Government's view that these conditions were self-inflicted. It also agreed that the right to preferential status for certain category of prisoners was not guaranteed by the Convention. The Commission, however, was critical of the authorities (1980, 86):

> The Commission must express its concern at the inflexible approach of the state authorities which has been concerned more to punish offenders against prison discipline than to explore ways of resolving such a serious deadlock. Furthermore, the Commission is of the view that for humanitarian reasons, efforts should have been made by the authorities to ensure that the applicants could avail of certain facilities such as taking regular exercise in the open air and with some form of clothing (other than prison clothing) and making greater use of the prison amenities under similar conditions.

The decision, however, did nothing to end the protest. As the confrontation between the authorities and the protesting prisoners intensified, Provisional Sinn Fein began a political campaign in support of the prisoners' claim to political status. An H-Block information centre was established to supply local and foreign journalists with information. The authorities on their part increased their efforts to emphasise the criminality of the activities of the IRA. They issued numerous press releases as well as glossy brochures entitled 'H-Blocks: The Reality', 'Day to Day Life in Northern Ireland Prisons', and 'H-Blocks: What the Papers Say'. In August 1981, they began to issue 'fact files' on each of the hunger strikers. These included a brief description of the activities leading to conviction and a montage of selected newspaper reports on the case.

All these activities emphasised the extent to which the authorities were prepared to go to maintain its policy of criminalisation. They were largely successful in convincing the British media of its case as almost without exception all newspapers and the media accepted the government's position. (see Hillyard 1982; Elliott 1977; Schlesinger 1978; *Information on Ireland* 1979).

The policy of eliminating special category status, however, was fraught with contradiction. To begin with, those involved in political violence are dealt with in a very different way from the ordinary person who gets involved in crime. They are arrested under emergency powers and convicted in radically modified courts. Secondly, the motivations for their activities are very different from those of 'ordinary' criminals. They carry out their activities for deliberate political purposes. They do not regard themselves as 'ordinary' criminals, nor are they seen as such by the communities from which they are drawn. Neither does the law under which they are convicted define them as 'ordinary' criminals. Most were arrested under suspicion of being a 'terrorist'. 'Terrorism' is defined as 'the use of violence for political ends'. As Tomlinson points out, 'they are considered as political in the courtroom but criminal for the purposes of punishment' (O'Dowd, Rolston and Tomlinson 1980, 193).

Third, the abolition of special status category created the anomalous situation in which hundreds of prisoners who had committed similar offences, but at different times, were serving their sentences with special status category in compounds in the very same prison.

Fourth, the penological justifications for the elimination of special status category, namely that the compound system made it more likely that prisoners would 'emerge with an increased commitment to terrorism', was not supported by any empirical evidence. All the evidence which now exists tends to support the opposite conclusion. The 1979 Diplock Court study found that only 11 per cent of all those who came before the courts had previous convictions for scheduled offences (Boyle, Hadden and Hillyard 1980, 22). In other words, very few people who had been released from the Maze were subsequently reconvicted. Further support for the view that the compound system does not encourage 'terrorism' is presented in the only sociological study of the Maze, carried out by Crawford (1979). He found that of a cohort of prisoners leaving the compound between 1976 and 1979 only 12 per cent had been reconvicted for either political or non-political offences (Crawford 1979, 101).

Fifth, the claim that the prison system in Northern Ireland is the best in the world is only part of the truth. Certainly the facilities are better than most but the regime within the prisons, particularly the Maze, is repressive.

When the first hunger strike began, it received widespread support. There were huge demonstrations in Belfast and Dublin. In the north there were 1,205 demonstrations requiring two and a half million hours of police duty. The total cost of policing these parades and the ensuing order was over £12 million (RUC 1982, xii). During the period a hundred thousand rounds of rubber bullets were fired, sixteen thousand in one month alone. The hunger strikes and the authorities response did more to unite Catholic opinion than any other single event since internment in 1971 or Bloody Sunday in 1972.

One very significant feature of the rioting and marches which took place during this time was the extent to which they were confined to the Catholic areas and away from the centres of Belfast and other towns. Any attempt to march to the Belfast city centre was strenuously resisted. The Troubles and the protests have now become ghettorised. The barriers across certain roads and the huge security gates on the roads leading out of the city centre to the Catholic areas are physical reminders of the extent to which this process has taken place. It shows how possible it is for the authorities to confine the problem of street violence to specific areas while life goes on 'normally' elsewhere.

The struggle which developed out of the authorities attempt to deny the political nature of the conflict in order to curtail support for the paramilitaries had considerable unintended consequences. Ironically the policy had the effect of depoliticising the IRA campaign to the extent that it pushed the central aim of the IRA's struggle, its object of achieving Irish unity, into the background. But in its place it provided a powerful humanitarian issue around which to mobilise support. The H-Block issue to the Catholic community was yet another example of a long line of injustices which had been inflicted upon them by Unionist and British administrations.

Conclusions

From a broader perspective a number of the more important characteristics of the repressive response of the state to the conflict in Northern Ireland may be stressed. The first point to note is the extent to which the emergency laws have now become normalised. The emergency legislation is regularly reviewed, the Northern Ireland (Emergency Provisions) Act every six months and the Prevention of Terrorism Act every twelve months, with little or no opposition usually in a sparsely attended House of Commons. This is a product of parliamentary procedures, political compromise as well as government pressures to accept emergency powers as the norm (Smith 1982). It is also a product of the decline of general power of parliament to which I will return. The normalisation, however, goes further than the constant renewal of the emergency legislation, it also involves the extension of use of the emergency powers in circumstances for which they were never intended, such as their use for the arrest and trial of offences which have nothing whatsoever to do with the emergency.

The second feature has been the scant respect paid to the rule of law in all the strategies. During internment and the military security policy no attempt was made to observe the rule of law. Internment and, to only a slightly lesser extent, detention were executive responses and the army practices of screening and trawling were of dubious legality. More recent security policies have been little better. Notwithstanding Merlyn Rees' statements in 1976 when he emphasised that they conformed to the rule of law, the extensive abuse by the police of arrest and detention powers and the modifications in the rules of evidence provide ample evidence of the extent of legal arbitrariness. The dominant form of policing in Northern Ireland is not an arrest followed by a charge and prosecution for a specific offence known in law, but regular questioning on the streets or in custody of all those perceived as potentially subversive to the existence of the present constitutional arrangements.

This represents a fundamental shift within the criminal justice system from policing offences to policing people; a shift from crime to status. On the one hand it opens up the relationship between the citizen and the state, which had been abstracted in the apparently neutral and objective concept of an offence. On the other hand, it reintroduces the possibility of policing classes of people through the criminal law rather than, as under the Unionist strategy, special powers.

The third feature has been the increased bureaucratisation of the response. Instead of a relatively informal system of the administration of the criminal law, there are a number of separate and relatively autonomous agencies with responsibilities for different aspects of the process. The setting up of the Director of Public Prosecutions in 1972 represented the beginning of the bureaucratisation.

The fourth feature has been the decline in the power of the legislature in the development of law and order policies. The policies are increasingly being developed by the executive in conjunction with the higher echelons of the police and the army. They are frequently helped in this task by judges who redefine traditional problems in technical and operational terms. All the recent policing policies, for example, as has been shown, have been developed through internal reviews. The public are never consulted and members of Parliament are simply presented with the formulated policies. They have little or no impact on them.

The fifth feature has been the mobilisation and routine employment of other state agencies in the exercise of informal control. Planners and social workers and other professionals are slowly being drawn into the general task of controlling particular sections of the population.

These changes in the strategies of control have run alongside broader economic and social developments in Northern Ireland. Economic intervention has taken place on a vast scale to aid both productive capital and also projects such as the Local Enterprise Development Unit. One feature of this intervention has been the extent to which it has been antinomian in the sense that the intervention has not been guided by rational-legal norms, the rule of law, but by its effects upon capital accumulation. These developments have paralleled the disrespect for the rule of law which has been a feature of the security strategies. Linked to these new forms of economic intervention has been the reorganisation of local government. The creation of a centralised Housing Authority and new administrative units to manage health and social services, education and planning has consolidated executive control of these services, led to the decline in formal representative democracy, which has, of course, also occurred at the higher level since direct rule, and an increased bureaucratic domination over civil society.

There is now much empirical data to suggest that the form of the state's repressive apparatus in Northern Ireland is not unique and that many modern capitalist states are evolving repressive apparatus with very similar characteristics. In the rest of the United Kingdom, while neither the army nor a paramilitary police patrol the streets, the movement towards the new form of a repressive apparatus is unmistakable. Over recent years in Britain, there has been an enormous growth in the technology of control and the military capabilities of the police have been greatly expanded. Moreover, there have been moves to reform the criminal justice system along similar lines as the changes introduced into Northern Ireland in the early seventies. Trial by jury has been constantly questioned in recent years and the Royal Commission on Criminal Procedure's recommendations in relation to police powers and rules of evidence were very similar to those of the Diplock Commission (see Hillyard 1980). Other state agencies are being mobilised to exercise greater informal control. And as in Northern Ireland all these developments are taking place not in Parliament but in the offices of those responsible for law and order.

Similar developments are taking place elsewhere. Poulantzas (1978, 203–204) has argued:

> In western capitalist societies, the State is undergoing considerable modification. A new form of State is currently being imposed—we would have to be blind not to notice (and passion always blinds, even if it springs from the noblest motives). For want of a better term, I shall refer to this state form as *authoritarian statism*. This will perhaps indicate the general direction of change: namely, intensified state control over every sphere of socio-economic life *combined with* radical decline of the institutions of political democracy and with draconian and multiform curtailment of so-called 'formal' liberties, whose reality is being discovered now that they are going overboard.

While the political struggle in Northern Ireland is obviously unique, the form in which the state, in general, and the repressive apparatus, in particular, has developed in recent years, follows closely transformations elsewhere. The principal difference is that the Northern Ireland state appears to have the unenviable honour of having its repressive apparatus transformed somewhat sooner than some other modern capitalist states.

3

Political Parties: Traditional and Modern

Ian McAllister

Despite Northern Ireland being constitutionally a subordinate part of the United Kingdom, it sustains a party system that differs in most important respects from the parent state—notably in the number of parties that are active, in the political cleavage that divides them, and in the political system within which they operate. In contrast to the British two-party system, Northern Ireland has a multi-party system, with the number of parties prepared to contest elections fluctuating constantly. The political cleavage that divides the parties is the constitutional future of the Province, underpinned by religion, whereas in Britain the cleavage is socio-economic. As a result, electoral outcomes are largely pre-determined and there is consequently no alternation of parties in office. As McCracken notes, 'there is no floating vote on the constitutional issue' (quoted in Darby 1976, 80). Finally, Northern Ireland has had a history of possessing a devolved legislature and government, with control over a wide range of important functions; Britain has a centralised government, with only limited administrative devolution to Scotland and Wales.[1]

Three themes run through party development in Northern Ireland and help to account for its unique evolution within the United Kingdom. Firstly, there is the *numerical balance between the two communities*, with Protestants constituting two-thirds of the population, Catholics one-third. Thus, so long as religion remains the basis of partisanship and a model of government used that confers power on the majority, the Protestant community are guaranteed political power *sine die*, while the Catholics are consigned to permanent political opposition. Historically, therefore, the Ulster Unionists, as the party political representative of the Protestants, have had every incentive to engage in electoral competition, to maintain an effective political organisation, and to ensure the loyalty of a mass party membership. By contrast, without the prospect of political power, the Nationalists, representing the Catholics, had no incentive to maintain the basic functions of a political party, and as a result failed to contest constituencies that did not have a secure Catholic majority.

Secondly, the *main parties are confessional* in so far as they strive for religious exclusiveness and class inclusiveness. Thus the Unionist and Nationalist parties had everything to gain from exacerbating the religious cleavage to ensure the maximum support for their community, while concomitantly muting intra-communal differences, such as class. Consequently, both parties emphasised the single issue of union with Britain versus the reunification of Ireland to the exclusion of other, often pressing, socio-economic issues.

The final theme which helps to account for the evolution of the party system is the element of *parochialism in politics.* Northern Ireland's political culture emphasises ascription, local attachment, and a form of clientelist politics common in many rural countries, including the Irish Republic and many Mediterranean countries. The style of politics that has evolved looks to the power of personality and politicians perform a brokerage role by mediating between the constituent and the government (see Sacks 1977; Bax 1976). Politicians therefore rely on their personal charisma rather than on a party label for election, and internal party disputes are swiftly settled by a resignation, rather than by utilising internal party channels to argue their case.

This chapter seeks to explain the unique development of the Northern Ireland party system from the rest of the United Kingdom through these three themes. It also groups the party system into three conceptually clear tendencies—Unionism and Loyalism, Bi-Confessionalism, and Anti-Partition. Each tendency has demonstrated a remarkable stability over a long period in the votes it wins, whatever the different party labels that are used to define them.[2] The Unionist and Loyalist tendency has encompassed the major Protestant party, the Ulster Unionist Party, and its splinter parties. The Bi-Confessional tendency was filled, before 1969, by the Liberal and Labour parties, but since 1970 has become synonymous with the Alliance Party. The Nationalist Party, the traditional vehicle for Catholic aspirations, was the largest component of the Anti-Partition tendency prior to 1969. It gradually became moribund after 1969, and was replaced by the Social Democratic and Labour Party (SDLP). Traditional nationalist and republican groups have periodically mounted an electoral challenge to the SDLP, but have normally been unsuccessful.

Since the start of the Troubles in 1969, academic writing in Ulster has represented a growth area. A bibliography published in 1980 listed no less than 780 academic works, not all of enduring quality, dealing with Northern Ireland politics (Pollock and McAllister 1980). The best background histories of Northern Ireland politics are to be found in Buckland (1980) and Farrell (1976), the latter having well-researched sections on pre-1969 Catholic politics. The operation and subsequent development of the Northern Ireland political system is outlined with perception by Arthur (1980). Rose (1971) provides an important analysis, based on a 1968 opinion survey, of political attitudes in the Province, and a subsequent work (Rose 1976) concentrates on events between 1969 and 1976. Bew *et al.* (1979) give a well argued Marxist account of the development of the Northern Ireland state. On Unionist politics, Harbinson (1973) gives an account of the party's organisation and development, while Buckland (1972) presents a thorough and highly readable exposition of its origins. On the politics of the Catholic community, Rumpf and Hepburn (1977) give a valuable summary of Nationalist politics before 1969, and McAllister (1977) describes the emergence and development of the SDLP.

Unionism and Loyalism

Throughout the half century between the founding of the Northern Ireland state in 1920 and the outbreak of the Troubles in 1969, the Ulster Unionist Party won a majority of both votes and seats in every election to the Stormont parliament. As Table 1 illustrates, the number of Unionist and Loyalist MPs never fell below 34 in a chamber of 52 members; over the 1921 to 1969 period as a whole, it averaged 38 MPs. The numbers of Nationalist and Republican MPs, by contrast, fluctuated from a low of 6 in 1969 to a peak of 12 in 1921 and 1925. This peak reflects the fact that these elections were conducted under proportional representation, and with its abolition in 1929 and replacement by the simple plurality method, it became harder for minority parties to secure representation relative to their strength in votes.

Because the Ulster Unionist's permanent electoral majority guaranteed it perpetual political power under a Westminster model of government, internal unity was obviously crucial for party survival. Notwithstanding its overall majority across the Province, the Unionists successively attempted to retain control of local government in areas where they constituted a narrow or even a clear minority. This they did through the manipulation of electoral boundaries and a

Table 3:1

ELECTORAL SUPPORT AND PARTY REPRESENTATION IN THE NORTHERN IRELAND HOUSE OF COMMONS, 1921–69

Election Year	Unionist and Loyalist		NILP		Nationalist and Republican		Other		Total	
	MPs	% Vote	MPs	% Vote	MPs	% Vote	MPs	% Vote	MPs	% Vote
1921	40	66.9	0	—	12	32.3	0	0.8	52	100
1925	36	64.0	3	4.7	12	29.1	1	2.2	52	100
1929	40	64.9	1	8.0	11	13.0	0	14.1	52	100
1933	39	64.5	2	8.6	11	26.9	0	—	52	100
1938	42	85.6	1	5.7	8	4.9	1	3.8	52	100
1945	35	55.4	2	18.6	10	9.2	5	16.8	52	100
1949	39	63.3	0	7.2	9	27.2	4	2.3	52	100
1953	39	60.3	0	12.1	9	15.5	4	12.1	52	100
1958	37	52.6	4	16.0	8	17.5	3	13.9	52	100
1962	34	48.6	4	26.0	9	15.4	4	10.0	52	100
1965	36	59.1	2	20.4	9	8.4	4	12.1	52	100
1969	39	67.4	2	8.1	6	7.6	5	16.9	52	100
Mean 1921–69	38	62.7	2	11.3	10	15.0	3	8.8		

Source: Adapted from Elliott (1973, 96).

restricted franchise which tended to disproportionately reduce the number of Catholic voters (Cameron Report 1969, Ch. 12). The imperative of maintaining political control in as many areas as possible meant that the party organisation which evolved formed an important cross-local framework, interlocking with and complementing other organisations dealing with the security and survival of the Protestant community, notably the 'B' Specials (part-time paramilitary police) (see Hezlet 1972; Farrell 1978) and the Orange Order.

Historically, the Orange Order has been an important institutional factor in the political mobilisation of Ulster Protestants. It emerged in the late eighteenth century as the latest in a tradition of sectarian secret societies which had terrorised the countryside since the early seventeenth century (see Williams 1972). It was relatively unimportant politically until 1885, when it was used as a base for organising Protestant opposition to the first Home Rule Bill (Savage 1961). With the emergence of the Ulster Unionist Party and the formation of the Northern Ireland state in 1920, it provided an ideological framework for justifying opposition to Irish nationalism and Catholicism, and for maintaining Protestant political unity. During the period of the Stormont system of government, the Order also played a latent political role by ensuring that the Unionist Party did not implement any policies it felt were not consonant with Protestant dogma (see Roberts 1971;

Bonnet 1972). Rose (1971, 257) found that 32 per cent of Protestant male respondents in his 1968 survey were Orangemen, giving the organisation a very substantial membership of around 90,000 across Northern Ireland.

Despite the potential divisions caused by drawing support from all social classes, political divisions in the Ulster Unionist Party, prior to 1969, were relatively rare. Overall, Unionists of various backgrounds and persuasions were united on the single issue of maintaining the constitutional link between Northern Ireland and Britain, but on little else. In sum, they represented 'an unhappy and unholy alliance of people thrown together by what they were fundamentally opposed to rather than by any positive or co-operative principles' (Arthur 1980, 65). What challenges were made to the authority of the parent party usually concerned individual issues, and came from working class organisations which combined a strong class identity with traditional unionism. The precursor of this tradition was the Belfast Protestant Association, founded in 1901 to oppose official Unionists on the grounds that they treated the working class simply as voting fodder (Boyle 1962). This tradition of popular Protestant radicalism was carried through after 1920 in the Independent Unionists, who ranged from groups concerned with furthering temperance to blatant anti-Catholicism and the 'view that politicians should be vigilant in defending the socialising institutions and practices of Protestant society' (quoted in de Paor 1970, 114). Less manifest were intra-Unionist dissidents: Whyte's study of the issues Unionist backbenchers voted against during the Stormont government indicated that most opposition came from the right, but that there was a strain of economic populism which criticised government bureaucracy and inadequacy in meeting the needs of the socially disadvantaged (Whyte 1972).

This mild pattern of Protestant dissent to the Unionist Party was overturned by the violence of 1969. Historically, Protestants have seen the Ulster Unionist Party as one guarantee of their political security in times of crisis—the concept of the 'public band' (Miller 1978)—but the Ulster Unionist Party's failure to halt the violence precipitated vocal opposition to its policies both from inside and outside the party. Two groups emerged from within the Unionist Party itself. Firstly, there were the majority of Unionists who remained party members but were committed to policies that were often at odds with the leadership. Secondly, those dissidents who demanded more stringent security measures and better constitutional guarantees grouped themselves as a pressure group within the party in 1972, leaving to form their own party, the Vanguard Unionist Progressive Party, in 1973. A third group wholly external to the Unionist Party were the Protestant Unionists (called the Democratic Unionist Party after 1971 to underline their populist roots) who established themselves as a vociferous opponent of official Unionism in the Independent Unionist tradition.

The breakup of the Ulster Unionist Party was crystallised in the 1969 Stormont general election, in the then prime minister Terence O'Neill's own phrase, 'the crossroads election' (see O'Neill 1969, 140). Fractionalisation within the party over the question of O'Neill's leadership was extreme: 29 constituency associations favoured O'Neill, while 15 opposed him. In addition, 15 unofficial pro-O'Neill candidates were nominated. The election result failed to silence Unionist opposition to O'Neill and forced his resignation as premier in April 1969, thereby enabling most of the anti-O'Neill Unionists to return to the party. However, opposition to the prevailing constitutional and security policies of the Unionist government continued. In February 1972 many of these dissidents helped to form Ulster Vanguard, an umbrella pressure group within the Ulster Unionist Party; in March 1973 Vanguard became a political party, approximately half its 10,000 membership opting to leave the parent party. The party's main platform was the need for stronger security measures against terrorism, and to that end it was less discriminating in including leaders of paramilitary groups within its ranks.[3]

Vanguard, under the leadership of a former Unionist Home Affairs minister, William Craig, followed a distinctive, if erratic, course for four years. Craig expressed a strand in Unionism which saw the Province more as an independent state than as a subordinate regime, and saw the Stormont parliament as not only an expression of identity, but also as a safeguard of Protestant security. This apparent militancy evaporated during the 1975–76 Constitutional Convention, when Craig advocated voluntary coalition with the main Catholic opposition party, the SDLP, in order to persuade the British government to return a devolved parliament to the Province. This *volte-face* split the party, and a year later Craig announced that he and the rest of his supporters were returning to the Official Unionist Party.

The alternative tradition of dissent to the Ulster Unionist Party— Independent Unionists—also became electorally important from 1969. This tradition has been channelled through the Rev. Ian Paisley since 1969, whose personal appeal represents a cross-fertilisation of fundamental biblical Protestantism and economic populism. Paisley's Democratic Unionist Party has consistently emphasised the mainstream unionist values of loyalty to Britain, stronger security against terrorism, and opposition to a Catholic presence in government. The DUP has consolidated a secure electoral position within the Protestant community as the major alternative to the Ulster Unionists—after 1977 reunited with its erstwhile Vanguard competitors. The DUP thus articulates the views of a significant Protestant minority who start from a fundamentalist religious standpoint in opposing social and political change—whether it be constitutional links with the Irish Republic or the legalisation of homosexuality.

The paucity of Protestant dissent to the pre-1969 political hegemony of the Ulster Unionist Party illustrates how well the balance of forces that helped to ensure its unity worked. Unionists could point to the negative uncompromising stance of the Nationalist Party, coupled with periodic physical threats to the integrity of Northern Ireland from the IRA. In return for loyalty, they could hand out patronage at the local level in the form of government employment, and also provide a ladder for the politically ambitious. To Unionists, the attitude of the British government and politicians appeared unsympathetic, a feeling which dated from the founding of the state in 1920, and which further served to isolate Protestants (Buckland 1975, 219–222). Finally, the Unionist leadership was able to manipulate natural Protestant deference and re-align the Protestant electorate along the constitutional-religious cleavage when it seemed as if its salience was declining—most notably, during the outdoor relief riots in 1932 (Bew and Norton 1979). This balance enabled the party to accommodate a remarkable diversity of support encompassing almost the entire spectrum of normal political views.

After 1969 this fragile balance of forces altered, and the Unionist Party began to fragment. Through the SDLP, Catholics became more conciliatory and prepared to participate in normal political activity, although the IRA threat continued. The ability to deliver patronage declined after the 1969–70 local government reforms and vanished totally after the imposition of direct rule in 1972, while the authority of the two Unionist prime ministers to succeed O'Neill—James Chichester-Clark and Brian Faulkner—was constantly eroded by divisions within the Unionist Party. Perhaps most importantly, the British government gradually increased its responsibility for Northern Ireland, culminating in the imposition of direct rule from London, which made the Unionists merely one of a number of competitors seeking to influence British policy.

Bi-Confessional Parties

Although groups which have sought support from both religious communities have had relatively little electoral success compared to the confessional groupings, bi-confessional parties have regularly won around one-tenth of the vote in Provincial elections. Prior to 1969 the main bi-confessional party was the Northern Ireland Labour Party (NILP). The party initially emerged from the trade union base which was a by-product of the growth of ship-building in Belfast in the late nineteenth century. Formally, the labour movement opted in 1923 not to take a stand on the constitutional question (previously it had been in favour of home rule) and a precarious balance was maintained on the issue until 1949. In April 1949 a special NILP conference decided 'to maintain unbroken the connection between Great Britain and Northern Ireland as part of the Commonwealth...' (Harbinson 1966, 232), a decision which precipitated the departure of many Catholic members who formed other republican and socialist political groups.

The split had one immediate benefit. Freed from its constitutional ambivalence, the NILP was able to make a direct appeal to the Protestant working class. The strategy was to emphasise two aspects. Firstly, the party underlined its constitutionality through the policy of preserving the British link, which acted as a safeguard for Protestants. Secondly, the party promoted its qualities as an effective opposition, ready to criticise the Unionist Party on economic grounds and undertake the role of Her Majesty's Loyal Opposition, a role the Nationalists were understandably loath to fulfil. Overall, the intention was to gain a secure power base within the Protestant community before crossing the religious divide to actively recruit Catholic support (Graham 1973).

In the late 1950s and 1960s, it seemed as if this strategy might have a chance of success. In the 1958 Stormont general election, the party won 4 of the 52 seats, all of which were retained in the succeeding 1962 election; between the two elections the party's share of the poll correspondingly rose from 16.0 per cent to 26.0 per cent. However, the fragility of the party's support was demonstrated by the loss of 2 of the 4 seats in the 1965 general election. At the same time, traditional religious attitudes began to reassert themselves within the party, initially over the sabbatarian issue, later in response to the reassertion of sectarian attitudes in the Protestant working class. Socially, these incidents illustrated how much the party owed its limited gains 'to evangelical Protestant influences rather than orthodox socialist ones' (Rumpf and Hepburn 1978, 206). Politically, it demonstrated that the party could not compete with the Unionist Party on economic issues when the constitutional question appeared to be at stake (see Rutan 1967).

The deepening post-1969 conflict, coupled with the formation of a competitor for the moderate vote, the Alliance Party, hastened the NILP's decline. Up until 1973 the party endeavoured to maintain a conciliatory position in the face of increasing religious militancy within its potential political base, the Protestant working class. The May 1974 Ulster Workers' Council strike, which brought down the power-sharing Executive, marked a turning point. The strike highlighted the impotence of the official trade union movement, to which the NILP is linked, when matched against loyalist working class leaders. The strike suggested that the party's only hope in retaining support lay in promoting loyalism at the expense of bi-confessionalism. As a result, the NILP's manifesto for the 1975 Convention election opposed both institutionalised power-sharing and any form of association with the Irish Republic. This provoked dissent from many of the remaining Catholic members, some of whom left the party.

The NILP's pro-union stance after 1949, coupled with the Nationalist Party's post-war withdrawal from contesting Belfast constituencies, created a vacuum which was filled by a number of schismatic anti-partitionist labour groups competing for the Catholic vote. All contained elements what had split from the NILP, but saw themselves sustaining the labour tradition within a nationalist or republican framework; none succeeded in gaining any significant electoral support. Some NILP dissidents persuaded the Dublin-based Irish Labour Party to organise in Northern Ireland, and it elected one MP (Jack Beattie) to Westminster in 1951, but fell apart shortly after due to personality clashes. One of the Irish Labour organisers, Frank Hanna, left and formed Independent Labour in 1958, a highly clericalised group that had some success in Belfast Catholic areas. Another Irish Labour member, Gerry Fitt, helped form the Republican Labour Party in 1962, with Harry Diamond. Fitt had been elected to Stormont in 1962 and was subsequently elected to Westminster in 1966. In 1970 he left the Republican Labour Party to become a founder member and first leader of the SDLP.

Although almost all of the factions splitting from the NILP after

1949 have been anti-partitionist, for the obvious reason that pro-union elements have been happily accommodated within the NILP, one Unionist Labour group is worthy of note. The Commonwealth Labour Party was formed by Harry Midgley in December 1942 to protest against the NILP's then ambivalent stance on the constitutional question. The party was committed to maintaining the British link and to mildly social democratic policies. In 1943 Midgley became the first non-Unionist cabinet minister as Minister for Public Security. In 1947, without consulting his party colleagues, Midgley decided to join the Unionist Party because, he declared, there was now 'no room for divisions among those ...who are anxious to preserve the constitutional life and spiritual life of our people' (Farrell 1976, 192). As a result Commonwealth Labour disintegrated.

Since 1969 the Alliance Party has dominated the bi-confessional tendency. The fragmentation of the Unionist Party in the February 1969 Stormont election, plus the intervention of independent pro-O'Neill candidates, provided the political base for the Alliance's formation. The party was formed in April 1970 from O'Neill supporters, Northern Ireland Liberals, and unaligned elements who had been active in the New Ulster Movement, a pressure group formed in 1969 specifically to mobilise support for O'Neill and his policies. The Alliance Party immediately established itself as a deviant within the Northern Ireland party system. The failure of labour bi-confessional groups to replace religion with class values had shown that there was little future in trying to emphasise a cleavage not coterminous with, or closely adjacent to, the religious divide. By contrast, Alliance placed its central appeal firmly on religion, so far as the issue became uniting Catholics and Protestants within a common political framework.

That Alliance has succeeded in achieving its fundamental aim of uniting Protestants and Catholics in a bi-confessional framework has been demonstrated by a survey of Alliance activists (McAllister and Wilson 1978). For Protestants the party offers a strong constitutional stand on retaining the British link; for Catholics, the party emphasises anti-discrimination issues and social reform. To some extent, Alliance represents the 'extreme' point to which individuals of each community will move, rather than an actual bridge for individuals to cross the sectarian divide (Laver 1976, 23). Survey evidence has however suggested that, rather than uniting the two religious communities simply on the religious dimension, the membership has a homogeneity of opinions on a wide range of social, economic and political issues (McAllister and Wilson 1978).

Tactically, Alliance's conciliatory appeal has led it to support power-sharing, and the party leader, Oliver Napier, held a portfolio in the ill-fated 1974 power-sharing Executive. Generally, the party has endorsed the SDLP's demand for power-sharing, an association which was strengthened during the 1975–76 Constitutional Convention when both opposed the Loyalist Coalition's demand for a return to majority rule. This close liaison effectively ceased in the late 1970s with the SDLP shift towards a stronger nationalist stance. The party's overall influence has been limited by its weak electoral support, and in particular by its singular failure to penetrate either the Belfast working class areas or the rural areas west of the River Bann, where religious tensions are highest. Alliance's appeal finds its strongest response in the middle and upper socio-economic groups, making its support disproportionately concentrated in the prosperous conurbations surrounding Belfast.

Nationalism and Republicanism

By virtue of their numerical minority, the Catholic community in Northern Ireland has never had the opportunity to win political power, so long as the principle of majority rule pertains, and consequently party unity has never been imperative. Two broad groups have vied for Catholic support between 1921 and 1969: constitutional nationalists and physical force republicans. While constitutional Nationalists have exclusively oriented their activities towards electoral competition, physical force republicans have used every means at their disposal, from electoral activity through to civil disobedience and armed assaults on the state.[4]

Since 1921 constitutional nationalism has been the dominant political strain within the Catholic community. Because of the electoral thresholds set for candidates in Stormont elections (for example, candidates had to declare their intention to take their seats if elected), republicans have tended to focus their electoral excursions on Westminster elections where no such thresholds apply, leaving Provincial elections free to constitutional nationalists, unhindered by the threat of competing Catholic candidates splitting their community's vote. This informal division of electoral activity was one mutually agreed between the two groups, at least at the level of an unspoken understanding (see Coogan 1966, 309). The Northern Ireland Nationalist Party was in fact the surviving Ulster remnant of the Irish Parliamentary Party, under Redmond, which had been crushed by Sinn Fein in the

1918 Westminster election. Catholic adherence to the Nationalist Party
was cemented after 1922 by the Ancient Order of Hibernians, the
Catholic equivalent of the Orange Order, which was headed by the
Nationalist Party's first leader, Joe Devlin. Although organised
throughout Ireland, the Order was strongest in Ulster and boasted the
highest membership in the rural west.[5]

The use of the title 'Nationalist Party' demands two caveats. Firstly,
the title was a broad one encompassing most of the groups which
espoused Irish unity to be achieved by constitutional means. Formally,
the Nationalist Party utilised the title except for two periods: between
1928 and the mid-1930s it was known as the National League of the
North, which was linked to a similar neo-Redmondite group in the
south; in 1945, it was known as the Anti-Partition League, a body
which gradually disappeared in the mid-1950s. Secondly, the Nationalist Party was not a political party in the generally accepted sense of
the term. It has no formal organisation or structure (annual conferences were not held until 1965) and no formal statement of policy
was ever issued until November 1964. In effect, the party operated
only at the parliamentary level and consisted of 'a loose alliance of
local notables' (Rose 1971, 221). The most sophisticated organisation
it ever developed was that of Catholic registration committees, a form
of political organisation common in societies on the threshold of
universal suffrage.

Because of the Nationalists' lack of organisation, and because of the
close identification with the Catholic community, clerical influence in
nationalist politics was strong. Nationalist candidates were frequently
selected by meetings chaired by Catholic priests, and until the 1950s,
nomination papers for Nationalist candidates were often signed by a
priest: in the 1924 Westminster general election, for example, 8 of the
12 Nationalist candidates were proposed by priests (Farrell 1976, 103;
see also Fahy 1971). Overall, this clerical influence tended to equate
'Catholicism with hostility to the state (and) detracted from the effectiveness of opposition criticism of the government even on issues which
had no bearing on the constitutional question' (McCracken 1967, 154).
Although committed to constitutional politics, the Nationalists frequently employed parliamentary abstentionism as a political tactic.
They abstained from 1921 until 1925, and after an unproductive return,
from 1934 until the late 1940s. Abstention highlighted the Catholic
community's political dilemma: to contest elections and voice grievances in parliament could gain minor concessions, but doing so would

effectively consolidate the legitimacy of a state they were pledged to oppose.

Throughout the 1950s and 1960s the Nationalist Party became increasingly anachronistic. Its electoral base was entirely rural; it emphasised the reunification of Ireland to the exclusion of all socio-economic issues; and it was periodically abstentionist, thereby robbing Catholics of what limited representation they might already have. Attempts by such groups as National Unity and the National Democratic Party to force reform on the Nationalists failed dismally (see McAllister 1975b). In the event the party was completely by-passed by another form of political expression, the Northern Ireland Civil Rights Association (NICRA), which began to mobilise mass support on the streets behind limited aims after 1968. NICRA won such concessions from the Unionist government that they were, in sum, 'greater than Catholics had won in 47 years of parliamentary opposition' (Rose 1970, 124). The Nationalist Party rapidly declined and was replaced in 1970 as the political mouthpiece of the Catholic community by the SDLP.

Although filling the place of the Nationalist Party as the major anti-partitionist group representing the Catholic community, the apparent continuity belied three fundamental differences between the SDLP and the Nationalists. Firstly, while the Nationalists refused to recognise the state and were abstentionist, the SDLP accepted that there would be no change in the Province's constitutional position without the consent of a majority. Since a permanent majority has always existed to retain the British link, in practice the SDLP thus accepted the constitutional status quo—a hitherto unprecedented position for a Catholic party in Northern Ireland. More significantly, it enabled the SDLP to participate in the institutions of the state, something the Nationalists were committed never to do. Secondly, the SDLP created political organisation with branches, constituency machinery, an executive and an annual delegate conference. Thirdly, it adopted a coherent set of socio-economic policies in a wide variety of areas.

The SDLP's experience in the Northern Ireland party system has been unique. In its short history it has occupied a variety of party political positions. For example, in 1970 and 1971 it acted as a constitutional opposition in the classic British context, waiting to win an electoral majority and hence accede to political power; in 1971 and 1972 it was an anti-system opposition, employing parliamentary abstentionism and civil disobedience to bring down the regime; and in early 1974 it participated in a power-sharing government, contributing 6 ministers to a total administration of 15. Throughout, the party has remained the sole electoral representative of the Catholic community; in both the 1973 Assembly and 1975 Convention elections, no other party or individual basing its support on the Catholic community succeeded in gaining election. This apparent Catholic unanimity can be traced to two factors. Firstly, there has been undoubted Catholic support for the aim of power-sharing between the two communities at the executive level of government. As power sharing requires Catholic participation in government, it gives them an incentive to engage in constructive political activity. Secondly, the party's political organisation has absorbed dissatisfaction into various forums within the structure and preserved party unity at times when the pressures to fragment have seemed irresistible—notably after the fall of the power-sharing Executive in May 1974 and the failure of the Constitutional Convention to find an agreed settlement in March 1976.

Despite the apparent resilience afforded the SDLP by these two factors, the party has been subjected to acute strain in recent years. Of the original six founding MPs, two have resigned, including the party leader for nine years, Gerry Fitt. A majority in the party refused to participate in the 1979 devolution talks organised by the then Conservative Northern Ireland Secretary, Humphrey Atkins. Fitt argued that participation was imperative to maintain the party's credibility within the Catholic community, and resigned to protest when the decision went against him. A more serious challenge to the party was the 1981 hunger strike by imprisoned Republicans. Ten prisoners died during the protest, radicalising popular Catholic opinion towards the IRA. One of the IRA hunger strikers, Bobby Sands, won a Westminster by-election for Fermanagh and South Tyrone in March 1981, shortly before his death. The SDLP had failed to fight the seat both against Sands, and in August 1981 against his Republican successor, Owen Carron. By twice failing to oppose militant Republicanism through the ballot box, the party forfeited much credibility among moderate Catholics, while gaining no corresponding support from more extreme Catholics.

Republican politics (as opposed to Republican military activity) has been consistently cast into a secondary role by the dominance of constitutional nationalism, both before and after the radical disjuncture of 1969. Typically, Ulster Catholics have been distrustful of physical force republicans, feeling that they do not understand their vulnerable position vis-a-vis the majority Protestant community. Political activists have therefore gravitated towards constitutional nationalism, leaving the republican movement the preserve of a small core of dedicated militarists. Republicans have, however, had infrequent electoral success. In the 1921 Stormont election, Republicans won more votes than Nationalists; in 1955 they had two candidates elected, both serving terms of imprisonment for terrorist offences; and, as already noted, in April 1981 a jailed IRA hunger striker, Bobby Sands, was elected at a by-election, and subsequently died of his hunger strike while still technically an MP.

After the failure of the 1956 to 1962 IRA border campaign, the republican movement took on a political aspect and emphasised housing, welfare and employment issues over the perennial partition question. However the movement's inability to protect Belfast Catholics from attack in the 1969 civil disturbances split the organisation in two. One group, the Republican Clubs (linked with the Official IRA) have enthusiastically contested elections on a Marxist platform; the other group, Provisional Sinn Féin (linked with the Provisional IRA) have based their appeal on a rudimentary combination of Catholic conservatism and orthodox physical force republicanism, and equally enthusiastically urged abstention in elections. Neither group has secured sufficient support within the Catholic community to enable it to mount a potential electoral challenge to the SDLP.

Traditionalism and Modernity in the Northern Ireland Party System

The Northern Ireland party system contains elements of both traditionalism and modernity. It is *traditional* by virtue of the permanent majority–minority balance between the two communities, because of the confessional nature of the parties, and because of the parochial and personalistic nature of the political culture. It is *modern* in so far as the political parties organise themselves around elections, operate relatively sophisticated machinery, and resemble parties that can be found in other advanced Western European democracies. The history of Northern Ireland parties can be viewed as a balance between these two themes: each party contains elements of both, to a greater or lesser degree, and each sustains a constant conflict between them.

Up until the 1960s, the party system was essentially dominated by traditionalism. There was little challenge to the accepted *status quo*, the parties maintained their confessional bases, and there was no attempt to introduce anything other than strictly constitutional issues into political debate. The limited attempts of the labour movement to raise such issues in the 1920s, and the dramatic but brief unity between working-class Catholics and Protestants in Belfast over outdoor relief in 1932 did not disturb this pattern (Bew and Norton 1979). Traditionalism first seriously came under attack when Terence O'Neill became prime minister in 1963. O'Neill's long term objective was to undermine the political and social basis of these traditional attitudes, and force through modernisation in the Province.

O'Neill's strategy was to achieve reform in three key areas which would eventually challenge the nature of the political system. Firstly, he sought to change the party system to resemble British two-party competition, with two parties competing for votes on socio-economic platforms. The initial stage was to get the Nationalists to participate constructively in the institutions of the state. This step was tentatively accomplished in 1966 when the Nationalists agreed to become the Official Opposition in the Stormont parliament, although they withdrew from the position in 1968. Secondly, O'Neill sought to undermine the confessional basis of the political parties. In the Ulster Unionist Party, his attempts to gain formal acceptance for Catholic membership were thwarted. Thirdly, by attracting industry and commerce and thereby stimulating affluence, he hoped to erode the parochial rural attitudes which suffused political debate.

In the relative economic prosperity of the mid 1960s, it appeared as if these policies might have some chance of success. However, O'Neill's central dilemma was that he was moving too slowly for most Catholics, who were seeking an end to discrimination and looking for upward social mobility in the growing economy, while many Protestants viewed reform as marking an end to their traditional supremacy. His problem was his inability to win sufficient Catholic backing to balance defections from the intransigent Unionists who were distrustful of his conciliatory approach. The paradox of O'Neillism was that its 'moderation lay in avoiding bigotry. It did not extend so far as to endorse change sufficient to dispel the Catholic sense of grievance' (Rose 1972, 124). In the event, O'Neill's attempt at modernisation failed and Catholics turned to the civil rights movement for remedial action on their grievances.

The civil rights movement represented another potentially modernising influence. NICRA presented the Unionist regime with a novel threat. Previous threats had invariably been violent, ephemeral and universally ineffective: faced with the threat of physical force, the government could easily retaliate in kind. But non-violent street protest presented a novel challenge, since it could neither be ignored, nor broken by undue force. The Unionist response was initially to concede some of NICRA's demands, while the popular Catholic response was a strong endorsement of street protest as a legitimate political tactic. While the civil rights movement achieved most of its short-term demands, its long term impact on Northern Ireland has been profound. Its reformist demands engendered a violent loyalist response, which in turn stimulated the growth of the Provisional IRA, initially as a Catholic defence organisation. It also had the effect of tipping the party system, particularly on the Catholic side, into turmoil. The extent of the changes wrought by post-1969 events can be illustrated by the fact that only two of the parties active today—the Ulster Unionists and the NILP—existed before 1970, and both have been subjected to frequent schisms (Rose 1976, 33).

Post-1969 Ulster has been dominated by two themes: firstly, the gradual withdrawal of powers from local elected representatives by the British government, and secondly, the emerging of extra-constitutional groups willing to use violence as a political means. The initial withdrawal of powers took place in local government and involved the transfer of housing, planning, and certain other contentious powers to a central authority. The process continued with the abolition of the Stormont parliament in 1972; the legislative assembly that was intended to replace it boasted considerably less powers than its predecessor, most notably it did not have control over security and the administration of justice. The result of this process has been to reduce the importance of political activity and hence of the parties themselves, and simultaneously shift the focus to Westminster, which to most Ulster people still remains a remote and unsympathetic forum.

The growth of extra-constitutional groups willing to use violence has further reduced the saliency of political activity. Agreements reached between elected politicians can have little legitimacy when they can be wrecked by non-elected gunmen. There is an ambivalence to the use of physical force in politics which transcends religious affiliation and party label. Each community expresses its fear of the other by the maintenance of an armed faction, which gains latent support as the last guarantor of the community's safety in the event of a disaster. The IRA has filled this role for Catholics; Protestants traditionally looked towards the 'B' special paramilitary police as their guarantor until their disbandment in 1969, after which time more traditional armed groups such as the Ulster Volunteer Force became active.

After more than a decade of civil disturbance and violence, Northern Ireland politics still displays the conflict between traditionalism and modernity. The political parties still personify the constitutional conflict over the Province's future, and the British government, by virtue of its role as the main arbiter in the conflict, still withholds political power from elected politicians in the absence of inter-communal agreement. The various attempts to impose modernisation through political elites—from O'Neill's reforms in the 1960s, to the imposition of the 1974 power-sharing Executive—have largely failed because the social and political attitudes within the two communities were unresponsive to change. Any hope of future progress must come from a change in these attitudes, and from no other source.

Notes

1. For introductions to the Northern Ireland party system, see Arthur (1980, 52–65), Darby (1976, Ch. 4) and McAllister and Nelson (1979). On the relationship between the Northern Ireland and British States, see Rose (1982).
2. For example, in the 1973 Assembly election, the three tendencies—Unionism and Loyalism, Bi-Confessionalism and Anti-Partitionism—received 61.9 per cent, 11.8 per cent and 25.3 per cent of the first preference vote, respectively. In the 1975 Convention election, each received 62.5 per cent, 11.2 per cent and 26.2 per cent of the first preference vote, respectively. See McAllister (1975a, Table V.1).
3. For example, at least three of Vanguard's 1973 Assembly candidates had connections with paramilitary organisations: Tommy Herron and Glen Barr were associated with the Ulster Defence Association; George Green with the Ulster Special Constabulary Association.
4. There is no separate history of the Nationalist Party, but the best accounts are to be found in Rumpf and Hepburn (1977) and Farrell (1976). The best account of republicanism and the IRA is Bowyer Bell (1972). On the SDLP, see McAllister (1977).
5. For example, in 1892 the AOH had just over 1,000 members in County Armagh, but only 70 in County Down. See Foy (1976, 18–19).

4

Economic Development: Cause or Effect in the Northern Irish Conflict

John Simpson

Northern Ireland has an unenviable record as the least affluent region of the United Kingdom and one of the least prosperous areas within the European Economic Community. Within the EEC, Northern Ireland is one of five areas qualifying, because of the scale of the local problems, for various forms of priority treatment from, for example, the European Regional Development Fund. However, as later evidence will show, the regional economy has, in some ways, shown significant improvements in the past two decades.

Economic issues are not new to any discussion about Northern Ireland. Professor Lyons summarised the position when he argued:

> The history of Northern Ireland has been dominated by three principal problems which have changed extraordinarily little throughout the entire period of its existence. These are, first, the problem of the triangular relationship with the rest of the United Kingdom and the rest of Ireland; second, the problem of the deep and continuing internal division of the population between, in the main Unionists and Protestants on the one hand, and Nationalists and Catholics on the other; finally the problem not only of developing a viable economy in such a small area, but of securing for the people public services and standards of welfare comparable with those in Britain. (Lyons 1972, 695)

After more than a decade of physical violence, any assessment is complicated by the undoubted consequences of this violence on the economy. It is perhaps helpful, for analytical purposes, to examine the state of the economy, and its underlying characteristics, as it was revealed in the 1950s and 1960s and then to make some tentative suggestions on the changes during the violent decade of the 1970s.

Naturally, any examination of the Northern Ireland economy must acknowledge that the state of the economy may have contributed to the emergence of community disorder. The discussion cannot prove any causal relationships. Indeed from the evidence, since the assessment is subjective, different observers would, and do, draw different conclusions. Anticipating the discussion which follows, this writer would not subscribe to the view that the state of the economy was the *main* factor in explaining the emergence and continuation of violence. However, in an explanation of the development of the economy in the 1970s, there can be little doubt that political instability and continuing disorder have had a major effect of the economy. Since the divisions, based on differences in the cultural and political identities in the island of Ireland, have been of sufficient strength and duration, it is at least credible to argue that relative economic disadvantage within Northern Ireland, if it is accepted that it existed, was not a *necessary* element in an explanation of the causation of violence.

An assessment of the state of the Northern Ireland economy can be attempted in different ways. The absolute scale of the economic problems has been well documented in the several official reports on the economy such as those by Isles and Cuthbert (1955), Wilson (1965) and Quigley (1976). The discussion which follows sets out, first, to examine the performance of the Province as a region of the United Kingdom where the main comparisons are made with the United Kingdom as a whole, and areas such as Scotland and Wales; in this first part of the discussion, comparisons with the Republic of Ireland are omitted in order to emphasise how Northern Ireland compared with other United Kingdom regions. Later, however, because of the obvious relevance of North–South comparisons, the discussion focuses on how the two parts of the island have been faring. Towards the end of the chapter, the examination turns to factors internal to Northern Ireland. Has the distribution of economic change within Northern Ireland been such as to illustrate any unnatural bias in the results in recent years?

Each of these elements is analysed with incomplete data. In fact, sometimes, for the best of reasons, data on the contentious issues are not available. How can an observer quantify whether a 'fair' proportion of new jobs or government investment was attracted to, or allocated for, areas of high unemployment? For this chapter reliance has had to be placed on the information which is available. It is, therefore, in some cases not as adequate or directly relevant as might be wished.

Northern Ireland: as a region of the United Kingdom

The long standing evidence is that Northern Ireland has experienced higher unemployment and lower average incomes than the average for the rest of the United Kingdom. Such a situation certainly predates the second world war and probably dates back earlier than the creation of a devolved administration in Northern Ireland in 1920. Statistical comparisons on a pre-1939 basis are not available in the forms which are now current, but the basic indicators of unemployment and incomes confirm these statements. In 1922, on the basis of the unemployment insurance scheme then in operation, Northern Ireland experienced an unemployment rate of 22.9 per cent compared with a United Kingdom average of 14.3 per cent. In the years up to 1937, the absolute difference in annual unemployment percentages fluctuated but at no time was it less than 3.4 per cent (1927) and at one time (1925) it widened to 12.9 per cent. In 1938 the difference increased again to 13.3 per cent. (British Labour Statistics, 1886–1968, table 160)

Comparisons of relative income levels, pre-1939, are even more primitive. Using some early estimates of personal income, prepared by Isles and Cuthbert (1957, 457), and comparing these with early estimates for the United Kingdom, it seems that in 1938 personal income per head of the population was about 55 per cent of the United Kingdom average. By 1950, Northern Ireland incomes, per head of the population, had improved, mainly because of the impact of war on relative pay levels, to some 68 per cent of the United Kingdom average. These differences, which are discussed further below, stemmed in part from lower average earnings in similar occupations, but more significantly were also caused by differences in the sectoral structure of the economy and differences in the proportion of the population in the labour force. Greater proportionate dependance on textiles and agriculture, as well as a higher proportion of dependents in the population would both have contributed to such a difference.

Unemployment is the most conspicuous sign of the economic problems faced in Northern Ireland. Even in the post-1945 era of full employment in the United Kingdom, the levels of unemployment remained high in Northern Ireland. Only rarely, and for short periods, has unemployment fallen below 6 per cent of the insured employees, whilst a figure of less than 2 per cent was commonplace for the United Kingdom in the 1950s and 1960s.

Although unemployment in the period from 1945 to the early 1970s was, in absolute terms much lower than the general earlier experience of the 1920s and 1930s, there are two ways in which the relative position can be argued to have worsened. First, by comparison with the improved position in the United Kingdom as a whole, Northern Ireland's relative position was worse. Second, in a comparison with the experience in Scotland and Wales, which are used here to make an illustrative inter-regional comparison with other less prosperous regions, Northern Ireland fared badly. This is illustrated in table 4:1, which shows, for each area, the distribution of unemployment in these regions of the United Kingdom. If a region had an unemployment experience the same as that for the whole country, the ratio would be equal to 1.0; a ratio of 2.0 therefore means that unemployment was twice as high as the national ratio. Table 1 brings out clearly that pre-1939, unemployment in these regions, although high in percentage terms, was usually less than double the national average. In the 1950s and 1960s, Scotland and Wales did not experience the same relative deterioration as Northern Ireland. In other words, full employment in the United Kingdom was shared more adequately in Scotland and Wales than in Northern Ireland. Only with rising national unemployment in the late 1970s has Northern Ireland's relative experience seemed better!

Table 4:1

UNEMPLOYMENT AS A PROPORTION OF THE
CIVIL LABOUR FORCE
(expressed as a multiple of the average U.K. ratio)

	N. Ireland	Scotland	Wales
1923	1.3	1.5	0.6
1929	1.2	1.2	2.0
1935	1.4	1.5	2.1
1938	2.1	1.4	2.0
1947	3.9	2.0	3.2
1950	3.4	2.1	2.2
1955	5.3	2.1	1.4
1960	3.6	2.2	1.4
1965	3.7	2.0	1.6
1970	2.5	1.6	1.3
1975	1.9	1.3	1.3
1980	1.9	1.4	1.3

Source: Derived by the author from British Labour
Statistics, 1886–1968 and later editions of the Department of Employment Gazette.

Unemployment in the 1950s and early 1960s remained a serious problem and was more noteworthy because of the relative improvement in the position in other regions of the United Kingdom. The easy explanation offered for this situation was to point to the importance of three sectors in the regional economy, all of which were contracting in employment terms throughout the United Kingdom. Agriculture, shipbuilding and textiles, in the early 1950s, accounted for over 35 per cent of the labour force, three times higher than the national average. Consequently, with a higher dependence on industries where employment was contracting, maintaining or increasing total employment was necessarily a continuing process of seeking expansion in other sectors. Because of the technical changes in production methods and the relative increase in the availability of competitive imports, the fall in employment in these sectors was unavoidable. For the Northern Ireland economy the absence of adequate alternative expansion, in a period of national full employment, was a feature of greater concern.

Attempts to encourage the expansion of manufacturing industry developed in Northern Ireland in the 1930s and increased rapidly in the 1950s. However, the government policies, which were gradually increased in scope and scale during the 50s, 60s and 70s have not been such as to have the effect of reducing unemployment to acceptable or desirable levels. The analysis which lay behind the efforts to expand the manufacturing sector as the means of securing wider economic development was unexceptional. Similar analytical conclusions formed the basis of Development Area policy in Great Britain, were a prominent part of the Irish programmes for economic expansion and were reflected in other countries in western Europe.

Government policies and/or inducements do not necessarily make a dramatic change in the pattern of location decisions for new industrial projects. Basic economic factors such as distance, material availability and costs, energy costs and labour costs are often influenced only marginally by government actions. Isles and Cuthbert (1957) summed up the position by saying:

> Because of Northern Ireland's geographical situation and its lack of raw materials, together with its smallness as a market for most goods, industry encounters transport and other situation costs which ... are a strong deterrent to the expansion of economic activity.
>
> ... the ratio of pay demanded by the workers and the ratio of profit on capital and enterprise required by investors and entrepreneurs, tend to approximate to those obtainable elsewhere in the

United Kingdom. In consequence, the amount of new investment undertaken in Northern Ireland . . . always tends to fall short of the amount required to yield enough jobs. . . Unemployment is therefore not merely a passing phase but a chronic tendency.   (p. 346)

If industry is normally to expand fast enough to keep the unemployment rate down to about the same average level in Great Britain, costs of producton must somehow be lowered enough to offset the retarding effects of the higher costs due to the natural handicaps . . . there would appear to be some scope for action . . . if (workers) were able and willing to reduce labour costs, per unit of output, so as to offset part of the higher costs arising from the disadvantages of location.   (p. 347)

Central to the assessment of the 1950s and 1960s is some evidence on the effectiveness of Northern Ireland in securing, or failing to secure, adequate industrial expansion and some conclusion on the factors affecting profitability, particularly labour costs, as outlined by Isles and Cuthbert. This should include the efforts by the Northern Ireland Government to stimulate expansion both by direct financial incentives to industrial projects and by indirect measures to improve the quality of manpower available (and incidentally help to ensure more efficient production, with lower labour costs per unit) and the wider infrastructure.

Industrial Employment

The basic strategy adopted by successive Government policies in Northern Ireland implicitly argued that if the industrial structure could be changed by attracting new modern industry to replace the sectors where employment was contracting, this new industry, after overcoming the initial disadvantages during a start-up period, might be able to operate on a continuing viable basis. Government direct assistance, as in other regions, has been (and is) heavily weighted to reduce the setting up costs: advance factories are available with an initial rent free period of tenancy, as are percentage grants on fixed capital costs and grants based on employment numbers in the early years. Without going into detail, (interested readers should consult the Wilson Report (1965), the Development Programme (1970) and the Quigley Report (1976)), the evidence is that Northern Ireland has had a scale of financial inducements somewhat higher than the other United Kingdom Development Areas since, at least, the mid 1950s, and in the past 25 years these inducements have, generally, been increased.

In view of the policies adopted and the expenditure incurred in their implementation, the evidence in terms of manufacturing output and employment is, at first sight, not very encouraging. Over the past 25 years manufacturing employment has, with fluctuations, tended to fall. Between 1956 and 1979 the number employed in manufacturing in Northern Ireland fell from 185,000 to 140,000, a decline of 24 per cent; the decline in the United Kingdom as a whole for the same period was 19 per cent. Only for the period 1961–1970 did manufacturing employment in Northern Ireland increase relative to the United Kingdom position.

Output levels from manufacturing industry compared somewhat more favourably: Output in Northern Ireland, from 1956 to 1979, increased by 96 per cent whereas in the United Kingdom the comparable increase was of 65 per cent. The decade of the 1970s is not adequately reflected in this comparison. Production peaked in 1973 in both areas and the subsequent contraction has been larger in Northern Ireland, down 9 per cent, than in the United Kingdom which experienced a fall of 4 per cent.

The period when output grew more quickly than that in the United Kingdom did not commence until the early 1960s and ended in 1971.

The overall picture is, therefore, one of decreasing industrial employment, increasing output and therefore increasing output per person employed. The evidence is consistent with a gradual improvement in Northern Ireland's relative position in the 1960s, after a fairly static period in the 1950s, followed by a significant deterioration in the 1970s. From this evidence alone, however, it would be simplistic, and possibly incorrect, to conclude that, because the experience of the 1960s showed that progress was being made and that this ended in the early 1970s, the later deterioration can solely be attributed to the impact of local disorder. The post 1973 international oil price rise and the emergence of unemployment more generally in Western Europe gives at least a *prima facie* argument that other factors may have played a part, even if a small one, in this reversal.

The gradual relative improvement in the 1960s can also be documented with reference to the figures published by the Department of Commerce on new projects announced as intending to provide extra industrial employment. From the limited official evidence available, the years when industrial expansion was most rapid (measured by the number and prospective size of the projects announced by the Department of Commerce) continued from the mid-1960s to the early 1970s.

Isles and Cuthbert quoted (p. 390) figures for the late 1940s and early 1950s of announcements of about 2,000 prospective new industrial jobs per annum. The figures from the mid 1960's rose to an average of 7,000 jobs per annum and this improvement was maintained into the early 1970s. However, by 1974 a distinct fall was in evidence and the low point was reached with only 3,000 jobs promoted in 1976. Some recovery took place in the later years of the 1970s.

Two cautionary points should be made on these figures. First, these are project announcements. There is always some shortfall in the numbers of jobs actually created. Many projects do not meet the optimistic targets set at the date of their launch. Second, allowing for the gradual process of industrial change, inevitable in any setting, it must be emphasised that the *net* change in total industrial employment would be much lower and in some years it has even been negative.

The gross and net characteristics are illustrated in the table below.

Table 4:2

MANUFACTURING EMPLOYMENT ('000s)

	Total	Assisted projects	Remainder	New jobs announced	Change in No. of jobs in assisted projects
1960	181	34	147	5(4) year totals	
1965	174	49	125	N.A.	15 (1960–65)
1970	177	67	110	32	18 (1965–70)
1975	156	70	86	31	3 (1970–75)
1979	140	64	76	19	—6 (1975–79)

Sources: Department of Manpower Services Gazettes, Department of Commerce Facts and Figures.

The picture is, therefore, one of:

(1) an overall decline in industrial employment.

(2) an improvement, relative to the overall United Kingdom average in the 1960s.

(3) a major contraction in employment in the 'non-assisted' firms.

For Northern Ireland, the inflow of new industrial employment has been inadequate to offset the contraction in existing firms. This contraction, as evidenced earlier, has to a significant extent been a reflection of the existing structure of industry with its particular dependence on textiles and shipbuilding. (A more detailed examination is to be found in Appendix 3 of the Northern Ireland Development Programme, 1970.) However, the amount of 'new' industrial employment, although inadequate to offest this contraction, was not small by the evidence of the success or otherwise of other United Kingdom regions.

One of the earliest attempts to assess how different regions fared in the search for new industrial projects was undertaken by R. S. Howard of the then Board of Trade (1968). This quantified the number of jobs promoted in regions by firms which moved into those regions in the period 1945-1965. As a percentage of 1966 employment, Northern Ireland's new employment, at 21 per cent of the jobs existing in 1966, was better than any other region, except Wales where the comparable figure was 29 per cent. Scotland's figure was much lower, at 14 per cent of the total industrial jobs.

In a more refined analysis of the period 1952-1965, Howard (1968) shows that Northern Ireland's experience was even more marked. Northern Ireland had a higher ratio of new jobs to existing employment than any other United Kingdom region. The results were some 50 per cent better than those for Scotland, the next highest region. The same analysis (Howard, 1968, 11) shows that the ratio of job losses to existing employment in industry was also much higher in Northern Ireland (−13 per cent in 13 years) than elsewhere. The region with the nearest comparable figure was the North West of England (−8 per cent).

Not only did Northern Ireland do, relatively, better than other regions in the attraction of new employment, but the evidence (Howard, 1968, Appendix B-E) is that the situation improved in the 1960s. The proportion of the new jobs in the United Kingdom coming to Northern Ireland compared to the Scottish record was as follows (per cent):

	N.I.	Scotland
1945–1951	3.8	13.0
1952–1959	2.6	7.3
1960–1965	8.0	15.4
1945–1965	4.6	11.9
% of U.K. industrial employment in 1966	2.1	8.2

More recent evidence, on a different basis, comes from the work of Moore and Rhodes and was summarised by Marquand (1980, 47). Moore and Rhodes have estimated how much employment, in industry, has been created by regional policy, in the period 1960-1976. Until 1971 Northern Ireland was estimated to have, relatively, done much better than Scotland or the North of England and the nearest comparable result was that for Wales. Again the evidence confirms that the mid 1960s were the best period.

Table 4:3

EMPLOYMENT EFFECTS OF REGIONAL
POLICY 1960–1976 ('000s)

	N.I.	Scotland	Wales
1960–1963	10	13	10
1963–1967	16	28	22
1967–1971	14	16	30
1960–1971	40	57	62
1971–1976	0	19	14

Source: Marquand (1980) p. 47
Note: Employment in Scotland is some 4 times
that in Northern Ireland; in Wales it is nearly
double.

The above table also includes the dramatic conclusion that the efforts to attract new industry to Northern Ireland produced little or no result in the early 1970s. (i.e. although some new projects were announced, these did not reflect a positive gain solely attributed to regional policy). A more recent study (Pounce, 1981) of industrial movement confirms that in the period 1972–75, the amount of employment promised in new projects fell dramatically when compared with other United Kingdom regions.

The argument in this section can now be put into perspective: The worst feature for the region was that in spite of efforts to expand the industrial sector, employment contracted. However, this contraction would have been considerably higher without the gross inflow of a large number of new plants. The records suggest that Northern Ireland's rate of employment turnover (job gains and job losses) was much higher than in any other United Kingdom region. In the years prior to 1971, and particularly during the 1960s, the rate of job promotion in Northern Ireland was better than in any other region. The evidence suggests that although Northern Ireland was the most successful region in attracting new industrial employment, the *net* result, in employment terms, was slightly worse than the United Kingdom average which, in itself, was poor by comparison with some other European economies. Overall, this result was disappointing and inadequate to meet the needs of the region. The only short period when significant net gains were recorded was from 1963 to 1970 approximately.

Industrial Investment

The loss of employment in textiles and shipbuilding was a major factor in offsetting the employment growth from new industrial projects. It was, however, given the *national* position of these industries in the faces of international trading changes, not surprising. The critical factor for Northern Ireland was the scale of new industrial investment and its determinants. Northern Ireland, as a United Kingdom region, did well, but not well enough. Since the 1950s and 1960s were a period of national full employment, why did Northern Ireland not attract a larger fraction of the new investment? The deflection of an extra 2 per cent of the national industrial investment total (about a 40 per cent increase in the amount which located in Northern Ireland) would have made the position radically different.

The first point of interest is whether Northern Ireland was sufficiently attractive as a location. Its disadvantages in terms of geography and domestic market size are and are constraints. Industry will not locate new projects in Northern Ireland if they would be conspicuously more profitable elsewhere. Yet there is no easy way of assessing, and no satisfactory way to make general statements about, the viability of plants in the province.

In any scrutiny of the factors affecting relative viability compared to another region the main elements are probably transport costs (on materials and final products), fuel costs, wage levels (*not* simply *rates*), efficiency in use of labour, and capital costs.

As Isles and Cuthbert (1957, 346) make clear, these must combine to give a rate of return which is preferably better than, or as good as, alternative locations. Using the only information available on profits (the figures on gross profits before depreciation in the regional GDP estimates for the early 1970s), it is of interest that gross profits in manufacturing were estimated at between 2 per cent and 2.2 per cent of the UK total. Since employment was, at the same time, about 2.1 per cent of the United Kingdom total, this is not inconsistent with the hypothesis that the average rate of return on capital invested for the new projects in Northern Ireland was not much in Northern Ireland's favour. Admittedly, this is not a very firm piece of evidence.

Transport costs are, in any average comparison, a disadvantage to location in Northern Ireland. Capital costs, because of government grants on capital spending are an advantage. Fuel costs, until 1974, were a relative advantage which, with oil price increases, swung to disadvantage and by 1981 had become more nearly equalised by government subsidies; some regions, notably Scotland, still have a small advantage. The major cost element, as elsewhere, is the labour cost per unit of output. A 20 per cent extra transport cost is often less than the equivalent of a 1 per cent extra element in labour costs.

For continuing viability, industry locating in Northern Ireland probably examines how its labour efficiency and costs compare with elsewhere. Government incentives and inducements, mainly paid at the time of establishment, would be less effective if labour efficiency and costs compared adversely.

For this reason, comparison of labour costs and costs per unit may give an interesting indication of how Northern Ireland's relative viability has been changing. The simple presumption that wage costs are and were relatively low in Northern Ireland, and that this is evidence in favour of location in Northern Ireland, is not justified.

Average hourly earnings (*not* rates) for adult males in industry were, in 1960 (the earliest comparison readily available) 83 per cent of the United Kingdom average. However, on an industry by industry basis, and for occupations within industries, such a figure is misleading. The greater part of this difference is explained by differences in the structure of industry in Northern Ireland. Isles and Cuthbert (1957, 230) even in the early 1950s emphasised that many national wage agreements, or their equivalent, produced near parity of rates particularly for skilled occupations.

From 1960 to 1980 the average hourly earnings 'difference' had narrowed from the 83 per cent in 1960, to 89 per cent in 1970 and 94 per cent in 1980. This narrowing of the gap reflects both the changing structure and the further reduction in any remaining occupational differences between Northern Ireland and the rest of the United Kingdom. A similar trend can also be observed in, for example, Scotland.

The earlier evidence was that Northern Ireland's ability to attract new industrial investment was most effective in the early 1960s. With hindsight this may be explained in terms of:

(1) full employment elsewhere in the United Kingdom.

(2) some difference in earnings levels or labour costs.

(3) government inducements.

(4) lower energy prices (as a mainly oil-dependent region).

By the mid 1970s, factors (1) and (4) had been reversed. Government inducements (3) had, however, been increased. Average earnings (2) have tended to catch up, but this is partly a feature of structural change.

If it is assumed that Northern Ireland had a wage cost per unit of industrial output which was slightly below the United Kingdom average in 1956 and that the increase in average earnings was not affected by structural components (which is unfavourable to the comparison), then in the period up to 1973 the relative position improved slightly.

INCREASE IN WAGE COSTS
PER UNIT OF OUTPUT

	U.K.	*N.I.*
1956–1973	+88%	+69%
1973–1979	+134%	+148%

Source: Author's calculations from indices of production, employment and earnings.

The relative position deteriorated slightly in the mid 1970s. Although Northern Ireland's relative competitive position, in terms of earnings, marginally improved within the United Kingdom, it is also relevant to note that allowing for exchange rate changes, the relative comparison with continental labour markets improved more dramatically. Germany is the extreme example.

INCREASE IN WAGE COSTS PER UNIT
OF OUTPUT

	Northern Ireland	*Germany (in sterling equivalent)*
1956–1973	+69%	+186%
1973–1979	+148%	+100%

Source: as above

The major change in the 1970s is therefore *not* between Northern Ireland and the United Kingdom, but between the United Kingdom and other countries. Exchange rate changes have not compensated for the faster domestic inflation and therefore the position of all regions in the United Kingdom in trying to attract external investment was, in the late 1970s, despite the advantages which EEC membership might have added much less favourable. On top of this, Northern Ireland had its own local difficulties as an unquantifiable disadvantage.

Consequently, the main factors, (not necessarily mutually exclusive) which eroded the net advantages of the mid 1960s were:

(a) the rise in national unemployment.

(b) the rise in energy prices after 1973.

(c) the rise in U.K. costs relative to other countries.

(d) the deterrent effect of the local disorder.

The Role of Government Spending

The earlier discussion suggested that it is possible to show, with justification, both that Northern Ireland, pre-1970, was perhaps the most successful region of the United Kingdom in attracting additional industrial investment and that the overall result was a relative *net* reduction in industrial employment greater than that for the United Kingdom.

Analysing the role of government produces another apparent contradiction. During the whole period of devolved government in Northern Ireland, but especially in the years after 1945, government spending was justified by the principle of 'parity' with Great Britain, and balancing the Budget of the Stormont government was often argued to be more a presentation issue than a sharp practical problem. The Treasury effectively ensured that agreed spending, based on parity principles and making up 'leeway', could be financed. This led to an appreciation, still accepted in 1981 and reinforced because of the impact and cost of the local disorder, that Northern Ireland's living standards were greatly increased by the scale of the net inflow of Exchequer funds. Reviewing the evidence now available, it seems that this conclusion needs to be presented more carefully.

Two contrasting statements illustrate the different interpretations of the issue. First, it is indisputable that Northern Ireland, as a relatively unprosperous region, has received a net inflow of government funds, over and above its own tax payments. This has obviously added to the total of personal incomes in the province. Second, and more surprisingly, the scale of government financial transfers to Northern Ireland has, by specified standards, not always reflected what might be considered the degree of fiscal redistribution justified by objective or comparative criteria. If the latter point is confirmed, it is an important restraint on any argument that Northern Ireland's violence should not be explained, even partially, by suggestions of unfavourable treatment in terms of government spending. If government spending, pre-1968, was in some sense below parity, then the question of any causation through regional disadvantage is at least relevant if not necessarily proven.

The statistical evidence on this problem is readily assembled (see Simpson, 1981). The accounts of the Northern Ireland Government, until 1972, and the Direct Rule administration since then, are published and presented to Parliament. There is no dispute that during the 1950s and 1960s government spending was (if public corporations and nationalised industries are excluded) higher in Northern Ireland, on a per capita basis, than the national average. In the late 1960s, before the impact of extra spending because of the civil disorder, Northern Ireland was spending 15 per cent more on a per capita basis (Simpson, 1981, Table 2). Since then the relative figures have increased and increased by more than the amount linked to directly offsetting the cost of violence. In 1978–1979, the ratio was over 50 per cent higher per capita than in the United Kingdom as a whole.

There are, however, at least two other possible approaches to this issue. The first asks not whether Northern Ireland government spending is comparatively higher or lower than in Great Britain, but whether, if such expenditure is measured in relation to some criteria of need, Northern Ireland compares as favourably. This question is conceptually of relevance but, in practice, harder to quantify. The United Kingdom Treasury has, however, for the six main social functions of government (including housing, education, health, social services, transport and roads, environmental services, and law and order) attempted such an exercise (H.M. Treasury, 1979). This study concluded that, in 1976–1977, in Northern Ireland, public sector spending was, relative to England, slightly higher than indicated by need (5 percentage points), but for earlier years the position was less favourable. Need was assessed at 131 per cent of the level in England; the actual figure was 136 per cent.

Table 4:4

PUBLIC SECTOR SPENDING

(In each year England = 100)

	N.I.	Scotland	Wales
1959–1960	88	105	95
1962–1963	92	118	99
1965–1966	97	111	94
1968–1969	103	134	101
1971–1972	111	125	104
1974–1975	112	118	97
1976–1977	136	123	101
1977–1978	141	128	100

Source: Treasury: Needs Assessment Study (1979) Table 2

A second approach is to compare the additional Exchequer transfers to Northern Ireland to the transfers in Great Britain to local authorities through the Rate Support Grant and to ask, if Northern Ireland were to receive a separate Rate Support Grant for the local government type services in the province, how would this compare with the total recorded financial transfers. (Such an approach is not fully justified since it presumes that Northern Ireland's taxable capacity is so low that the whole Rate Support Grant would be an extra flow of funds. However the over-statement may not be too misleading!) Estimating a hypothetical Rate Support Grant on a crude proportion of that paid in Great Britain gives a somewhat unexpected result.

Before 1973, Northern Ireland, by this standard, was not particularly favoured. Since then, local disorder and, it must be emphasised, a rapid relative expansion in public sector spending in many other areas (see Simpson, 1981) has produced a much more favourable result. The difference between a hypothetical Rate Support Grant and the actual financial transfers was almost non-existent before 1971. Since then subventions to Northern Ireland have risen, above the Rate Support Grant, to meet some 20 per cent of public sector spending.

Public sector finances in Northern Ireland have, over the years from the mid 1920s, been supplemented by transfers from the United Kingdom Exchequer. By the 1960s these were the equivalent of some 16 per cent of total public sector spending; this is the basis of the argument that Northern Ireland was treated favourably. However, the degree of social and economic need in Northern Ireland, stemming from higher unemployment, a greater proportion of family dependants, a poorer stock of social capital in housing and health, and lower living standards, was such that the scale of government financial transfers was, until the early 1970s, below the level which might have applied if Northern Ireland had 'enjoyed' the scale of spending justified by need. This is a significant conclusion, both in terms of the remedial action taken in the early 1970s to expand public sector spending and in terms of the continuing major social problem in the housing sector where, it is argued, the current (1980–1981) spending programmes may still be inadequate on a comparative basis.

Comparisons within the United Kingdom

Despite the efforts made to improve Northern Ireland's relative position in the United Kingdom, unemployment and emigration remained at higher levels than would be indicative of economic prosperity.

More reassuring evidence is given by the basic indicators of living standards. Whether measured by Gross Domestic Product or personal income levels, the evidence is that in the past twenty years the difference in standards between Northern Ireland and the United Kingdom, as a whole, has narrowed. Indeed on the less elaborate evidence, for example, from Isles and Cuthbert, this process has gone on since, at least, 1939. The following crude comparisons, with dates chosen because of the limitations of comparable statistical evidence, illustrate the change since 1961.

Table 4:5

INDICATORS OF LIVING STANDARDS
(as % of U.K. average)

| | Gross domestic product per head | | Personal income per head |
	Northern Ireland	Scotland	Northern Ireland
1961	61	87	71
1978	77	97	80
Gain	+16	+10	+9

Sources: Derived from National Income Blue Book, Regional Trends, Scottish Abstract of Statistics and Wilson Report

No single indicator gives a 'best' indication of relative prosperity. To illustrate both the range of possible answers, and the differences which they bring out, the following comparisons of Northern Ireland with the United Kingdom, for 1978, are relevant:

Table 4:6

COMPARATIVE INDICATORS

1978	*% of U.K.*
Gross domestic product per head	77
G.D.P. per person in labour force	86
G.D.P. per person at work	91
Personal income per head	80
Personal income per person in labour force	91
Personal income per person at work	96
Personal disposable income per head	82
P.D.I. per household	90
P.D.I. per person in labour force	93

P.D.I. per person at work	98
Consumers expenditure per head	88
C.E. per household	96
C.E. per person in labour force	100

(*Source:* Regional Trends, 1981. Adapted by the author)

The political reader now has evidence either of a 23 per cent gap or a parity of spending, depending on motivation, interpretation and purpose. For those who are unemployed or who have involuntarily emigrated such comparisons may, very reasonably, seem somewhat academic!

Northern Ireland and the Republic of Ireland: economic comparisons*

The preceeding sections were deliberately constructed with no reference to the Republic of Ireland. The intention was to try to assess the Northern Ireland economy in a United Kingdom context only. Of course, this was incomplete if only because one of the hypotheses for debate by all political groups in Northern Ireland is that Northern Ireland has, or has not, done better as a region of the United Kingdom than it might have done if it had been part of an enlarged Irish state. Not many political parties would suggest that their views on the unification of the island of Ireland or the retention of Northern Ireland as part of the United Kingdom are based solely, or even mainly, on the economic issues. Nevertheless, attempts have been made to use the economy as a supportive issue for the different viewpoints.

The arguments, in terms of the comparative performance of the two economies, Northern Ireland and the Republic of Ireland, do not readily lend themselves to one particular political viewpoint. Some of the quantifiable indicators can be presented and are listed here in two obvious contrasting groups.

Table 4:7

NORTH–SOUTH COMPARISONS, 1978

	N.I.	R. of I.	Relative N.I. position
Gross domestic product per head	£1,949	£1,744	+12%
G.D.P. per employed person	£5,316	£5,186	+2%
Personal income per head	£2,034	£1,837	+11%
Personal disposable income per head	£1,647	£1,471	+12%
P.D.I. per employed person	£4,493	£4,329	+4%

* The statistical sources in this section are, for Northern Ireland, as indicated earlier, and, for the Republic of Ireland, are drawn from the parallel official publications.

(1) Northern Ireland, on average, enjoys a higher standard of living than the Republic of Ireland and has done so continuously since the two units were created, although this did not occur *because* the island was divided. For 1978, the comparisons are illustrated in table 4:7.
(2) Although unemployment in Northern Ireland has been high, the position has, until recent years (which may be partly a reflection of the local problems), tended to be slightly lower than that in the Republic of Ireland. The published unemployment rates differ conceptually, in a manner which understates the position in the Republic relative to that in Northern Ireland, but still confirms this point.

Table 4:8
UNEMPLOYMENT RATES (%)
(annual average)

	N.I.	*R. of I.*
1951	6.1	7.3
1956	6.4	7.7
1961	7.5	5.7
1966	6.1	6.1
1971	7.9	7.2
1975	7.9	12.2
1979	11.3	9.3

(3) Emigration rates, pre 1971, were much higher for the Republic of Ireland than from Northern Ireland. In the period 1937–61, emigration rates from the Republic were almost double those from Northern Ireland. In the 1960s, both areas experienced similar emigration rates (see table 4:13, below).
Figures for the 1970s will be, when published, very different, showing a higher emigration rate from Northern Ireland and a net immigration flow into the Republic of Ireland.

(4) Living standards have, since the late 1950s or early 1960s been rising faster in the Republic of Ireland than in Northern Ireland.

Table 4:9
LIVING STANDARDS COMPARED

Gross domestic product per head (as % of U.K.)	*Northern Ireland*	*Republic of Ireland*
1961	61	40
1978	77	69
Gain	+16	+29

Personal income per head
(as % of U.K.)

	N.I.	R. of I.
1961	71	50
1978	80	71
Gain	+9	+21

(5) The growth of employment in the Republic of Ireland has, when the contraction in agricultural employment is taken into account, been better than that in Northern Ireland. This has been most conspicuous in the industrial sector. Employment in manufacturing has tended to decrease in Northern Ireland; in the Republic of Ireland there has been a general increase.

Table 4:10
EMPLOYMENT IN MANUFACTURING
('000s)

	N.I.	R. of I.
1956	185	167
1961	171	180
1966	179	197
1971	172	214
1976	147	219
1979	140	239

(6) The number of new industrial jobs promoted in the Republic of Ireland has increased both in absolute terms, and in comparison with the achievements in Northern Ireland.

Table 4:11
NEW JOBS PROMOTED

	N.I.	R. of I.
1966–1970	32,000	44,000
1971–1975	36,000	78,000
1976–1980	30,000	142,000

Sources: I.D.A. reports, Department of Commerce Facts & Figures
Note: I.D.A. 1966–70 = April 1966 to March 1971; N.I. includes Local Enterprise Development Unit.

The statistical comparisons, if they are to be summarised, present a picture of the economy of the Republic of Ireland expanding more quickly than that in Northern Ireland. The process of 'catching up' has been accelerated in the 1970s and, to a significant degree, can be attributed to the effect of the civil disorder in Northern Ireland. However, it would be misleading not to acknowledge that the evidence of a faster growth rate and a 'catching up' process pre-dates the emergence of the civil problems in Northern Ireland.

The faster expansion in the Republic of Ireland, pre-1970, was not particularly to be credited to a difference in the ability to attract investment. The experience of the 1960s was that, proportionately, Northern Ireland did rather better in securing new projects, but that this was counterbalanced by the contraction in the older industries. This 'declining sector' problem was less significant in the Republic of Ireland because, before 1960, it had a much smaller industrial sector than Northern Ireland.

In the 1970s the major difference has been the continued industrial expansion in the Republic of Ireland, contrasting with Northern Ireland's relative contraction. A further major difference has been the increased scale of the support for public sector spending in Northern Ireland which is not paralleled in the Republic. The net result has been that employment in both areas has expanded in similar proportion in the 1970s but in very different sectors of the economies.

Comparing the factors which contribute to the generation of economic expansion, the net gains for the Republic of Ireland in the past twenty years can possibly be traced to:

(a) the combination of full employment elsewhere and relatively cheaper labour supplies in the Republic attracting industry, together with a generous incentive package;

(b) the opening up, with guaranteed prices, both of the British and, later, EEC markets to Irish agricultural produce;

(c) the advantages, financial and economic, of EEC membership;

(d) the absence of the same dependence as Northern Ireland on textiles and heavy engineering industries where employment was contracting;

(e) the achievement, and retention of, a reputation for political stability.

Various points can be developed from these arguments. First, argument (a) is not so relevant in the early 1980s and is further weakened by the faster growth in wage costs per unit of output in the Republic of Ireland than elsewhere in Europe. Second, relative to Northern Ireland, arguments (b) and (c) are not now areas of significant advantage particularly if U.K. Exchequer transfers to Northern Ireland are taken into account. Argument (d) is still in the Republic's favour and argument (e) is certainly to Northern Ireland's disadvantage. Other factors in Northern Ireland's favour are, despite the earlier unfavourable comparison with Great Britain, the better provision of physical infrastructure and social facilities in Northern Ireland. It is not immediately obvious that, so long as both the United Kingdom and the Republic of Ireland remain members of the EEC, any of the direct *economic* factors would be moved in Northern Ireland's favour by changing its political relationship to take it out of the United Kingdom. Nor is it obvious how such a change would be arranged without prejudicing the large scale United Kingdom government financial transfers which are currently made to Northern Ireland. The major caveat to this conclusion is that the attainment of political stability is probably the most important factor in generating economic progress in Northern Ireland and this may have implications involving some elements of political change.

Variations within Northern Ireland: the issue of discrimination

There is, however, one further and important hypothesis which, even if the earlier arguments gave no part of an explanation of the tension in Northern Ireland (which is a more extreme statement than this writer would feel to be justified) would, on its own, link the civil disorder with economic factors. This is the suggestion that, *either* because of the scale of the regional problems *or* in spite of the scale of the problems, the distribution of the costs and benefits of the unemployment, new jobs and government spending, etc., falls unfairly within Northern Ireland. As a shorthand, with its admitted failings, this will be discussed in terms of whether the Roman Catholic community, either by the result of the interplay of market forces or by the result of deliberate acts of commission or omission, has done less well than the Protestant community.

This discussion is, if anything, even more difficult than the issues raised in earlier sections. In common with some of the earlier discussions, perceptions of reality or causation are often as strong, or stronger, factors than the reality itself in an analytical discussion. A *belief* that something is true can be an explanation of causation even if it is *not* true or cannot be shown to be true or false. The section is also made more difficult because certain evidence is simply not available. For example, the average incomes of Roman Catholics, or Protestants, is simply not recorded because the economic statisticians do not ask questions on earnings by religion and would not be encouraged or permitted to try.

In basic terms, there is no disagreement that unemployment and emigration have been higher in the Roman Catholic community than the Protestant. The problem of interpretation is one of what conclusions should be drawn from these facts. For some, these facts alone will be sufficient evidence. However, the geographical and structural factors determining the areas and occupations in which the communities are to be found may be an important determinant in any economic factors explaining the situation.

From the 1971 Census the Fair Employment Agency (1979, 8) has estimated the unemployment rates for Roman Catholics and Protestants and these are shown in table 4:12.

Table 4:12
UNEMPLOYMENT AND RELIGION, 1971 (%)

	Males and females	Males only
All Northern Ireland	8.5	10.4
Roman Catholics	13.9	17.3
Protestants	5.6	6.6

The Fair Employment Agency also presented evidence to show that unemployment (apart from within the inner Belfast area) tended to be higher the further the area was from Belfast, for both groups. In every District Council area, however, male unemployment for Roman Catholics was higher than for Protestants. This ratio, which on a Province-wide basis was 2.5 to 1, varied, between areas from the highest in Armagh (3.5 to 1), Castlereagh, Londonderry and Craigavon, to the lowest in Moyle (1.4 to 1), Ballymena, Coleraine and Newry.

Normal location theory would suggest that unemployment would be higher in the more rural areas of the Province and this, on a simple demographic relationship, would mean higher unemployment rates for Roman Catholics who are much more likely to reside in, what the Fair Employment Agency define as, peripheral areas (1979, 12). However, this is not adequate as more than part of this explanation.

The different unemployment ratios, by area, are not very consistent with an explanation which relies heavily on a pattern of deliberate discrimination in favour of one or the other community in some areas and not in others, although this does not rule this out as some part of the explanation.

One piece of evidence which seems to explain more of the difference in unemployment experience is the pattern of certain occupations being more heavily frequented by one group than the other. Whatever the historical explanation, Roman Catholics are more likely to be found in the occupations which have experienced the highest rates of seasonal and long term unemployment (Fair Employment Agency, 1978). For example 52 per cent of the Roman Catholic work force in 1971 was in the group classified as semi-skilled and unskilled, whilst the Protestant proportion was 40 per cent (Fair Employment Agency, 1979). This fact alone would explain a major part of the difference in unemployment rates, although the consequential question on the origins of this occupational structure then becomes relevant.

Emigration rates have also been higher in the Roman Catholic community. The evidence is summarised in the following table.

Table 4:13

NET EMIGRATION RATES FROM NORTHERN IRELAND
(Rate per 1000 per annum)

	Roman Catholics	Non-R.C.	Both Groups	R. of I.
1937–1951	6.5	2.3	3.7	6.9
1951–1961	10.8	4.6	6.7	13.8
1961–1971	6.9	2.8	4.3	4.8

Source: 1937–61 Barritt and Carter (1962), 1961–71 Author's calculation

The emigration ratios are consistent with an explanation that higher unemployment and emigration have been strongly correlated. One feature with possible relevance to the comparison with the Republic of Ireland is that in 1961–1971 the rate of Roman Catholic emigration from Northern Ireland became *higher* than the emigration rate in the Republic. In the earlier periods, emigration was higher from the Republic than even that experienced by Roman Catholics in Northern Ireland.

Given this demographic data which, whatever its causes, gives some insight into suggestions of 'unfairness', the question of economic policy is whether this situation was adequately assessed in the formulation and execution of government policies in the period under review.

As has been outlined earlier, the main thrust of government policy in attempting to generate economic development has been the expansion of industrial investment. This has been executed through a series of inducements and incentives to firms locating in the province, usually privately owned, from within or without the United Kingdom, supplemented by indirect policies of manpower training and infrastructure provision. Both in relation to infrastructure planning and industrial location there have, over the years, been allegations of inadequate recognition of the needs of the less prosperous parts of the province. Such complaints have focused on 'West of the Bann' or particular areas such as Londonderry, Strabane and Newry. Londonderry was a special focus for complaint when, in the late 1960s, it suffered a series of major economic setbacks. The then largest single male employing industrial firm (B.S.R.) closed completely in acrimonious circumstances; the rail link through Omagh to Belfast was closed; the New University was located at Coleraine and the decision to put extra resources into the development of Craigavon was seen as a diversion from the needs of the North–West of the Province.

Although government spending decisions may not be explicable in terms of 'pleasing all of the people all of the time' the underlying criticism was that government policy did not ensure an adequate, or fair, distribution of resources. This charge was particularly levelled at industrial projects. Successive governments relied on the strength of market forces to defend their position.

As far back as 1957, Isles and Cuthbert argued that

> Owing to the ...relationship between industrial density and distance from Belfast, this means also that most areas in which a large proportion of the insured workers are engaged in manufacturing are fairly near to Belfast, and most of those which have a small proportion in manufacturing industries are situated in outlying parts of the province   (p. 112)

Their evidence was that over 80 per cent of industrial employment was within 30 miles of Belfast and, by implication, that, given the characteristics of this area of $1\frac{1}{2}$m. people, this was not surprising.

The criticism of the past thirty years is that the areas of high unemployment in 1950 are the same areas that experience high unemployment in 1980. The defence of the situation is, first, that unemployment in total is still too high and that changes in its distribution (if they had occurred) would only have been a shifting of the problem. More positively, government would point to:

(a) the development of the growth centre strategy in the 1960s which resulted in New Towns legislation being used in Craigavon, Antrim–Ballymena, and Londonderry;

(b) the attempts to restrain the growth of Belfast in the 1960s;

(c) the co-ordination of infrastructure planning, manpower training and advance factory building to make various centres more likely to attract industry;

(d) the expansion of transport facilities through Larne and Warrenpoint;

(e) even during the disorder of the past decade, the efforts to ensure that physical development strategies evolve for the period to the end of the century (Regional Strategy, 1975–1995, published in 1975);

(f) the introduction of a differential in the scale of financial inducements to firms which locate in the areas of worst unemployment; usually a 5 per cent extra grant on capital spending (on top of the existing regional grants of some 40 per cent),

. . . and would add that a decade of disorder and the external image created by political uncertainty can be as powerful a disincentive as all the above positive efforts.

An analysis of the number of new projects by the district of location shows the spread of the new projects established since 1945. Employment figures are not available, to give a better indication of the employment impact, but the evidence is some indication of the combined effect of market forces and government policy.

New industrial projects have, in number, if not in employment terms, been widely spread throughout the province. Indeed a calculation shows that there is a close comparison of percentages unemployed in sub-regions and the number of new industrial projects.

Greater Belfast	37% of projects;	43% of unemployed in 1981
'East of the Bann'	66% of projects;	68% of unemployed
Londonderry	9% of projects;	10% of unemployed
Newry	9% of projects;	5% of unemployed
'West of the Bann'	33% of projects;	32% of unemployed

(For these purposes Newry and Armagh have been classified as West of the Bann)

Since the larger projects, in employment terms, may have tended to locate nearer to Belfast, this comparison is probably biased against the areas away from Belfast.

Another characteristic of the process of change is that the ratio of closures to new projects varies significantly. The worst records for closure rates (excluding Moyle) are in:

Newry	61%
Banbridge	57%
Ballymoney	55%
Belfast City	51%
Armagh	50%
Castlereagh	50%
Carrickfergus	50%
Londonderry	46%
Down	44%
Omagh	44%

against an overall average of 38%.

Another method of assessing the results is to examine the changes, if any, in the distribution of unemployment. This is done in table 4:14, which examines the position in 1955, 1961, 1968, and 1975. These dates have the common characteristics that the overall unemployment rate was at a similar level in each of these years, so that any changes would not be expected to reflect differences in the distribution of unemployment in periods of, for example, recession. 1981 has been added to show both the latest figures and to indicate whether the present recession has changed the picture, which it has.

Table 4:14

PROPORTION OF UNEMPLOYMENT IN DIFFERENT TRAVEL-TO-WORK AREAS

	June in each year				
	1955	1961	1968	1975	1981
Belfast	39	43	40	36	43
Ballymena	5	5	3	7	9
Downpatrick	5	5	4	3	4
Craigavon	8	6	6	6	5
Coleraine	7	5	6	6	5
Above areas	64	64	59	58	68
Londonderry	13	13	13	12	10
Strabane	5	4	5	5	3
Strabane	5	4	5	5	3
Omagh	2	2	3	3	3
Enniskillen	3	3	5	5	4
Dungannon and Cookstown	5	3	5	6	5
Armagh	4	4	3	3	2
Newry	4	7	7	8	5
Above areas	36	36	41	42	32
TOTAL	100	100	100	100	100

Source: Department of Manpower Services Statistics, adapted by author.

The location of new industrial projects is, however, only a part of the explanation of unemployment differences. No figures are available to show, for example, the spread of direct government spending throughout the Province. Areas of high unemployment almost always create a natural and understandable pressure for a reallocation of government spending in their favour.

A major part of the debate on allegations of discrimination in employment opportunities inevitably focuses on the unemployment problem in the city of Belfast. The 1971 Census of Population shows that unemployment was higher in Roman Catholic areas of the city than in Protestant areas.

During the 1960s, government would probably have argued that within a modern urban area, differences in unemployment could not be the basis of policies which were specific to particular suburbs. There was, in all the Government planning documents, an implicit assumption that Belfast could be treated as a single travel to work area. West Belfast was part of the city, with major social problems, but its economic welfare was treated as dependent on the overall welfare of the city as a whole.

This argument, which was not accepted by politicians representing the Roman Catholic areas of West Belfast, has been less defensible in the 1970s. Prior to the 1970s, the argument was vulnerable to the criticism that several major industries in the Belfast area had employment structures which reduced the opportunities for Roman Catholics. The law has since been altered to make deliberate discrimination illegal. Less amenable to legal action is the effect of the decade of violence on the preparedness of people to seek employment freely throughout the city. Violence, fear, and social tensions have themselves had a differential effect on the labour market.

The 1971 Census shows that unemployment is directly correlated with the social status of people in particular suburbs. This correlation is probably stronger than any other explanation of why employment rates vary. However, unpublished research into the Census results shows that when religion is added, unemployment experience for Roman Catholics, even when socio-economic status is taken into account, is, in the North and West of Belfast, about 50 per cent worse than in non-Roman Catholic areas. It is not yet possible to be sure of the basis for this difference. Contributory factors would include lack of preparedness to travel to some places to work, the historical consequences of discrimination, and demographic factors. It is a difference which is not easily reduced by explicit government policies.

The basic figures show a trend for unemployment in the period of relative success (the 1960s) to be alleviated proportionately more in the Belfast region. (In 1981, this has been sharply reversed.) The areas which did worst were Enniskillen and Omagh, but not, as might have been expected, Londonderry. In so far as a correlation between *worsening* unemployment and the emergence of civil disorder is being investigated, then this evidence is not particularly supportive of the thesis since the initial disorders were associated with Londonderry and Belfast. However, this is not to ignore the fact that the main sources of community tension and disorder have been in areas of *continuing* high unemployment.

Violence and the economy: the 1970s

The earlier discussion has continually emphasised the theme that, in the 1970s, economic analysis has been severely complicated by the interaction of local violence and disorder on the economy. The cost in terms of human suffering is, of course, unquantifiable and more important than the economic consequences in terms of finance.

The direct financial cost of more than a decade of violence can be presented in terms of Exchequer spending. Extra internal government spending for compensation and law and order, excluding the army, in 1979 probably was about £200m. Other government spending by 1979, in total, was some £350m. higher than it would have been by the (admittedly too low) standards of the late 1960s. In this sense government spending is now some 25% higher than by the relative U.K. standards of the 1960s.

Government revenue is down because of the tax loss from the loss of employment that might otherwise have existed. This, however, is a speculative area.

Among the other costs of the decade are the jobs lost, the investment deterred and the people who involuntarily emigrated from the Province. If Northern Ireland had managed to continue to increase industrial production at three-quarters of the rate in the Republic of Ireland, as was the position in the 1960s, then, at the end of the decade of the 1970s, production would have been 39 per cent higher. This is the equivalent of over 50,000 jobs. Even if this is an optimistic overstatement, as it seems, a loss of over 30,000/35,000 industrial jobs is a conservative estimate.

To estimate what might have been is always hazardous. However, even allowing for the 'ill-wind' effects of increased government spend-

ing, it would be hard *not* to conclude that the regional economic problems have been increased sharply in the past decade after an earlier
period when there were some small but significant improvements.

An Overview

In the late 1960s, the position of the Northern Ireland economy seemed
to be improving and, for a brief period, it seemed as if real long term
gains were being realized. In the main autonomous sectors of the
economy, reassuring trends or features could be cited.

In agriculture, the United Kingdom post-1945 price support system
had generally given Northern Ireland farmers a satisfactory set of
income guarantees and discussion of changes in the support system,
partly in anticipation of EEC membership, was not seen as a major
threat.

In industry, the rate of inward investment was meeting the targets set
in the Wilson report (1965) and seemed to be capable of offsetting the
loss of employment in existing firms.

The Government had devised financial arrangements to increase the
financial transfers from Westminster (the new Health Services Agreement and the Social Services Agreement, 1971) and the level of public
sector spending per capita was well above the United Kingdom average.

The effects of this buoyancy were, of course, transmitted to the other,
induced, sectors of the economy.

This is the structure of the argument that emphasized that Northern
Ireland had 'never had it so good' (to abuse the Macmillan description
of the late 1950s). However, the problems were far from being removed.

Agricultural employment, but not output, continued to contract.
Industrial employment did not expand as rapidly as needed or hoped.
Government spending was low when assessed by comparison with
relative needs, or certain other regions.

Developments in the 1970s have, with some exceptions, tended to
erode the gains of the 1960s. Agricultural incomes, at the end of the
decade have fallen sharply, and this is attributed to the problems of
financing the agricultural policy of the EEC. Industrial investment has
fallen sharply; it would have been deterred by the local disorder, but
wider economic forces would also have produced adverse consequences,
although on their own these would presumably not have been so severe.
The increase in Government spending programmes in the 1970s has, in
fact, been the major offset to a sharp contraction in the regional
economy. This increase was on a scale which may have increased total

employment (and incomes) by some 7–10 per cent in the decade. Even the restraints on public sector spending in 1980 and 1981 were small by comparison.

There is no doubt that Northern Ireland is still the least prosperous region of the United Kingdom. That fact alone may be relevant in an assessment of the origins of social tensions and violence, but has it been less prosperous because of neglect by government or because of defective government policies?

Earlier sections have shown how the Northern Ireland economy could be described as having had to 'run hard to stand still'. Industrial development was not large enough to offset the loss of industrial jobs. Government spending increased and was higher per head than in Great Britain, but was, until the early 1970s below the level assessed on the basis of 'need'. Although unemployment and emigration have remained at relatively high levels, the objective indicators of living standards showed a marked relative and absolute improvement.

The improvement in the performance of the economy of the Republic of Ireland was, even before 1970, more marked than in Northern Ireland. In the 1970s, the Republic has been catching up somewhat faster.

This evidence, if the arguments are accepted, does not *prove* the hypothesis that economic progress in Northern Ireland was significantly deterred because of factors inherent in the political structure of two separate units. There has been some political support for the suggestion that Northern Ireland would have benefited economically by being linked to the faster growing economy of the Republic. This argument, on the evidence cited earlier, is unproven unless it is presumed that the existence of 'one' economy might have somehow created conditions which would have avoided the indirect effects of violence on the economy. Put in a quasi-political style, what were the *economic* gains to commend a change (a) when both were members of the EEC and (b) when the main economic benefit of the existing framework was and is the continuing large scale government financial transfers to Northern Ireland from the United Kingdom Exchequer which would be difficult to sustain in an all-Ireland setting.

5

Informal Social Organisation
Hastings Donnan and
Graham McFarlane

Any assessment of the current state of Northern Irish society must deal with the relevance of being a Protestant and being a Catholic in the mundane areas of everyday life. While it is true that dramatic events can lay bare the dominant characteristics of a society, it is also true that any understanding of a society's make-up cannot be achieved without paying detailed attention to those aspects of life which appear trivial when set against the big issues of the day. Only too often a focus on the dramatic blinds the observer to the complexity to be found in a society's fabric.

This paper deals with the sociological and social anthropological literature which has focused its attention on the informal social relations which exist between Catholics and Protestants. The literature with which we will be concerned is all based on some kind of research using fieldwork, i.e. the active participation of the researcher in the day to day life of the people whose activities are being investigated. We will not discuss that research which uses the more depersonalised attitude surveys and questionnaires, even though this means that we will have to disregard the literature which looks specifically at Catholic and Protestant *attitudes* (the best of these are probably O'Donnell 1977 and Rose 1971). We believe that attitude surveys in general provide little more than a partial and sometimes distorted view of day to day life: in day to day life attitudes are fluid, and responsive to the exigencies of the situation. Consequently, attitudes and actions are not in any simple relationship with one another: not only do they interact but they often seem to be in apparent contradiction to one another. It is for these reasons, and not because of some simple professional preference or bias, that we consider the battery of techniques used most consistently (but not exclusively) by social anthropologists to be the most suitable for research on the social interaction between groups (cf. Harris 1982). These methods comprise, briefly, a blend of formal and informal interviews supported by, and dependent upon, lengthy periods of intensive involvement with a limited number of people (this latter aspect is vaguely described as 'participant observation'). All the literature with which we will be dealing is based on research using these approaches to varying degrees.

We will start by providing a brief overview of this literature, then go on to review in some detail what we know (or think we know) about the relevance of the Catholic-Protestant division in various areas of social life.

Informal Social Organisation in Northern Ireland: An Overview of the Literature

Although a somewhat impressionistic analysis of Catholic and Protestant relations was undertaken by a team led by Mogey in the 1940s (Mogey 1947; 1948), and although Barritt and Carter have provided a brief overview of social life in Northern Ireland (see Barritt and Carter 1972, chapt. 4), Rosemary Harris' research around the border town of 'Ballybeg'* in the early 1950s constitutes the most sensitive early attempt to get behind the public attitudes of Protestants and to a lesser extent Catholics. This research was the basis for her M.A. thesis (Harris 1954), but it was substantially reworked for her paper on political leadership in the area (Harris, 1961) and for her justly acclaimed book *Prejudice and Tolerance in Ulster* (Harris 1972). Since Harris' work has had great importance for later research, in that many of her themes are echoed there, it is worthwhile to spend some time looking at it in detail.

Harris sets about making explicit the attitudes of local Protestants towards Catholics and then tries to deal with what looks like a paradox: those Protestants with the strongest anti-Catholic attitudes were at the same time those who interacted most tolerantly with their Catholic neighbours. Harris' explanation of this apparent paradox has two parts. Firstly, the generally negative attitudes towards Catholics were intensified by the distrust the less prosperous Protestants felt towards the Protestant elite (both in the local and national context). The fear was of being 'sold out' to the Republic of Ireland, and it was this fear

---

*'Ballybeg' is a pseudonym for the place in which Harris carried out her research. We have put all such pseudonyms within inverted commas the first time they appear in the text but thereafter have not distinguished them. Concealing the identity of the area studied has long-been a commonplace anthropological practice.

which motivated the poorer Protestants' appeal to Protestant solidarity in their dealings with the elite in the local Orange Lodge (the only arena they had for interaction with them). Secondly, their behaviour towards their Catholic neighbours was guided by conflicting values relating to the proper behaviour between neighbours of whatever religion: the Catholic and Protestant identities were underplayed. These values were part of what Harris calls the 'common culture' which seemed to derive not only from being neighbours but also from sharing a similar class, or position on the economic ladder. Harris argues that the conflict built into the basic dichotomy between Catholic and Protestant was restrained by cross-cutting personal relationships and the norms which pertain to them. In short, Harris shows the amount of common ground which existed between members of each religious category at given socio-economic levels. The religious dichotomy did, however, remain basic, as evidenced especially by the limited number of marriages and hence kinship ties across the boundary.

Harris followed up her suggestion, that the lack of kinship ties across the boundary maintains social distance, with historical work which seems to show that where kinship networks did cross the boundary in Rathlin Island, they actually encouraged mixed marriages, and hence the creation of more kinship and affinal ties across the boundary (Harris 1979). Ultimately, she argues, such marriages across the boundary were engendered by a shared culture which itself had been generated out of mutual opposition towards the landlord class.

Harris has since returned to the paradoxes of Northern Irish life in a recent comparison between community relations in Ballybeg and 'Patricksville' in southern Eire (Harris 1979; Bax 1976). On the surface, according to Harris, political attitudes in Patricksville in the 1960s seemed to exhibit a kind of consensus, while on the surface in the 1950s Ballybeg political life showed signs of considerable disunity, to say the least. On the other hand, actual day to day life in Patricksville seemed to be replete with obvious tensions, clashes of interest and, indeed, violence; while among the population of Ballybeg there was a playing down of blatant hostility.

Other work mirrors much of what is to be found in Harris' material. The forces which operate, not only to divide, but also to integrate Northern Irish society are summarised by Leyton, in a paper written around the same time as Harris' *Prejudice and Tolerance in Ulster*, but based mostly on research in two communities in South Down in the 1960s (Leyton 1974a). Leyton has also elegantly demonstrated the importance of class, or one's relative position in economic hierarchies, for the understanding of patterns of inheritance (Leyton 1970a; 1970b; 1975) and for the understanding of attitudes towards, and interaction with, kin and friends in the Protestant village of 'Aughnaboy' (Leyton 1974b; 1975). Leyton has also looked at how disputes are channelled and contained in this Protestant village: here he argues that the shared values and the balance of power which were created by the community served to counterbalance the negative forces which operated within it (Leyton 1966). Similar mechanisms containing open hostility seem to be at work in the 'Upper Tullagh' (Buckley 1982). Extending Harris' remarks on the language of debate in the Ballybeg Orange Lodge, McFarlane's work in a predominantly Protestant north Down village shows how notions about Catholic, Protestant, and class identities and values functioned as part of the rhetoric used to wage the trivial and not so trivial disputes which are probably the stuff of everyday life in any community in Northern Ireland (and elsewhere). McFarlane has also taken up Harris' interest in mixed marriages, attempting to unravel the significant factors which people take into account when evaluating such marriages (McFarlane 1979). In an effort to get behind public responses to mixed marriages, Monaghan (1980) has attempted to detail the ways in which a small number of middle class couples coped with their stigmatised position. Bell has taken up Harris' interest in co-operation between farmers in a comparative study across Northern Ireland (Bell 1978). Finally, Blacking, Holy and Stuchlik's work in four rural communities (in north and south Down, Fermanagh and Antrim) returns to one of the central questions of Harris, though from a slightly different methodological angle (see Blacking *et al* 1978, and McFarlane 1980 for a brief summary). Unlike Harris, they do not attempt to account for the religious divide, but like Harris they do try to show exactly where, when and how the division was made relevant or irrelevant in the 'private' and 'public' domains of community life. Their findings seem to be very similar to Harris', so they add a 1970s dimension to her research.

Thus, Harris' work does seem to be a kind of touchstone for research into the informal social organisation in Northern Ireland. It is certainly the major text which has to be taken into account for any new research in this area. However, in setting the pace it has also been partly responsible for directing research on social organisation into small scale rural networks, probably because the very sensitivity of the approach precludes its application to large populations. No once can deny the usefulness of Boal's extensive and innovative analyses of territoriality and population movement in Belfast (see Boal 1969; 1970; 1971; 1972; Poole and Boal 1973), nor the value of Kirk's work on religious segregation in Lurgan (Kirk 1967), but urban research into Catholic and Protestant relations has, until recent years, been based on questionnaires or indirect social indicators rather than 'on the ground' reportage. It has missed out on the qualitative element. It is only recently that anthropological type research has been carried out in such areas. The most important recent text is based on research carried out in 'Anro', a Catholic enclave in West Belfast, over a period of eight months, between 1972 and 1973 (Burton 1978). Burton's work is another milestone, not only for its focus on an urban area but also because his book is the first to look at a completely Catholic community. Burton attempts to uncover the dynamic and fluid relationship which existed between the Provisional IRA and the embattled community, a community with a Catholic view built up around the three features of community solidarity, sectarianism and Republicanism. Most important for a consideration of Catholic-Protestant relations is Burton's analysis of sectarianism, According to Burton, the dimension of sectarianism is both demonstrated by, and is sustained to uncover or 'tell' the religious affiliations of new acquaintances prior to social interaction (see Burton 1978, chapt. 2; 1979). This practice is also discussed in Harris 1972, 148). Other enthnographic work which is now beginning to bear fruit has been carried out by Nelson on the world view of a group of Protestant activists in Belfast (see Nelson 1975; 1976a; 1980); by Jenkins who has researched into the problems confronted by Protestant youngsters entering employment in Belfast (see Jenkins 1978; 1981a; 1981b); and by Taylor who has looked at the interaction between religious and political ideas among Free Presbyterians (Taylor 1979; 1980; 1981). New research is being carried out by Blacking on Catholic and Protestant relations in Larne.

Informal Social Organisation in Northern Ireland: Detailed Research Findings

This section deals with the detailed findings of the research work which has been carried out on social relations between Catholics and Protestants. To provide some order in our presentation of these findings, we have used a range of easily identifiable areas of everyday life as a framework, assessing the relevance of the Catholic and Protestant division in each area. We have also made a broad categorization of these areas into two domains: public and private. We will turn to the private domain first.

The Private Domain

Economic Co-operation

One of the most important gauges of the social relevance of the Catholic and Protestant identities in everyday life is the extent to which they co-operate with one another. Co-operation may be of two types: primary co-operation for gaining a livelihood, and secondary co-operation like babysitting, lending ladders, etc. Most social anthropologists have concentrated on the first of these, and all the detailed investigation has been carried out in rural areas.

Harris (1972: especially chapt. 5), puts her emphasis on the different co-operation practices to be found among the Catholic and Protestant hill farmers and more prosperous (and mostly Protestant) infield farmers in Ballybeg in the 1950s. In the infield, co-operation was a matter of contributing labour: depending upon who was available, kin, friends or in-laws would form work teams (or 'swop') with one another. One of the consequences of this class difference in co-operation practices was the fact that some of this neighbourly co-operation went on between Catholic and Protestant; the fact that one did not have machinery nor kin or neighbours who were co-religionists tended to encourage 'swopping' labour across the divide. On the other hand, because most infield farmers were Protestant, co-operation between Catholics and Protestants there was limited; and when it existed, it had an element of imbalance in it, since machine owners (usually Protestant) expected labour from non-owners (usually Catholic) in return for the use of their machinery.

Harris does not assess the relative stress placed on different types of social relationship in co-operation practices in Ballybeg, although neighbourhood proximity did seem to have a primary role. Co-operation depended on some degree of geographical proximity: where kin were also neighbours, that was even better but if neighbours were mostly Catholic, that was not insurmountable. At first glance Leyton's work on Aughnaboy seems to contradict Harris' emphasis on neighbourhood. Leyton wanted to assess the role of kinship in the economic affairs in Protestant Aughnaboy. Despite the fact everyone in the village agreed (though for different reasons) that relatives and economic affairs ideally do not go together (cf. Bell 1978, 49), there were some differences in co-operation practices within the population. Leyton identifies two broad economic levels which he refers to as the working masses and the elite, each of which exhibited different attitudes towards such co-operation. The working masses needed kinsmen for information about jobs, and occasionally for obtaining jobs, while some of the elites in the area saw kin as an encumbrance to their social and economic mobility. The masses actively manipulated kinship relations, while the elites tried to prevent their kinsmen manipulating them. Those among the masses who had no kin in the area made up for this deficiency by making use of friends or, if they had married into the village, in-laws and other affines.

The difference between the Aughnaboy masses' emphasis on kinship and affinity for economic co-operation and the general emphasis on neighbourhood proximity in the Ballybeg area is probably a result of the different economic bases in the two areas (cf. Leyton 1977). In the hills around Ballybeg, co-operation was more direct and materialistic and it was rooted in space: in Aughnaboy, co-operation between kin was more a matter of exchange of indirect services and spatial factors counted for less. The two patterns have obviously different consequences for Catholic and Protestant co-operation. The importance of kinship and affinity for economics for the masses in Aughnaboy, together with the fact that kin and affines tend to be co-religionists, seemed to preclude any co-operation across the religious divide; in Ballybeg, as we have seen, the demands of proximity in farming allowed it to some extent. Buckley's conclusions from his work among the farmers of Upper Tullagh seem to be anomalous here (Buckley 1982). To Buckley, economic co-operation between Catholic and Protestant farmers is not a simple product of the economic necessity of co-operation with those living nearby; it is rather a matter of conscious design. Buckley argues that since any close relationship can be disrupted and contaminated by economic considerations, there are obvious dangers in co-operating with such people. Arguments with one person can lead to the severing of many ties. According to Buckley, the farmers in the Upper Tullagh therefore tended to cut their losses, and they chose to co-operate with those with whom any disruption of relations would have the least social costs, i.e. with neighbours of the opposite religion.

Although the argument is intriguing, the evidence advanced to support it is unconvincing. Moreover, can it be argued that people choose to co-operate with one another simply with an eye to the consequences of a disruption in that relationship, or do they mix these considerations with an awareness of the *positive* benefits of co-operation with particular people? For instance, it could be that one avoids co-operation with kinsmen in favour of neighbours, not out of a fear of spoiling good relations with kin, but out of a desire to extend one's sphere of co-operation outside the kinship network. One does not have to continually and deliberately foster good relations with kin (good relations are in a sense assumed), but one does have to invest in relations with neighbours if one wants to have an extensive sphere of co-operation. It is possible that co-operation with neighbours across the religious divide also has practical roots: if a Protestant/Catholic can obtain something from a Catholic/Protestant which he or she cannot obtain from a co-religionist then this will encourage cooperation.

While kinship and neighbourhood have different degrees of importance for primary economic co-operation in different areas and at different times, it can be gleaned from the available evidence that there is a strong tendency for people in local communities to rely chiefly on kin, if kin are available, for most *secondary* favours. This is the conclusion of Blacking *et al* (1978, 23-25) from their work in four villages, of Burton from his work in Anro (1978, chapt. 1), and of McFarlane from his work in a north Down village (1978, 141). Of course, non-kin were often involved in the exchange of such favours as babysitting etc., and people with no kin nearby had to rely on other people. Nevertheless, the emphasis on kinship still stands.

Blacking *et al* have some interesting things to say about the importance of the Catholic and Protestant division in this area. They point out that there were various strategic reasons for such a stress on kinship relations in the four villages they investigated—for instance, safe-guarding reputations, or the fact that direct or immediate returns of favours are not necessary; consequently such co-operation was quantitively less frequent outside the kinship field. Since most kinsfolk were of the same religion, given the small number of mixed marriages, this implies that such co-operation was almost certain to be between co-religionists. But the religious factor cannot then be used to explain such co-operation, since some people did have kin of the opposite religion and they *did* co-operate with each other. According to Blacking *et al,* the religious factor seems to be of only contingent relevance: as a subtle constraint on mutual aid between specific kin who are not co-religionists, and an *additional* constraint among people who are not kin.

Informal Visiting

Perhaps the safest generalisation one can make about social relations in Northern Ireland is that most inter-household and informal visiting goes on between close relatives. This is emphasised by most writers (see Blacking *et al* 1978, 25-26; Boal 1969, 43; Buckley 1982, 124-125; Harris 1972, chapters 5 and 7; Leyton 1974b; 1975, chapters 4 and 5; McFarlane 1978, 199; Harris 1972, 144-146). This is most important for women, and in many rural areas most inter-household visiting goes on between female relatives (Blacking *et al* 1978, 25-26). Given the importance of kinship, it is obvious that there is little to produce a definite pattern of visiting across the religious divide (cf. Harris 1972, 146). Nevertheless, in the case of the exchanging of small favours, with which visiting is closely tied up, it does seem that those who have kin of the opposite religion can justifiably maintain a visiting relation with kinsfolk: however, this is less frequent when kin of the same religion are equally accessible. Of course, visits with non-kin did occur in the areas studied, and not only with co-religionists, but this was most evident and important among those who do not have relations in the vicinity. Blacking *et al* have calculated that of all the visits between unrelated Catholics and Protestants, most were between individuals who had kinship ties to a particular locality and individuals on the other side who lacked such ties. Visiting relations across the divide were also often established between people who both lacked kinship connections in a given locality, especially among incomers to that locality.

It would seem, therefore, that the informal visiting pattern is based on close relations of kinship and friendship, ties which are usually to be found among co-religionists, but which do, of course, occasionally cross over the divide. As in the case of exchange of small favours, in this sphere religion seems to be contingent in two ways: it is a restriction on the relative frequency of visiting between Catholic and Protestant who have accessible kin of the same religion, and it is an additional constraint on the amount of visiting undertaken by non-kin. To counterbalance this emphasis on religion, it is important to point out that differences in the perceived class of individuals can operate in a similar way. Differences in perceived class did seem to limit interaction with secondary kin (cousins, uncles etc.) among the elite of Aughnaboy (Leyton 1975, 44-45), and it operated similarly in the four communities investigated by Blacking *et al* (1978, 25). Further perceived differences in class operated to preclude informal visiting between non-kin.

Personal disputes

Not so much of a systematic nature has been written about involvement in personal disputes, apart from Leyton's paper (1966) on his data from Protestant Aughnaboy, and Blacking *et al* (1978), which includes some material on interpersonal disputes across the religious divide. This area is a crucial one, since disputes are probably the most obvious indication of 'on the ground' social strain. What does this material tell us?

It is probably safe to say that there is a value put on harmony in most communities in Northern Ireland: practically every observer has commented on this. However, this value on harmony is not enough either to contain disputing, nor does it help us to understand the regularities or patterns to be found in disputes. Leyton argues that involvement in disputes among the Protestant villagers in Aughnaboy was determined by the different mixes of costs and benefits built into the relationships between the disputants and others. The weighing up of these costs and benefits account for variation in the intensity and number of disputes between different types of people: among kin, benefits outweigh costs (especially among kin related through women, between whom conflict over property was unlikely), so disputes were on an individual level and were relatively easily settled. With non-kin the potential for social strains outweighs the benefits which are built into such relations, so disputes were more likely. However, these disputes were also kept at an individual level, and were usually easily settled, since if whole families were to be involved, numerous valuable cross-cutting social ties would be disrupted; there was pressure on the disputants either to settle, or to maintain a low key in the dispute. With people who did not have a dense network of kin to support them, these disputes could last longer. Most disputes were between people related by marriage, where costs usually outweigh benefits, and they were at their most severe when, as was usually the case, in-laws lived in different communities. These findings are very similar to those of Blacking *et al* (1978, 27).

Given the logic to be found in this dispute pattern, it would seem likely that disputes which break out between unrelated Catholics and Protestants should be both common and difficult to settle. Moreover, they should escalate into a group confrontation between members of different kinship networks, if not whole religious blocs. In fact, there does not seem to be any evidence that disputes between unrelated Catholics and Protestants are more frequent than they are within each bloc. Nevertheless Blacking *et al* argue that, when such disputes develop, they are not settled quickly. This is logical enough, since there are usually few direct benefits in settling quickly, or in putting pressure on others to do so. This is also because such anti-social behaviour can be easily defended. One can challenge the value placed on harmony and escape sanctions by arguing that one is fighting from a Protestant corner. This is especially the case when the dispute is not about control over people or about breakdown in reciprocity, but about resources like land (cf. Barritt and Carter 1972, 61). However, in no case recorded by Blacking *et al* did disputes escalate into a conflict between Catholics and Protestants as groups; in the four rural communities investigated, the network of supporters of those involved seemed to cross over the religious border.

Life Cycle Events

Buckley has neatly summed up one aspect of Northern Irish social life when he describes it as 'endoritualistic', a piece of anthropological jargon which means that Catholics and Protestants do not participate directly in each others' rituals (cf. Barritt and Carter 1972, chapt. 2 and p. 64; Harris 1972, 132; and Leyton 1974a, 192-193). Here we are concerned with rituals pertaining to the life cycle, baptisms, weddings and funerals, all of which are principally the concern of kin (see Blacking *et al* 1978, 28-29, 31 for detailed data on the parts played by kin in these rituals). However, when it comes to less direct involvement in rituals, this clear boundary around those who should be involved seems to become a little blurred.

In Ballybeg, Aughnaboy and in the four communities investigated by Blacking *et al*, local morality emphasised that community member-ship entailed an interest or concern for the passage of all co-residents through the life cycle. Harris stresses the obligation felt by all people in the Ballybeg area to show respect at funerals; and she shows how in the hill area at least, it was important to attend *all* neighbours' wedding parties: in the more prosperous infield, invitations to wedding parties were more restricted (Harris 1972, 79-80, 108-110). Leyton refers to the obligation of community members to help bury the dead (Leyton 1975, 11). Blacking *et al* reiterate that it was the obligation of all senior adult males at least to walk behind the coffins of all fellow villagers, but they point out that greatest emphasis was placed on relationships based on kinship, neighbourhood, friendship and affinity. This was symbolised by the fact that only people in these relationships attended pre-funeral wakes and returned to the house for post-funeral snacks and meals. Where such relationships cross the religious divide, the duties built into such relations are played up, and the Catholic and Protestant identities are underplayed.

This section is probably a suitable point to bring up the question of mixed marriages. Although Buckley argues, somewhat controversially, that the conventions prohibiting mixed marriages are decreasing in importance in the Upper Tullagh (Buckley 1982, 127), most of the available evidence suggests that mixed marriages are still the ultimate challenge to the rules defining proper relations between Catholics and Protestants. The material collected by Blacking *et al* in the 1970s does not suggest that attitudes towards or practical responses to such marriages among the population at large were much different from those of the residents of Ballybeg in the 1950s (Blacking *et al* 1978, 29-30). Harris argues that mixed marriages were very rare indeed (Harris 1972, 143-144, 171). Leyton argues that in Protestant Aughnaboy in the 1960s there was a total prohibition on marrying Catholics (Leyton 1975, 57), while elsewhere he refers to the threat of violence from the prospective bride and groom's families, (Leyton 1974a, 191).

While all mixed marriages seem on the face of it to be anathema to the lay population in Northern Ireland, commonsense tells us that this is not all there is to it: it is likely that some mixed marriages are worse than others. McFarlane (1979) has indicated the factors which people seem to use to evaluate different types of marriage. There are different types of mixed marriage in the sense that there are different likely outcomes for the future children of various marriages: these outcomes depend upon the sex of the spouse who is of the other religion and upon which spouse has decided to change religion. Out of this McFarlane has devised a cultural scale dealing with the relative unpopularity of different types of marriages.

The Public Domain

Political Involvement

It almost goes without saying that political support and opinion in Northern Ireland has for the most part been based on the Catholic-Protestant division. Each side has its own political parties and movements. We are not concerned here with the factors lying behind this sectarian division in politics. Our concern is rather with putting politics into its social context (the approach advocated by Harris 1979): to assess what is known about grass roots political activities and what is known about the relations between political groupings and surrounding community structures and attitudes. We will start by looking at what is known about the activities of local branches of official political parties.

Surprisingly not very much has been written on this, and some comments which have been made raise more questions than they answer. A lot of disparate pieces of useful information are hidden behind the statement that in the Aughnaboy area 'virtually all Protestants are members or supporters of the Unionist Party, and virtually all Catholics are members or supporters of the various Catholic parties such as the Nationalists, the Republicans, or Sinn Fein' (Leyton 1974a, 191). Who are members? Who is involved? What are their attitudes? Harris refers to the great deal of distrust felt by the poorer Ballybeg Protestants for the Belfast Unionists (1972, 189-190), but she does not give many details about political activities in the area, either by the poorer hill farmers or by the infield farmers. One would expect that the infield farmer population would have included a few local political activists.

There are only a few suggestive remarks made elsewhere. McFarlane's data (1978) indicates that it was only a small core of middle class Protestants who were members of, and actively participated in, the affairs of the local branch of the Unionist Party in the north Down village in which he did his research. Moreover, the same people are prominent in other organistions. Blacking *et al* also note that in the four communities which they studied, active involvement in both Orange and Green political parties was mostly restricted to the categories of businessmen, professionals (especially teachers), farmers (especially large scale farmers in the Unionist case), retired members of these groups, and spouses of those belonging to these groups. There is obviously a considerable variation in the factors which might be used to account for low levels of direct political involvement: for instance, where a party's seat is considered safe, party supporters may be too complacent to become actively involved, while opponents may see activism as pointless (see McFarlane 1978, 280). However, in general terms it could be argued that the low level of popular involvement has at least something to do with the easily discernible set of popular attitudes towards politics and political activity. Blacking *et al* report (like Harris 1961; 1972, chapt. 11) that those who become involved in political affairs were both distrusted and ridiculed as upstarts.

As far as we can tell, the rural studies focus their attention only on the political parties whose legitimacy is not in question. Burton's analysis of the relationship between the Provisional IRA and the community of Anro presents a picture of the struggle for legitimacy faced by paramilitaries. Burton anchors the ideology of the activists in a divided society, but, more important, he assesses the mainsprings of support for the IRA in its local social milieu of Anro, rather than in any broad commitment to Republicanism or Nationalism. Support was fluid and waxed and waned within the community: it responded to outside forces which affected the community, it responded to the periodic challenges of other parties (for example, the Catholic Church) and it took into account that activists were known 'in the round' as someone's kinsman or neighbour. The debate about the rights and wrongs of IRA activists was contained within Anro: it was seen by the local people as an internal debate and only members of the community had the right to be involved.

Burton's focus on the claims and counterclaims of the various parties to this internal debate demonstrates as neatly as possible the potential of the ethnographic method and the importance of examining the broad social backcloth against which politics is played out. The fact that there was a debate about the legitimacy of the IRA in Anro meant that support could not be attributed to a given section of the population in a simple way. The fluidity of the situation meant that there were shifting allegiances over time, and it meant that support could be given to different arguments even at the same time. Despite what a recent critic has suggested (see Patterson 1979), Burton does not seem to deny that there were other traditions, or other rhetorics, operating in the community: he just suggests that it is superficial to view support as somehow fixed and a limited resource which can be given to only one organisation or movement. Commonsense tells us that support can be given to different organisations, for different purposes. This fluidity of support also seemed to characterise relations between working class Protestant communities in Belfast and Protestant paramilitaries in the early 1970s (cf. Nelson 1976b).

The political importance of the Protestant Orange Order and, to a lesser extent, the Catholic Ancient Order of Hibernians has been stressed by virtually every commentator on Northern Ireland. There is virtually nothing in the literature on the local organisation of the Ancient Order of Hibernians and virtually nothing on the urban Orange Lodges. However, there is some evidence of a distinct pattern in membership in rural Orange Lodges. Blacking *et al* report that overall membership of the lodges in their rural communities amounted to between 30 and 40 per cent of the total adult male Protestant population (Blacking *et al* 1978, 36). In addition, many spouses of Lodge members belonged to ladies' committees (emphasising the Lodges' social role) and many sons belonged to Junior Lodges or bands attached to Lodges, prior to becoming members of the local Lodge. Most members of the rural Lodges belong to the skilled, semi-skilled or unskilled manual occupational categories, while there were very few professionals involved (cf. Barritt and Carter 1972, 62; Buckley 1982, 147-148).

The class composition of at least the rural Lodges is understandable when we consider attitudes towards the Lodges. Harris reports that the Ballybeg Lodges were regarded with disdain by the more prosperous infield farmers in the area (Harris 1972, esp. 191-193), while the Protestants in the less prosperous hill area regarded it as the last bastion of Protestantism. Similar attitudes have been recorded by McFarlane (1978, 225-226).

Voluntary Organisations

The intensification of conflict in urban areas in the early 1970s brought in its wake a proliferation of local community associations, many of which were formed initially to offer protection and to alleviate housing intimidation (see Burton 1978, 29; Darby 1976, 159; Griffiths 1978). With the failure of the authorities to deal satisfactorily with the demands from both communities and with their increasing inability to provide even basic social amenities (such as refuse collection and transport to and from the city centre) in some areas, living conditions could be maintained or improved only when local residents tackled the problems themselves. Consequently, self-help seemed the only solution and many new tenants' associations were founded to operate in this capacity. As the Troubles intensified the role of these associations broadened and in some cases even matured into experiments in self-government (see, for example, Burton's discussion of the Anro Community Council and Relief Committee 1978, 29ff).

In urban areas membership in these associations was almost entirely religiously homogeneous. This seems to have been partly a consequence of the fact that they were formed initially to protect the areas in which they emerged (and like Anro's Relief Committee were therefore sectarian by definition), and partly also the result of residential segregation (cf. Darby 1976, 160). Such segregation, and so such homogeneity of membership, seems likely to continue despite efforts to change it; though the Anro Redevelopment Association itself intended to rehouse the original Protestant inhabitants in dwellings which it had restored within Anro, its attempts have so far been unsuccessful (Burton 1978, 30). The situation with regard to membership in such associations in rural areas is not so clear and the available literature tends to give them scant attention. Exceptions here are the work of Blacking *et al* (1978), and McFarlane (1978). In all four of the communities investigated by Blacking *et al* there were tenants' associations, all of which were established as a result of the centralization of local government functions, especially those concerned with housing and planning. These have marked a change in the traditional leadership pattern described by Harris (1961); the minister, priest, doctor and teacher no longer have a monopoly of influence. However, membership in each was low and, despite the fact that they were *de jure* open to all comers, they were dominated by businessmen, farmers and professionals. It would be extremely difficult to argue that there was any sectarian basis to recruitment into these organisations; membership of the association in the largely Protestant north Down village investigated included middle-class Catholics. (Blacking *et al* 1978, 34). Much more significant was the low level participation by both Catholics and Protestants. Both Blacking *et al* and McFarlane (1978, 231) argue that low participation is a consequence of a general reluctance to set oneself up as a spokesman for the community and to leave oneself open to ridicule if one does not perform well at meetings. This is the 'modesty' syndrome discussed by Harris (1972, chapt. 6). Its consequences are exactly the same as those described by Harris (1961); only those who have little or nothing to lose from criticism, or who are confident enough to be active, take part. As Blacking *et al* point out, the fact that one can be denigrated for participation only dignifies those who are able to participate effectively. These people tend to be in a different league; they are middle-class, and very often middle-class immigrants to local communities.

Information on other kinds of voluntary associations does not seem to have this urban bias, and most writers give at least some attention to membership of organisations like the Women's Institute, Young Farmers' Club, Lions' Club and so on. The avowed aim of many of these associations in both rural and urban areas is to transcend the sectarian divide and most of them actively try to recruit members along non-sectarian lines (Buckley 1982, 150; Darby 1976, 155: Harris 1972, 138).

However, though expressed policies may be consistent it is less easy to generalise about actual membership. Thus while membership in the Women's Institute was predominantly Protestant in Ballybeg in the 1950s (Harris 1972, 138), it was entirely Protestant in Aughnaboy in the 1960s (Leyton 1975, 12), and mixed in 'Kilbeg' in the 1970s (Buckley 1982, 150). Similarly, while membership in Young Farmers' Clubs in some areas might have been drawn from both communities (see Barritt and Carter 1972, 146; Buckley 1982, 150), in Ballybeg it was once again predominantly Protestant (Harris 1972, 138). Certainly in Belfast, and in some provincial towns, membership in voluntary organisations has often reflected the religious divide and, in some places such as Lurgan, parallel associations have existed for both Catholic and Protestant (Darby 1976, 155; Kirk 1967). Perhaps not surprisingly, such religious homogeneity of membership has been particularly characteristic of youth clubs, since many of these are connected to particular church congregations (cf. Barritt and Carter, 1972, 146; Buckley 1982, 145).

While the difficulties of making generalizations are therefore apparent, certain kinds of voluntary association seem to be consistently quoted as examples of organisations which do have cross-cutting membership. Thus Barritt and Carter note that both Catholic and Protestant participate in societies associated with the Arts, in Rotary Clubs, the Round Table and in Business and Professional Women's Clubs (Barritt and Carter 1972, 142, 144); Leyton notes that in Aughnaboy voluntary associations like the 'Perrin' Development Board and the Golf and Country Club did cut across the division (Leyton 1974a, 196); and Buckley comments on the religious mixing characteristic of the Kilbeg Historical Society and Camera Club (Buckley 1982, 150). What is striking about these particular associations and societies, however, is that their membership is drawn primarily from the middle-class. In Belfast and Lurgan, for example, while those associations with a predominantly working-class membership tended to recruit only Catholic or Protestant, those associations with middle-class membership were frequently mixed (Darby 1976, 156; Starling 1970); thus in Lurgan links were fostered among the professional classes of both communities in the town's art club, film society and local history society (Kirk 1967). Membership of similar associations in Kilbeg was also drawn from the farming, business and professional classes (Buckley 1982, 150). Indeed, in certain areas it appears to have been only the wealthy who were considered to make suitable members of some associations, and low economic position was often the reason for the reluctance of both poorer Protestants and poorer Catholics to join local associations (see Harris 1972, 138).

The danger here, therefore, is in making generalizations about the nature of Protestant-Catholic interrelations within voluntary associations which are valid only for people in certain socio-economic positions. While working-class Protestants and Catholics may have their separate associations this does not seem to be so true of middle-class Protestants and Catholics. Before we make generalizations about voluntary associations, we must first consider what kind of association we are talking about, and specify the class position of those involved.

Recreation and Leisure

Many writers have noted that, in general terms at least, there exist in Northern Ireland sports which are distinctively 'Protestant' and sports which are distinctively 'Catholic' (see for example, Barritt and Carter 1972, 148-151; Blacking *et al* 1978, 37; Darby 1976, 152-153; Harris 1972, 134; Leyton 1974a, 191 and 1975, 12). Interest in a particular sport frequently derives from schooldays, though Darby has warned us against overemphasising the dichotomy in sport at school level (Darby 1978, 218-219). In many areas, however, Protestants do learn to play soccer, rugby, hockey and cricket at school, while Catholics learn to play Gaelic football, hurling and camogie. The political associations of these sports are historically based: while rugby and cricket are often associated with the rich and the Protestant 'Ascendancy', the Gaelic games are encouraged and promoted by the Gaelic Athletic Association founded in 1884, which now, as then, has close links with political and cultural nationalism. Any possibility of participation in both has been effectively precluded by a ban imposed by the Gaelic Athletic Association on playing or watching certain non-Gaelic 'foreign' games, until the ban was removed in 1971.

In some cases spectators have also tended to be recruited along sectarian lines (see Boal 1969, 38; Darby 1976, 153). Until it was disbanded in 1951, Catholic soccer fans supported Belfast Celtic while Linfield received the encouragement of a predominantly Protestant following. However, rugby internationals, which are held in Dublin and which are organised on an all-Ireland basis, have tended to attract both a Protestant and Catholic following from north and south of the border. Though not all sports are organised on an all-Ireland basis, occasionally the organisation of international teams and matches gives rise to disagreements over the correct protocol (see Darby 1976, 154, for some examples of this).

Even though boxing, soccer, athletics and darts are among a number of sports played by members of both religions, obviously this does not always mean that both sets of players and spectators will meet on and off the field of play. Frequently sporting activities revolve around the church and teams formed on this basis will more than likely be involved in different church leagues. Furthermore, the venue for sporting activities may not always be considered equally suitable by both sides. For example, the bowling club in Kilbeg met in the Orange Hall (Buckley 1982, 148).

However, it is not always clear when support and interest in a particular sport is based purely on sectarian grounds and when it is the result of differences in social class. Though few Catholics play rugby or cricket it is also true to say that so do few working-class Protestants (cf. Darby 1976, 153), and cricket in particular seems to have a predominantly middle-class following among members of both communities (Barritt and Carter 1972, 150). Golf also seems to be played by the more wealthy and, when Barritt and Carter note that the golf course is often cited as 'a prime example of a place where Protestant and Catholic meet in friendship', it may only be the middle-class who are able to meet in such circumstances (*Ibid*, 151; see also Harris 1972, 134).

Despite the separation of Catholic and Protestant sports, a separation apparently almost so complete in some areas that no one sports club could unite Ballybeg even in the event of a match with outsiders (Harris 1972, 9), common residence does seem to promote a certain degree of interest in the fortunes of *any* teams representing a given community (see also Blacking *et al* 1978, 37). Here there seems to be a rural-urban difference. For example, while most Belfast Protestants are apparently ill-informed about what goes on in Gaelic football, there seems to be more Protestant interest in the success of a local club in rural areas (Barritt and Carter 1972, 150). However, partly because the games are played on Sunday, and partly because of their symbolic significance, this interest does not seem to extend to active participation as either player or spectator (cf. Darby 1976, 152; Harris 1972, 135). Thus Harris notes that in Ballybeg attendance at Gaelic matches was 'almost as much a purely Catholic activity as was attendance at Mass' (1972, 135). Nevertheless, though Protestants may not turn up to watch a Gaelic match, many do take an interest in the result, this tendency having been noted in several rural areas (Buckley 1982, 166; Harris 1972, 135).

Perhaps the most important meeting place everywhere in Northern

Ireland during leisure hours is the public house. While in general terms it may be true that Protestant and Catholic each prefer to drink in the establishment of a co-religionist, it is difficult to assess from the existing evidence exactly to what extent this is actually the case. Certainly it seems to vary with time and place. The Republican associations of the drinking clubs which replaced the burnt-out pubs of the predominantly Catholic Anro district of Belfast in the seventies and eighties ensured that their clienteles were exclusively Catholic (Burton 1978, 12-13). A consequence of the increase in open conflict during this period was that it was no longer safe for the Anro residents to patronise the facilities in the neighbouring Protestant areas, and by the same token of course, Protestants were excluded from Anro. On the other hand, in Tyrone in the early fifties, though the town of Ballybeg could boast two pubs one of which was Protestant-owned and the other Catholic-owned, patrons of each were not segregated on the basis of religion. While 'in general, groups of men composed of Catholics only went to the Catholic pub, and Protestant groups to the Protestant pub' it was by no means uncommon that groups of mixed religion would drink in either pub (Harris 1972, 141). Particularly on occasions such as Fair Days, either bar would be used by traders of both religions to conclude a sale. The more contemporary situation in Upper Tullagh seems to be similar. Here the groups which drank together were based on ties of kinship, neighbourhood, work, leisure or co-membership of voluntary associations (Buckley 1982, 155). Similarly for the four communities in north Down, south Down, Fermanagh and Antrim studied in the mid-1970s (Blacking *et al* 1978, 32). It would be difficult to argue that Catholics and Protestants in mixed rural areas deliberately select co-religionists as drinking companions. It would seem that drinking groups are recruited not in terms of religion *per se,* but rather in terms of other relationships which may cross the divide even if to a limited extent. To conclude that the situation is clearly one where Protestant and Catholics drink exclusively in their own bars, therefore, would be a misleading over-generalization.

Since they are much more anonymous, it is difficult to make reasonable generalizations about the degree of segregation to be found in cinemas and dance halls. Nevertheless, the main factors which seem to determine the religious composition of participants are the loyalties of the organiser and the venue of the event. Where such activities are organised as private enterprises it would seem that some mixing is inevitable, and Barritt and Carter note that the youth at least have an opportunity to meet in commercial dance halls (Barritt and Carter 1972, 146). However, in many rural areas in the past, such amenities were unorganised on a commercial basis, and those that existed tended to be organised by bodies with religious or political associations and centred in their halls. With only one television and no cinema in Ballybeg in the early fifties, for example, the screening of a film every Sunday in the Catholic parochial hall assumed some significance. Nevertheless, because Sunday was considered to be an unsuitable day to pursue such pastimes, and because of the location, few Protestants attended, while those who did attend were severely criticised by other Protestants (Harris 1972, 135). Elsewhere Protestant attendance at Catholic dances was similarly frowned upon, and for similar reasons (see Barritt and Carter 1972, 64). Even more recently, in many smaller towns it would seem that the church and associated political bodies occupy a central position in the organisation of social activities, particularly those that concern the young (see for example, Buckley 1982, 145 and Kirk 1967). In Aughnaboy, for example, the adolescent's '"courting" begins and continues at dances held throughout the Perrin region, Protestants dancing to Scots music in Orange Halls and Catholics dancing to Irish Show Bands in Hibernian Halls and Catholic auditoriums' (Leyton 1974a, 191; see also Leyton 1975, 12). Here, apparently, one of the main reasons for church involvement in the organisation of social activities was to encourage contacts among those of the same faith, and at the same time to reduce the opportunities for contact between boys and girls of the opposite religion. These contacts would have opened up the possibility of permanent relationships of mixed marriages (cf. Darby 1976, 152; Harris 1972, 136).

As in the case of sporting activities, class differences again seem to affect the religious composition of those attending a dance. However, this is only hinted at in the available literature. Thus Harris notes that the more middle-class Catholics and Protestants both went only to expensive formal dances held at the Hospital or Golf Club in a neighbouring town; and even though both communities here attended the same dance, they usually went as paired couples or in organised parties, so that there was not the same opportunity for mixing as at the local dances (Harris 1972, 136).

Shopping and Other Services

There is a certain amount of evidence to suggest that in a number of areas Catholics and Protestants patronise only those services owned or controlled by co-religionists. This practice tends to result in a duplication of certain facilities and ensures that no one owner will manage to acquire a monopoly in a single trade. Thus Harris notes that the pattern of sectarian loyalties in Ballybeg was largely responsible for limiting competition between shops, with the result that though the town was small, it was able to support a relatively large number of businesses. Indeed, in some places the moral responsibility to support one's own side seems to be so strong that for the Protestant owner to attract Catholic customers, or vice-versa, he must first offer considerable advantages over his rivals (Harris 1972, 6; see also Leyton 1975). Except in certain circumstances it is unacceptable to patronise the business of the other side. Thus, for example, only when the interests of the person providing the service are felt to be inherently incompatible with one's own interests, as when Ballybeg farmers traded with cattle and sheep dealers, or when none of one's co-religionists provide a particular service, can one seek the service of a member of the opposite religion without embarrassment (cf. Harris 1972, 139, 142). Yet other situations may give rise to a conflict of loyalties as when a co-religionist newly provides a service previously provided only by someone of the other religion. This seems to have been the case when the Protestant doctor, who for years had been the only doctor in Ballybeg, was joined by a Catholic counterpart; many Catholics felt it was their duty to transfer allegiance, though apparently only against their better judgement (*Ibid,* 142). Such conflict of loyalties seems less often to be an issue in areas like the largely Protestant Aughnaboy, where there were high expectations that members of each religion would support their own side (Leyton 1974a, 193; 1975, 12).

However, it should be emphasised that, even in areas dominated by a single religion, the tendency to patronise co-religionists is not always clearly defined but can vary from time to time. This seems to be true even of the religiously homogeneous districts in Belfast and Londonderry. While in the early sixties it was noted that 'Catholics now shop in the Protestant area of the Shankill Road, because it is known to be a good shopping centre' (Barritt and Carter 1972, 76), by the late sixties this pattern was less obvious; and factors like geographical proximity to shops were often less inducement to do business there than was the religion of the owner (Boal 1969, 41). While it does seem that Catholic and Protestant often do patronise only their co-religionists, it would again be misleading to obscure the variations which can and do occur.

Annual Festivities and Other Occasional Events

It is well known that every year each of the two religious communities in Northern Ireland hold their own separate, special commemorative events. While the Protestants commemorate the Battle of the Boyne and the Derry Apprentice Boys, Catholics celebrate the Easter Rising and certain feast days such as the Feast of the Assumption and Lady Day. This seemed to be as true for urban Anro as it was for the rural Aughnaboy (Burton 1978, 14; Leyton, 1974a, 192). Both sets of celebrations are accompanied by street processions, bands and bunting. Participants in either set of events belong exclusively to one religion or the other to such an extent that participation in the Twelfth of July celebrations, for example, can be taken as an indicator of Protestant territoriality in urban Belfast (cf. Boal 1969, 34). Catholic solidarity is similarly reaffirmed in their celebrations; thus Burton notes that 'internal coalescence . . . (is) . . . vividly portrayed within Anro during its ceremonies and celebrations' (Burton 1978, 16). However, there is some indication of a slightly ambivalent attitude towards the celebrations of the other side, and they are not always and not everywhere as mutually exclusive as they might at first seem. For example, while some Kilbeg Catholics expressed resentment at the march on the Twelfth of July, and while no bunting or flags were displayed in this largely Catholic village on this date, other Catholic villagers supported and even helped to organise a concert to raise money to pay for instruments for the accordian band which lead the parades on this day (Buckley 1982, 148-149). Elsewhere Catholics have made similar contributions to support local bands (McFarlane 1978, 253).

Some annual village festivals do not seem to be of sectarian interest and are not organised along sectarian lines, but are held solely with the intention of bringing the whole community together. The annual festival in Kilbeg seems to be of this type. For a week during the summer months the Festival Committee, headed by a working-class Catholic and including both Catholic and Protestant members, arranged a variety of outdoor events and activities which not only attracted tourists to the area but also drew together the local residents. This is an event, it is argued, at which 'religion and politics are absent' (Buckley 1982, 153). Fair Day in Ballybeg seemed to be another occasional event at which sectarian loyalties were superseded; on this occasion economic interests usually took precedence. Indeed , Harris notes that the question of moving the Fair to a new site was the only important issue over which sides were taken on an entirely non-sectarian basis (Harris 1972, 3).

Several authors have remarked that both Catholic and Protestant support each others' occasional fund-raising activities, fetes and bazaars (Barritt and Carter 1972, 63; Blacking *et al* 1978, 38; Buckley 1982, 149; Harris 1972, 137). This seems to be particularly true of small country towns and villages where perhaps, Barritt and Carter suggest, there are few alternative attractions (Barritt and Carter 1972, 63). However, residents of Ballybeg apparently made a distinction between different kinds of fund-raising events, and they did not lend support indiscriminately to all events arranged by the other side. Thus, while they considered it neighbourly to support the other side's collections for religious causes, they believed it to be entirely inappropriate to support the fund-raising efforts of their political organisations (Harris 1972, 137; see also Blacking *et al* 1978, 39). Nevertheless, actual attendance at a sale or fete even for religious causes was a different matter and such attendance was almost entirely restricted to members of one religion or the other. In Ballybeg fund-raising was never undertaken for charities of a non-sectarian or non-political nature (Harris 1972, 136).

Conclusions

On the basis of the evidence presented above there are some deceptively simple generalizations which can be made about the day to day relevance of being a Catholic or a Protestant in Northern Ireland.

First, it would seem that the degree of everyday segregation seems to be more acute in working-class urban areas than in the small towns and villages of the countryside. Recent conflict at territorial boundaries and population movements seem to have re-emphasised working-class residential segregation in urban areas. Consequently, they have reinforced the tendency for community life in these areas to be centred in single religion enclaves. In rural areas and villages, geographical proximity has given rise to a *modus vivendi* which has found expression in a value on community harmony and in the underplaying of Catholic and Protestant relations in middle class suburbs.

Second, within the mixed areas studied in detail (unfortunately almost entirely in rural areas) the relevance of the religious division varies to a certain extent according to the areas of life being investigated. There is a logical system to be found however. It would seem that in most areas segregation in the *private* domain does not derive simply from a desire to maintain close relations with co-religionists: in most rural areas the religious divide seems to be underplayed (at least explicitly in attitudes). Actual segregation derives much more from the fact that people emphasise the importance of kinship and to a lesser extent neighbourhood relations for ordering everyday contact and co-operation. In the *public* domain, on the other hand, segregation seems to be an aim: the concerns here are the political and economic well-being of one side or the other. Mixed marriages seem to be a link between the two domains. They are seen as political actions as much as matters of personal or family concern: as such they are viewed with antagonism by both sides. Consequently, few marriages are contracted across the divide. This feeds back into the private domain: the lack of mixed marriages means that family ties, so important for everyday life in rural areas, do not cross the divide.

This is what the available literature seems to tell us. However, we have suggested that these generalizations are deceptive; as our review shows, there seem to be some contradictory findings even within the body of literature discussed. Moreover, these generalizations are probably open to objections not only from professional social scientists but also from all the casual observers who seem to be the bane of those who do research in Northern Ireland. For instance, everyone can give examples of occasions when rural areas seemed as sharply divided as any urban areas (as we write, this seems to be the case in some border communities). Furthermore, people can point out that not every area in working-class Belfast is riven by sectarianism.

Given the co-existence of different views on Northern Irish society the relations to such local level research can be envisaged. First, it can be argued that the small community or network of people whose affairs are investigated is not representative of Northern Irish society, or even representative of urban or rural Northern Ireland. It is doubtful whether this can be resolved completely satisfactorily, because it is doubtful whether there is such a thing as a representative community. The nearest thing to a solution is to add more studies of local areas or of different sectors of the population (the middle class is virtually unresearched, for example) to add more evidence for any generalization. We should emphasise again that this work could not be done in pursuit of the truth or the final word on Northern Irish society: there is no magical number of studies which would provide the truth. All we can ask for is more research. But how should this be carried out?

This brings us to the second line of objection to a given set of observations: they might derive from inappropriate methods. We pointed out in our introduction that we were not going to discuss research which used questionnaire surveys because they are too unreliable. However, even in the research carried out by more personalised methods, there are certain to be differences in emphasis. It is perfectly reasonable to conjecture that the tolerance and harmony to be found in many reports is simply a product of using interviews more than any other research tool. Everyone in Northern Ireland knows that few people are willing to be frank and open about their strong opposition to the other side, especially to seemingly educated researchers. The solution here is probably to carry out more research using the more informal methods *and* to be more explicit about the methods which are used.

A third objection to pieces of research on relations between Catholics and Protestants derives from the fact that they are often carried out in communities without an eye to events which are taking place outside the community. One could argue that apparent harmony in local relations can give way to apparent conflict in response to events in Northern Ireland. Hence a study carried out in one community in one year might give rise to different results from a study done the next year in the same community. Is there a solution to this? It might be possible to do research *in* a community, but to focus on the community's reaction to events *outside* the community. It might even be possible for researchers to extract such material from their existing data.

This problem of the interaction between the local community and events outside it brings us full circle. We noted in our introduction that dramatic events and the big issues of the day can do two things: they can lay bare the true fabric of society or they can cover up and blind us to the true fabric of society. Opting for one of these alternatives is a product not only of observation but also of the set of assumptions (or ideology) of the researchers. Any piece of research on Catholic and Protestant relations in Northern Ireland can be challenged in terms of two sets of assumptions. One set, usually held by sociologists, is that Northern Ireland has a core problem which hides beneath a veneer of superficial good relations. This core problem erupts at certain times and in certain places, and subsides beneath the veneer at others. The other set of assumptions, seemingly shared by most social anthropologists, is that Northern Irish society has a reasonable balance at its core, which is only temporarily disrupted by dramatic events. As assumptions these can obviously not be proven or disproven, though further detailed research on informal social relations might suggest which is the more likely.

6

Schools and Conflict

Dominic Murray

In order to more readily appreciate any relationship which may exist between educational segregation and broader community divisions in Northern Ireland, it is essential first to consider the conception and historical development of the separate systems of schooling.

The Development of a Segregated System

In 1921, the original Government of Northern Ireland *inherited* a segregated system of schooling. The National (primary) system of education, established in 1831, had continued to provide the only education experienced by the vast majority of children in Ireland until the formation of Northern Ireland as a separate political entity. Although originally conceived as a non-donominational system, it rapidly evolved into segregated schooling, usually under the management of the local parish priest or minister.

Secondary education in 1921 was provided in the main for Catholic pupils within the religious school which came into being during the nineteenth century as a result of the Catholic Relief Act of 1782. Protestant secondary education was provided almost exclusively by the Anglican Diocesan schools, Royal schools, or the Presbyterian established academic institutions. There were few free scholars in the secondary sector as a whole. Thus it catered mainly for the children of middle class Catholics and Protestants.

This then was the segregated nature of educational provision at the onset of the State of Northern Ireland in June 1921.

One of the major problems experienced by Northern Ireland's new Minister of Education was the refusal of a large number of Catholic schools, both primary and secondary, to recognise his authority. In border areas some continued to claim, and receive, salaries from the Government in Dublin. Their position collapsed in 1922 when the

Southern authorities, prompted it would seem more by pragmatism than by patriotism, announced the cessation of such payments.

The reticence of clergy and teachers to accept the authority of the Northern Ireland Ministry of Education had a significant effect on the educational interests of Roman Catholics in general. Akenson (1973) claimed that

> At the very moment when the Ulster Government was establishing the new educational system, the Church's already weak bargaining position was being destroyed by the non-co-operation policy.

As a consequence, no Catholic clerical representatives were included in the educational policy committees which had been set up. Nonetheless, despite the abstentionist position of Catholics, the initial machinations of the Ministry of Education under the able leadership of Lord Londonderry, was characterised more by fairness than chagrin. Inevitably, however, the resulting educational structures catered for Protestant rather than Catholic concerns.

The Lynn Committee (1921) commissioned by Londonderry, recommended *inter alia* that schools which were handed over to the Ministry should receive 100 per cent grants for both capital expenditure and maintenance. Such schools were termed Controlled schools.

Those schools whose managers wished to remain entirely independent were to receive only grants for heating and cleaning. These were called Voluntary Schools.

It was also suggested that in Controlled schools the Bible should be taught without note or comment. Londonderry baulked at this latter suggestion since he perceived it to be an implicit endowment of Protestantism in Controlled schools. However, an amendment to the original (1923) Act, introduced by the then Prime Minister Sir James Craig, reinstated Lynn's suggestion.

It would seem that requiring Bible instruction, while prohibiting comment, did in fact reflect the teaching of Protestantism, since the Catholic Church insists on interpretation in the light of Church teaching. It was this amendment which sowed the seeds of the perception of Roman Catholics in Northern Ireland that Controlled schools are *de facto* Protestant institutions. This view still prevails today.

The 1930 Education Act made concessions to both Protestant and Catholic concerns. To the former it increased guarantees about the selection of teachers, i.e. only Protestant teachers would be appointed to Controlled schools. The latter were more or less appeased by the raising of grants to Voluntary schools (50 per cent of capital expenditure, 50 per cent towards maintenance). These grants to Voluntary schools were increased in The White Paper of 1944 to 65 per cent for capital expenditure and 65 per cent for maintenance. By 1947 almost all Protestant schools had transferred control to the Ministry to become known as Controlled and, more recently, State schools.

Catholic schools remained 'voluntarily' aloof until an Amendment Act (1967) produced increased incentives for them to concede one third of the seats on their management committees to public representatives. In return, 80 per cent grants were offered towards capital expenditure together with 100 per cent grants for maintenance. The less suspicious Catholic managers soon acquiesced and by the late 1970s almost all Catholic schools had accepted the new '4 and 2' or Maintained status.

The present situation is that State (formerly Controlled) schools are perceived by Catholics as being Protestant while Maintained schools are seen by all as being Roman Catholic institutions. One must ask, however, how much quantative or objective evidence exists to support these generally held perceptions.

Research on Segregation

Surprisingly, in the light of the perennial debate on the deleterious social effects of segregation, little research has been carried out into the segregated nature of schools in Northern Ireland. Akenson (1973) commences his bibliography,

> The most striking thing about the historiography of Northern Ireland is how little historical writing of any real quality there is . . . there is as yet no satisfactory general history of Northern Ireland since 1920.

Akenson was especially concerned with the dearth of writing on education in the Province. In fact a good deal of historical research has been carried out on the Northern Irish educational system (Dent 1965; McElligott 1969; Musson 1955; Robinson 1967; Spence 1959). However, little has been made available in the form of published works. In fact most early available material seems to have been preoccupied with global structures and political influences on schooling in Northern Ireland. Akenson for example has written an illuminative account of education in Northern Ireland between 1920 and 1950. His book is essential reading for anyone with an interest in educational structures in the Province especially during the formative years of the State itself. Campbell's (1964) slim volume is perhaps the best existing exposition of the Roman Catholic viewpoint on education with Cardinal Conway's (1971) pamphlet also of interest in this context.

Barritt & Carter's (1972) fine sociological survey of Northern Ireland seemed, for the first time, to direct attention not only to the segregated nature of structures in the Province, but also to its ramifications. This shift in emphasis can be argued to have engendered a novel approach to research in education and especially its effects upon children attending religiously (and therefore culturally) segregated schools.

Typical of this new approach was the work of Robinson (1971) and Russell (1972). The former, a case study carried out in Derry in 1969 demonstrated interesting differences in perception between Catholic and Protestant school children. 62 per cent of Catholic children named either Bishop Farren or John Hume as Derry's most important citizen while 70.9 per cent of the Protestant children named Northern Ireland's Prime Minister or the Lord Mayor of the city. When asked to name the capital city of the country in which Derry was situated, more than half the Catholic pupils named Dublin while more than two-thirds of the Protestant children cited Belfast. While it would be erroneous to attempt to attribute such variance to school experience alone, Robinson concludes that the schools seem to do little to moderate them.

Russell's (1972) research demonstrated a greater liklihood for Catholic children to exhibit negative attitudes towards Government, although it is again difficult to determine the extent to which schools can be deemed responsible for the formation of such attitudes.

Research which has been carried out on the effect of schooling on children's attitudes and cultural identity in Northern Ireland has tended to concentrate on the curricular areas of religious instruction and history teaching. Greer (1972) in a study of Protestant sixth form boys describes a notable gap in most religious instruction courses. He claims that while Hinduism, Buddhism and other religions are studied in both types of school, 'little reference is made to the problem of comparative religion which lies at the root of so many social problems in Ireland, the Protestant-Roman Catholic division'.

This selective approach also applied to history teaching. In describing history teaching in Northern Irish State schools, Magee (1970) pointed out that, 'Irish history was taught only where it impinged in a significant way on the history of Great Britain'. Hadkins (1971) describes the deliberate use of emotionalism in some Nationalist text-books. Darby (1974) has voiced the concern that bias in presenting (especially) history to school children may help to propagate two hostile cultural traditions. (For a fuller account of curricular practices within segregated schools see Darby (1972)).

All of these studies provide information about the effects upon children of school curricula and materials. Little evidence exists, however, which provides insight into the extent to which the overall process of, or experience within, segregated schools may contribute to the attitude formation of children. For this type of information we have had to rely on autobiographical or semi-fictionalised accounts. Devlin (1969) for example, describes the secondary school which she attended as, 'a militantly Republican school'. The Principal is portrayed as a women to whom everything English was bad and who, 'although she did not hate Protestants (unlike the English whom she did hate), believed they could not be tolerated because they were not Irish'. *No Surrender* is an appealing, auto-biographical account of experiences of growing up in a Protestant district and attending a Protestant school (Harbinson 1960).

In this context, one research project is worthy of a more comprehensive description. *Schools Apart?* (Darby *et al* 1977) attempted to blend quantative evidence about segregated schools with more illuminative data obtained within them. The underlying objective of the project was to attempt to, 'fill the gap between the wide general interest in the subject of integrated schooling in Northern Ireland and the shortage of information about segregated schools'.

Segregation and its Effects

It must be said that the bulk of public debate on the subject of integration seems to be carried on without any apparent appreciation of either the nature or magnitude of segregation in schooling. This has tended to sterilise such debate. In order to ensure that future discussions are more fruitful, three vital aspects must therefore be addressed.

1. The actual extent of segregation in Northern Irish schools.

2. The degree of difference between the two types of school.

3. The possible relationship between educational segregation and broader community divisions.

1. How extensive is segregation?

Barritt & Carter (1962) claim that as far as can be discovered at least 98 per cent (and probably more) of all Catholic primary school children attend Catholic schools. Data obtained in the *Schools Apart* project infer that 95 per cent of State schools have less than 5 per cent Roman Catholic enrolment and over 98 per cent of Catholic schools have less than 5 per cent Protestant children attending them.

The *Schools Apart* data demonstrated a similar polarisation in the employment of teachers. Of the 1,521 secondary teachers studied in the survey, only 29 were employed in schools where the predominant religious affiliation was different from their own. Of 480 Grammar school teachers studied, only 9 were thus employed. Polarisation is even more extreme at primary level where only 3 teachers (out of 750 surveyed) were employed in schools of a different religion from their own.

Apart from the confessional preponderance among pupils and teachers, there is also historical evidence to demonstrate that schools in Northern Ireland can be described with accuracy as either Protestant or Catholic. In the latter case the schools are self-avowedly Catholic and acclaim rather than resent the title. In the former the claim is often made that State schools are open to all and therefore should not be described in religious terms. Nonetheless, State schools have always been perceived as Protestant establishements.

In September 1981 the *Sunday News* published official documents from the PRONI (Public Record Office of Northern Ireland) which had become available under the fifty year rule. Some of these demonstrate clearly the official perception of State schools prevailing at the time. For example, Dr. Hugh Morrison, a member of Parliament for Queen's University, referring to the possibility of regional educational committees being established in 1923 and their possible influence on schools, claimed that, 'in some areas where Catholics were in the majority, they would have the power to appoint teachers to Protestant (sic) schools . . . This is a situation which the Protestant Church will not submit to'. Dr. Morrison was in fact referring to State schools. Another member of Parliament, Joseph Morgan, was even more outspoken in a Government debate in 1946: he asked, 'Is it too much to ask that a Protestant Government elected by a Protestant people, should maintain that we should have Protestant teachers for Protestant children?'

It is also noteworthy that the passing of the 1930 Education Act (N.I.) was acclaimed by the joint education committees of the main

Protestant bodies as the conception of a state system of education which would, 'maintain the Protestant nature of the State'.

More recent events suggest that the general perception of State schools being Protestant establishments is no less strong. In August 1981 a petition was prepared for submission to the Minister responsible for education, Lord Elton, asking that the Western Education and Library Board should restrict its representation on management committees of State schools to non-Roman Catholic members because, 'in the vast majority of cases, pupils at State schools are Protestant'. This petition was organised by parents of Protestant children and members of management committees of State schools in the area.

There is also evidence of at least tacit acceptance by official bodies of a denominational school system on religious lines. Few people in Northern Ireland would deny that some schools are overtly Catholic. It is not surprising therefore that statutory bodies deal directly with the Roman Catholic Church when a new Maintained (Catholic) school is being built. What is significant is that when a new Controlled school— a State school entirely financed by public funds—has been built, the main Protestant Churches are asked to contribute nominees to its management committee, but the Roman Catholic Church is not. It is of course, possible that the Roman Catholic clergy would not wish to be consulted. That they are not, however, demonstrates an acceptance that State schools are *de facto* Protestant schools and are acknowledged as such by statutory bodies.

2. *How different are the two systems?*

Implicit in the arguments of both sides in the debate about segregated schooling is the belief that there is a real difference in the experience undergone by Catholic and Protestant children within their denominational schools. The Roman Catholic case for retaining their schools rests on a conviction that they provide a religio-moral ethos which is integral to Catholic education. Those opposed to segregation usually base their case on the belief that separate schools encourage a divisiveness by propagating different and perhaps hostile cultural heritages. Both of these stances are premised on the conviction that schools attended by Protestant and Roman Catholic children are significantly different kinds of institutions.

The differences between the two systems of schooling are often overstated and overemphasised. Obviously no two schools, whether they be Catholic or Protestant, will ever be identical. Each will have its own unique character constructed by a myriad of interrelating influences. One should therefore evaluate any differences existing between the two sets of schools in the context of the many similarities in their day-to-day procedures.

It is fair to say that in the majority of schools, the single most significant factor affecting curricular procedures is the existence of external examinations. The transfer assessment at primary level, and G.C.E. and C.S.E. at secondary level, are all common to Catholic and Protestant schools.

Again, although Gaelic games are played exclusively in Catholic schools, there is in fact a wide variety of sports which are equally popular in both sets of schools. These include athletics, soccer, netball basketball and hockey.

At a curricular level, the *Schools Apart* project recorded a high degree of commonality of practice across a broad range of activities:

> In both (types of) schools the educational qualifications of staff were roughly similar; the work profiles of principals were almost indistinguishable; most classroom procedures are common to both systems—they stream pupils to similar extents and are equally likely to practise some form of integration within the curriculum.

In addition, the authors claim the possibility of an acceptance by both school systems of a shared heritage. This conclusion is based on the wide use by both types of school of broadcasts and project materials which deal with value-laden areas such as religion and history. They went on to argue:

> The popularity of such venues within Northern Ireland as The Ulster Folk Museum, The Ulster Museum and The Ulster Transport Museum is of a sufficiently high level in all schools to suggest the existence of a shared Ulster culture.

It must be questioned whether participants in such activities perceive them in terms of culture or heritage or simply as outings away from the school. Therefore, the claim that they represent some form of shared heritage may have been overstated. Nonetheless, it must be emphasised that there are many more similarities of practice within Protestant and Catholic schools than there are differences between them. Why then does the conviction, that a high correlation exists between segregated schools and community conflict, continue to flourish?

3. *Is there a relationship between educational segregation and broader community divisions?*

The high degree of polarisation of both staff and pupils in State and Maintained schools inevitably results in State schools being perceived as Protestant institutions and Maintained schools as Roman Catholic establishments. However, if religion is the sole criterion used to demonstrate the divisive potential of Northern Irish schools, then how much more pernicious must be the separate churches themselves? If community division is seen exclusively in religious terms, then the various churches must be seen as the most divisive structures in society. Nevertheless, when churches are referred to in debates about community conflict in the Province, the approach is invariably to ask why they are not doing more to stop it rather than in terms of how the separate churches may have caused the conflict. On the other hand, debates about segregated schools carried on in this same context inevitably stress their actual contribution to the perpetuation of violence and conflict. It would seem therefore that churches are accorded with less positive influence with regard to community conflict than are schools. One must ask therfore what are the aspects of schools which identify them as being the principal villains of the peace.

In order to answer this question with any degree of confidence, much information is required about the actual day-to-day practices within segregated schools. In this sensitive area, qualitative rather than quantative data is essential. In view of the widespread general interest in segregated schooling and its ramifications, it is quite amazing that so little qualitative information is available. In fact no research has attempted to isolate the specific influence of the school.

In a realisation of this dearth of information, Murray (1982) attempted to study the relationship between segregated schooling and community conflict. His objective was to investigate the claim that schools attended by Roman Catholic and Protestant children are significantly different types of institutions with real differences in experience being provided within them. His participant approach, entailing one year being spent in two primary schools (one Catholic, the other Protestant) reveals interesting insights into these segregated schools. The findings suggest that at a curricular level the schools were almost indistinguishable, the one significant exception being the content of, and approach to, religious instruction. In the Protestant school this was rigidly curtailed to the 'non-secular day' i.e. between 9.00 a.m. and 9.45 a.m. In the Catholic school however, at certain times of the year, religion and religious instruction took precedence over all other subjects. For example, the class being prepared for First Communion had, on occasion, two thirds of the day allotted to this preparation. School Mass, daily prayers, receiving the Sacraments and attending other religious celebrations all took up a significant amount of the school day.

It is difficult to relate such disparate emphasis on religion in the schools to broader community divisions in Northern Ireland. Different religious groupings proliferate in the Province, and will continue to do so irrespective of whether schools are segregated or not. No one would deny the right or desirability of such pluralism. It would seem therefore that we must consider other factors in an effort to identify specific relationships between separate schooling and community division. Murray has identified the concepts of culture and identity as being of most significance in this respect, claiming that schools, and individuals within them, can be distinguished to some extent by the dominant cultural ideology to which they subscribe. This culture of the school is constructed by such factors as history, tradition, pupil background and recreation.

Any cultural analysis of Northern Ireland must take into account the peculiar position which schools occupy in the Province, where religion, politics and culture are inextricably enmeshed. Most Protestants subscribe to a Unionist/British political ideological position and maintain their own cultural traditions, attitudes and values which are largely a function of an English or Scottish identity. Most Catholics, on the other hand, aspire, to varying degrees, towards a Nationalist ideal and possess a set of values and traditions emanating from and identifying with an Irish heritage.

Since it has been demonstrated previously that segregated schools in Northern Ireland can validly be described as either Catholic or Protestant, it is not unreasonable therefore to expect that each type of school will reflect the cultural aspirations of each religious group as a whole. However the problem with segregated schools, with regard to community divisions, lies not predominately in the fact that they reflect different cultures but rather in the meanings which are attributed by observers to the overt demonstrations of such cultural affiliation. Controlled schools in The North-Eastern Library Board area are required to fly the Union Jack daily outside. Individuals within these schools may see this as a natural manifestation for a State school. The response among Catholics however may be somewhat different. Murray cites a general reaction from staff in an adjoining Catholic school:

They fly the flag down there to show that they are more British than the British themselves. It's also to let us know that they are the lords and masters and that we (Catholics) should be continually aware of it.

Again, quite naturally, symbols abound in Catholic schools which emphasise their Catholicity (statues, Papal flags, crucifixes etc.). It might be difficult to imagine how these might cause offence. Indeed they can justifiably be seen as a *sine qua non* of Catholic education which has always posited salvation higher than education. However, this observation too can be transferred into a rather different reality, as it was by a Protestant teacher:

We play St. Judes often in games and visit their school regularly. I never fail to be impressed by the plethora of religious pictures and icons staring at you around every corner. It's hard to escape the view that a special show is being put on for our benefit ... This doesn't just apply to St. Judes of course, but they must know that these are the very things that we object to, yet still they are flaunted everywhere.

These two examples give insight into the gulf which exists between intention and perception in Northern Ireland. The two dominant cultures are so mutually antipathetic that any demonstration of one is perceived as an assault on the other. There is no doubt that the two separate systems of schooling do reflect the two dominant cultures in the Province. Murray has demonstrated this with regard to textbooks, library materials, ritual, symbols and general ethos. But is this necessarily an undesirable aspect of schooling? Can pluralism be undesirable in any society?

Hitherto the tendency has been to accept tacitly the undesirable effect of segregated structures, and debate has proceeded at this axiomatic level. However, such structural approaches have contributed little with regard to ameliorating divisions in society. Perhaps a phenomenological analysis is more likely to prove fruitful in this context.

Segregated schooling exists uncontentiously in other countries yet fails to do so in Northern Ireland. This may suggest that the problem lies not within segregated education but rather in the perceptions of the society in which it is operating. It could well be that the actual existence of segregation has less influence on community divisions than have the meanings which are attributed to it by members of that community.

Thus there may well be some kind of self fulfilling prophecy in operation—schools are perceived as divisive and hence become so in their consequences.

Structuralists would argue of course that if segregated schools are abolished and an integrated system (whatever the phrase is taken to mean) is introduced, then these societal perceptions will disappear. This argument is only tenable however if segregated schools can be demonstrated to be *intrinsically* divisive. This has yet to be shown. Indeed, in countries other than Northern Ireland, it seems not to be the case.

It would seem essential that social attitudes are tackled before social structures. However, Lagan College, the first officially integrated school in Northern Ireland, seems to have been founded on an opposite rationale. While its efforts can, and should be accorded both respect and applause, it can only have an effect on the relatively few children who attend it. Added to this is the possibility that only the converted will 'hear the sermon'. In other words it is likely that only those individuals who are already sympathetic to the concept of integration will support such an integrated structure. Thus when structural change precedes attitudinal change, it is probable that any impact will be restricted to within that structure only.

This analysis has been confined to the possible connection between segregated schooling and community conflict. It would seem however that a stronger argument can be made against segregated schools which is based on the harmful educational and cultural consequences of such structures. In the first place, most educationalists would agree that schools should present as broad a range of experiences as possible to children attending them. With two groups of children attending their own exclusive schools, such experience is necessarily curtailed. At a cultural level, segregation entails that both Catholic and Protestant children are denied a knowledge of elements of history, tradition and culture which should be common to them both.

Another aspect of segregated schooling more likely to contribute to community division than either culture or religion is the concept of identity, i.e. the extent to which individuals within separate schools accept, or identify with political or institutional bodies outside the schools. Russell's (1972) survey of children in Northern Ireland has suggested that Roman Catholic children are more likely to demonstrate negative attitudes towards the Northern Ireland Government. Robinson (1971) suggests that Protestant and Catholic children held very different views of the society in which they both lived.

The Schools Cultural Studies Project (1982) attempted to introduce into Northern Irish schools a programme which encouraged children to clarify their values, and especially cultural values. The experience of the project was that it was much more readily accepted in Catholic than in Protestant schools. A conclusion of the project team was:

> Any attempt to introduce an innovation which requires participants to question previously sacrosanct societal values will be likely to evoke different responses from the two existing educational systems. On the one hand, Catholic schools which may have no great empathy with such values may find it expedient to embrace such an innovation. On the other hand, staffs in State (Protestant) schools may see any such assault on the *status quo* as a positive threat to their position and as such to be opposed, or at least ignored.

Murray, in his study of two schools, also commented on this aspect of segregated education:

> It appeared that the Protestant school identified much more closely with the policy-making and administrative sections of the educational system. These were deemed to be natural and effective support structures which, through dissemination of information and close contact, moulded a kind of solidarity among all State schools. There seemed to be a sense of belonging to, and identity with, an extended educational family.

The Catholic school on the other hand, only contacted administrative bodies on occasions of dire necessity, 'Otherwise', as one teacher put it, 'they would be crawling all over us'. In fact one senior Library Board official claimed that his office received ten times as many enquiries of a relatively trivial nature from Protestant schools than from Catholic schools.

The disparity of approach to educational bodies between the two schools may well reflect the historical lack of empathy of Catholics with broader political structures in Northern Ireland. In this sense, educational policy-making may be being equated with a political power base to which Catholics have never subscribed. Whatever the reasons, the fact that such a disparity of practice prevailed in the schools is of significance with regard to community divisions. Of even more import is the possibility that other structures of society exist to which Catholics in general, and Catholic schools in particular, attribute similar negative responses.

A cameo from the Catholic school in which Murray researched suggested that this kind of negative attitude was not confined to educational bodies. It was noted that pupils in the Protestant school paid much more frequent visits to community organisations such as the fire station, post office, local Government offices, police station etc. The Catholic teachers agreed that this was probably so, but asked, 'What would be the sense in our kids going there? They will never get a job in any of them'. The inference was that they would be discriminated against because they were Catholics.

It is interesting that the Catholic teachers perceived these visits in vocational, rather than civic terms. If this perception is common to the Catholic sector as a whole, it seems inevitable that the two groups will relate to, and identify with, the ordinary day-to-day structures of their community in entirely different ways. More to the point, it may mean that Catholic teachers were not only curtailing the vocational aspirations of their pupils but also restricting their occupational possibilities. Again, a self-fulfilling prophecy may be operating. If pupils are advised, or given the impression, that they will not get a job in these establishments because of their religion, then it is hardly surprising that they will become underrepresented in these occupational sites.

This rationale therefore may contribute to and perpetuate community differences and divisions. The construction of behaviour based on a perception of division may in fact reify that division.

Conclusion

The religious polarity of both teachers and pupils within segregated schools has no doubt contributed to them being viewed as separate institutions. Unfortunately this separateness in itself has been equated with community division in Northern Ireland.

At the levels of religion and culture, the influence of the school seems to have been grossly exaggerated. Commentators have tended to assume that segregated schools create differences in society rather than reflect them.

The 'identity' aspect of segregation may give more cause for concern. It is possible that certain Catholic schools may see their occupational task as preparing children for what they perceive as a discriminatory society. They can therefore validly be said to perpetuate community division by directing their pupils either towards, or away from, certain sectors of their community. Perhaps this could be rectified by actively fostering increased communication between Catholic schools and statutory bodies. This might be facilitated through an emphasis of their common concern—the successful education of children.

There is evidence (Darby *et al,* 1977) to suggest that, presently, suspicion between the two systems of education in Northern Ireland is contributed to, in no small way, by the stereotypes of the members within them. These stereotypes are spawned largely in a mutual ignorance of each other's schools. It would seem, therefore, that fruitful debate can only take place in the future if it is supported, not only by in-depth studies of the schools themselves, but also an awareness of the perceptions and consciousness of the individuals for whom they exist.

7

The Demography of Violence

Michael Poole

Background

A survey of recent ethnic violence in a sample of nineteen different societies selected from all five continents has not only classified Northern Ireland as a 'high violence' society, but has bracketed it in this category with just four other geographical regions. These four are Zanzibar, Lebanon, Cyprus and Guyana. Clearly, Northern Ireland is by no means unique in suffering this form of violence—in fact, it ranked fourth or fifth in this survey, depending on the specific measure used— but, set in international context, it is one of a small group of societies with a much higher death rate from ethnic violence than any of the others considered (Hewitt 1977).[1]

The special significance, for this chapter, of Hewitt's international survey is the analysis he undertakes of the hypothesis that demographic structure is salient in the explanation of where ethnic violence occurs. The specific aspect of demography explored by Hewitt is the ethnic composition of the population.[2] The demographic situation is, in fact, one of three groups of factors whose possible effect on the incidence of this type of violence is considered by this author. The others are economic and political grievances, and he finds that all three are significant.

This evidence from Hewitt's investigation may be placed alongside the contention of Darby (1976, 26) that, within Northern Ireland, on a 'local level it is often religious segregation, especially in towns, which converts distrust and dislike into violence'. He considers that towns which have religiously integrated housing have escaped the worst 'community violence'. Darby does not support his contention by referring to any quantitative evidence, but it does constitute a plausible hypothesis relating the local demographic situation to the geographical places where violence occurs.

The common tie linking this observation of Darby to the conclusion reached by Hewitt is that there is a relationship between demographic characteristics and the most violent forms of ethnic conflict. The demographic characteristics receiving attention from both authors are concerned, more specifically, with ethnic composition. The principal difference, on the other hand, distinguishing Darby's suggestion from that of Hewitt concerns geographical scale. Hewitt's study-area is the whole world, and the individual places for which he analyses data are separate 'societies', of which Northern Ireland is the only one which has not been, at some stage in the study-period, a sovereign state. For Darby, however, Northern Ireland is the study-area, and the individual places about which observations are made are specific towns.

Indeed, the scale-level difference between the material quoted from these two authors is, in a sense, even greater than this, for, whereas Hewitt is not concerned with the geographical variation in ethnic composition within such a place as Northern Ireland, Darby is concerned with such variation within his towns. This is precisely what is implied by the latter's use of the concept of segregation in housing.

Objective

The idea of geographical scale-level is a sufficiently fundamental one in the context of the argument in this chapter to be used as a basic principle for its organization. We shall consider both the two extremes represented by the material referred to from Hewitt and from Darby and also certain intermediate scale-levels. As in the extracts already taken from these authors, the main element of population structure to be examined in this chapter at the varied range of scale-levels specified is the ethnic composition of the geographical areas in which people live.

This is not, however, a study of ethnic composition in isolation, for such general reviews are available elsewhere (Walsh 1970; Darby 1976, 25–47; Compton 1976; Compton 1982). Instead, an attempt will consistently be made in this chapter to relate this demographic characteristic to ethnic conflict. Such conflict takes many forms, including electoral contests and pressure-group struggles (Osborne 1982; Birrell and Murie 1980, 110–131), but the specific form examined in this chapter is the most violent one already referred to in the work of Hewitt and Darby.

Even this topic of violent conflict can take many forms. Schellenberg (1976, 10–17), for example, studied the statistics on shooting incidents, explosions, injuries and deaths, while Darby and Williamson (1978, 13) mapped the location of the last three of these, along with riots, gun-battles and armed raids. However, in this chapter only one aspect of violent conflict will be considered. This will be deaths directly attributable to the current spate of Troubles since 1969.

The reasons for concentrating on this aspect of violence have been succinctly summarized by Murray (1982, 310) in justifying the use of the data on fatalities, and also explosions, for his own inter-regional analysis: 'They are the incidents that arouse greatest public and political concern, they have the greatest impact on the community and, not least, they are the best documented.' To this set of reasons can be added the fact that most research on the relationship between demography and political violence in Northern Ireland has concentrated on deaths, so the only way of achieving consistency of subject-matter at all geographical scale-levels, without undertaking fresh empirical analysis at virtually every such scale-level, is to follow this other research by focusing on fatalities. Therefore, fresh analysis is restricted to just one of the several scale-levels considered, the inter-urban, and the attempt at an original contribution elsewhere in this chapter takes the form of a hopefully innovative interpretation of the relationship between violence and the demography of ethnicity, especially to take account of the effect of geographical scale-level.

The work of Hewitt and of Darby referred to in this introduction treated violence as a consequence of certain factors—including demographic factors—and this approach, Murray and Boal (1979, 153–154) have suggested, is common to almost all studies of violence. In fact, there is at least one exception to this general rule within the Northern Ireland context, in the set of contributions edited by Darby and Williamson (1978) investigating the effect of violence on the organization of social services in the province. Murray and Boal, in making their point, were especially keen to assert that violence is a factor affecting urban spatial structure, including what is particularly relevant to this chapter, the geography of ethnic composition. Their conclusion that violence, as both cause and consequence, is 'an inseparable component of the urban system', and probably of the rural system, too, is an inescapable one. However, it is one which will be almost ignored in this chapter.

The reason for ignoring that aspect of the relationship between demography and violence dealing with the effect of the latter on the former follows from our decision to limit the form of violence discussed, to deaths. The point is that there is little evidence that this aspect of the violent conflict, despite its seriousness, has had any significant effect on the demography of ethnicity by, for instance, the stimulation of population movement. In this respect, there is a strong contrast between this manifestation of violence and certain other forms, especially intimidation and property damage, which have caused a considerable movement of refugees, especially in Belfast (Poole 1971, 9; Darby and Morris 1974, 16–18). This movement, in turn, has had the effect of intensifying, albeit not on a vast scale, ethnic residential segregation since 1969. For example, 66 per cent of Belfast County Borough's households were located in streets in which they were in at least a 91 per cent ethnic majority in 1969, and this proportion has risen to 76 per cent by 1972 (Boal et al. 1976, 106), shortly after which there was a sharp decline in the numbers rendered homeless by violence (N.I.H.E. 1978, 15).

True, it is impossible to distinguish the separate components of violence and identify the contribution of each to refugee movement. However, there is no suggestion, either in the literature already quoted or in other studies of this type of movement (Black *et al.* 1971; Black 1972; Murray et al. 1975; Murray and Boal 1980), that the actual occurrence of deaths has had much impact on population mobility, whereas many of the other manifestations of violence are accorded a great deal of significance. Therefore, in investigating the relationship between violent death and ethnic demography in this chapter, we shall take what Murray and Boal identified as the most conventional approach, that of dealing with violence, not as a cause, but as a consequence.

A further narrowing of the subject-area is that the frequently-investigated hypothesis that the chronology of violence is a response to changing ethnic composition, such as the initial rapid rise, and subsequent decline, in the Catholic share of Belfast's population in the nineteenth century (Jones 1956, 168–170; Baker 1973) will be omitted. Rather than studying this essentially historical question, this chapter will tackle a problem which has received much less attention in the literature. This is the basically geographical one of understanding the location of violence.

National or International Scale

International Context

We shall begin this initial part of the analysis at the same point at which we began the introduction—at the extreme end of the spectrum of geographical scale-levels where Hewitt analysed international variations in ethnic violence. The specific variables involving demographic characteristics, which Hewitt hypothesized to be related to conflict, were two in number. These were the minority percentage, the term we may use to refer to the size of the minority ethnic group relative to the total population, and the rate at which this percentage is changing through time.

Firstly, he suggests that, the larger the minority percentage, the greater the likelihood of violent conflict, partly because small minorities are too vulnerable to get involved in conflict and partly because large minorities are a threat to the power of the majority in 'winner take all' democratic societies. This threat to majority power is particularly severe if a large minority shows signs of growing into a new majority, and this is the main reason why he suggests that the rate of change in the minority percentage is positively correlated with the level of conflict. In addition, however, any growth in the minority share of the population will create friction, Hewitt proposes, in those societies where the style of democracy practised involves some form of political power-sharing.

Having outlined these hypotheses, Hewitt classified the nineteen societies he examined into three groups according to the level of ethnic violence suffered, and he suggested that all five of the societies he classified as having a high rate of violence have demographic characteristics conducive to conflict. However, such a confident and unequivocal statement seems at odds with the quantitative evidence he presents. Only two of his high-violence societies, Lebanon and Guyana, satisfy his first hypothesis by having a large minority percentage. Northern Ireland occupies an intermediate position, with a minority share of 34 per cent, while the other two, Zanzibar and Cyprus, have much lower figures.

Hewitt's second demographic hypothesis, concerning the growth of the minority percentage, is again confirmed in the case of Lebanon and Guyana, where he states that the minority has now grown into a majority, and is again disconfirmed for Zanzibar and Cyprus, where no such demographic event is possible.[3] Northern Ireland is again intermediate, but, he suggests, it confirms his hypothesis because he maintains that the minority will become a majority within a generation if present trends continue. Thus, he argues, Northern Ireland is like Lebanon and Guyana in that one community is frightened by the population increase of the other.

The evidence for and against the two demographic hypotheses cannot be assessed solely by looking at the high-violence societies. We need to see whether any of the other societies have a demographic situation which would have led us to expect more violence than actually occurred. In fact, there are, as Hewitt acknowledges, deviant cases, such as Fiji and Trinidad, and their existence is an indication that his three groups of factors—economic and political grievances, and demography—are by no means perfect predictors of ethnic violence. In fact, a careful examination of his own evidence suggests that the demographic group is an even worse predictor than he maintains.

There is, however, one other variable he records for his nineteen societies which is a reasonably good predictor and which, though classified by Hewitt as a characteristic of the political situation, could be argued to be demographic. This is the occurrence of a difference between the majority and the minority over the constitutional identity of the state. Such a difference is a feature of no less than four of the five high-violence societies, including Northern Ireland, the only exception being Guyana. Moreover, the only other society amongst the nineteen studied in which there is said to be a conflict over the existence of the state in its present form is Israel, which Hewitt has classified as having only an intermediate level of violence after ignoring Palestinian guerrilla activity because he regards it as international violence, rather than domestic ethnic, a distinction which he concedes may be spurious.

The reason why it may be valid to reinterpret this constitutional difference as a demographic variable is that the redrawing of state boundaries wished for by one of the ethnic groups in each case results from that group identifying ethnically with a larger neighbouring political unit. Thus, to use simply the evidence from Hewitt's own commentary, Greek Cypriots identified with Greece, Northern Ireland Catholics with the Republic of Ireland, and Zanzibar Africans with the former Tanganyika, while Lebanese Muslims have links with Syria and Palestine.

Double Minority: Static View

In the case of Northern Ireland, this identification of one of its ethnic groups with the inhabitants of a larger neighbour has led to the conceptualization of the conflict situation in terms of what has been described as the 'double minority' model. Several recent academic writers have referred approvingly to this model (Stewart 1977, 162–163; Whyte 1978, 276; Douglas and Boal 1982, 3–4), all attributing it to the journalist Jackson. He had written, shortly after the start of the present Troubles, that 'within their own enclave the Protestants of Ulster, one million strong, outnumber their Catholic brethren two to one. But in the wider context of Ireland they themselves are easily outnumbered three to one. The inevitable result has been the disastrous advent of a ruling establishment... acting under the stresses of a beseiged minority'. (Jackson 1971, 4). For most of the Protestant community 'there has only been one issue—the preservation of the border with the Catholic Republic', for this has been viewed as essential to prevent their absorption into a political state in which, inter alia, their minority status would, they fear, deprive them of power. Correspondingly, Jackson suggests, it is the actuality of suffering, for several decades, such a deprivation of power consequent upon minority status which generates 'a burning sense of grievance' amongst the Catholic community of Northern Ireland. This is augmented by their awareness that they are part of the ethnic majority in the island of Ireland, which many see as the legitimate political state to which the region should belong.[4]

The academic writers who have endorsed the double minority model have differed significantly in their treatment of it. Whyte follows Jackson closely in referring both to the minority status of the two communities and to the consequent stress suffered by each, but Stewart places more emphasis on the stress felt by the Protestant community, tracing its historical continuity from 1886 to the present. Douglas and Boal, too, emphasize these Protestant fears, induced by being a minority, and they contrast them with the confidence and resolve given to the Catholic community by its perceived island majority status.

Above all, however, Douglas and Boal complicate the original double minority model by incorporating the United Kingdom dimension. Stewart (1977, 173) had pointed out that, before partition, the Protestant people of north–east Ireland saw themselves as part of the Protestant majority of the United Kingdom, but the implication of the reasoning presented by Douglas and Boal is that it is more relevant to argue that the Northern Ireland Protestant community is not only a minority within Ireland but, even within the United Kingdom, it is, on its own, 'again a minority with ultimate political power beyond its control'. It is, in fact, a mere 1.7 per cent minority at this scale-level (Compton 1978, 81; Paxton 1981, 1288–1366), with a consequent sense of powerlessness, especially since direct rule of Northern Ireland from London was introduced in 1972.

A further result of this minority status within the United Kingdom, stressed by Douglas and Boal, is the way in which it compounds 'the political uncertainty and territorial ambiguity of the Northern Ireland problem'. This is because the Protestant community is fearful not only of the anti-partitionist stance of Irish Catholics but also of the possible unreliability of the British government, despite its repeated pledges that 'in no event will Northern Ireland or any part of it cease to be part of the United Kingdom without the consent of the majority of the people of Northern Ireland' (*The government of Northern Ireland* 1980, 5).

It is curious that Douglas and Boal did not consider Northern Ireland's Catholic community in the context of the United Kingdom. Clearly, it, too, is a minority in an obvious sense: it constitutes a mere 1.0 per cent of the entire sovereign state's population, it is a component of what is a 10 per cent Catholic minority within this state (Compton 1978, 81; Paxton 1981, 1288–1366), and it is part of an approximately 4 per cent minority formed by the 'Irish Catholic community' in the United Kingdom.[5] Yet Northern Ireland Catholics are, in a certain political sense, part of a majority in the United Kingdom, for opinion polls in Great Britain throughout the present period of Troubles have consistently shown that a 60–65 per cent majority of those people with opinions have approved of Irish unification (Rose et al. 1978, 29; *Sunday Times* 21.12.80).

There thus exists a complex mosaic of alternative geographical frameworks for considering which of Northern Ireland's two ethnic groups is a socially and politically meaningful minority. And this mosaic could, in fact, be added to with further geographical frameworks of relevance from within Ireland itself. However, the most critical contemporary frameworks for identifying meaningful minorities are the ones we have discussed—Northern Ireland itself, the island of Ireland, and the United Kingdom.

Double Minority: Dynamic View

There is a further aspect of demography at the provincial scale-level to consider in the context of the double minority model. This is the problem of change over time, which has already been referred to when dealing with Hewitt's analysis of high-violence societies. His specific assertion that the Catholic community will become a majority of Northern Ireland's population within a generation if present trends continue is, at first sight, perhaps surprising in view of the remarkable stability over time in the Catholic share of the province's population.

Thus, from 1901, twenty years before partition, to 1961, this share was consistently recorded at between 33.5 and 35.2 per cent at every single census (Compton 1976, 434–436).

It has long been recognized that a higher Catholic emigration rate has just been sufficient to offset the higher Catholic birth rate and hence achieve this stability (Barritt and Carter 1962, 108; Park 1962–63, 12; Walsh 1970, 22). However, between 1961 and 1971, the differential between the two ethnic migration rates was no longer able to counter the further increased differential in rates of natural increase between the two ethnic groups (Compton 1982, 87–92). Therefore, the Catholic share of the total Northern Ireland population rose to 36.8 per cent in 1971 (Compton 1978, 80–81), and this rise has continued, it is estimated, to about 38 per cent in 1980 (Compton 1981, 3), caused by a continuation of the migration differential's inability to offset the ever-widening differential in natural increase (Compton 1982, 90, 93).

More specifically on the prediction of when the Catholic community might form a majority of the Northern Ireland population, several sets of projections have been made, differing somewhat in the degree of elaborateness and, above all, incorporating more and more up-to-date demographic trends (Walsh 1970, 22–23, 35–36; Compton and Boal 1970, 462–463, 471–475; Compton 1976, 446–447; Compton 1982, 98–99). The most recent of these projections suggests that the earliest possible year by which Catholics could form a majority of the total population of the province is 2020. However, if all the most recent demographic trends continue, which is the scenario referred to by Hewitt, a Catholic majority could not be expected until the middle of the twenty-first century.

In terms of the effect of demography on conflict, however, it is at least arguable that perception is more important than reality—that what people believe about population trends is more significant than the actual trends themselves. In this context, a special feature of the early paper by Compton and Boal (1970, 475–476) was the survey of student opinion, which showed that the average date by which these young people expected Catholics to form a majority of the Northern Ireland population was 1990. This is much sooner than any of the dates given by the projections, and the perceived imminence of this critical event fuels the fears of the current Protestant majority and the hopes of the current Catholic minority within the province (Rose 1971, 364; Cameron 1969, 55, 65).

This anticipation of the future leads Compton and Boal (1970, 455) to refer to 'the paradox of two minorities' in Northern Ireland which 'is explained, on the one hand, by the existence of the current Catholic minority, and, on the other, by a Protestant group, in the majority at present, fearing that in time it will become a minority'. Here yet again, therefore, is the double minority model, but this time solely in the context of the ethnic composition within the political boundaries of Northern Ireland.

Double Majority

We end up, in consequence, with no less than three totally distinct ways in which the Protestant community of Northern Ireland can be conceptualized, and indeed sees itself, as an ethnic minority. It is currently a minority both within the island of Ireland and within the United Kingdom, and it fears future minority status even within Northern Ireland. Moreover, the way in which all three of these minority situations achieve behavioural relevance is by generating apprehension about the future (Poole and Boal 1973, 11). The corollary of this is that there are also three distinct ways in which the Catholic community of Northern Ireland can be perceived as an ethnic majority, and its awareness of this gives it, one may suggest, an otherwise surprising confidence about the future.

Indeed, in the context of trying to understand violent conflict, it may be much more relevant to emphasize a remarkably ignored implication of the double minority model, which is that a society to which this model is applicable is also characterized by having a double majority. The significance of this is that, while minority status may generate conflict because of a sense of grievance and because of apprehension about the future, it may be argued that violence is more likely to be encouraged by the confidence and sense of strength associated with majority status, together with the feeling of moral righteousness resulting from that perceived status. This sense of righteousness, for example, is very apparent in Randolph Churchill's notorious phrase which was so enthusiastically adopted by the Protestant community towards the end of the nineteenth century, 'Ulster will fight, and Ulster will be right' (Buckland 1973, 10). If both ethnic groups have a sense of strength and a sense of moral justification, as in a double majority situation like Northern Ireland, an eventual violent clash may be very hard to avoid.

Whichever aspect of this model, however, double majority or double minority, is stressed, it must be applied in a rather more varied and complex way than any single writer seems to have suggested in the literature reviewed here. Moreover, when this complexity is reasonably fully explored, it appears that not only can both of Hewitt's two demographic hypotheses about the preconditions for violent conflict—concerning the present minority percentage and its rate of growth—be included in the double majority model, but so also, at least in some cases, can another of his hypotheses. This is the very successful proposition that a difference between the minority and the majority over the constitutional identity of the state is conducive to political violence. At the national or provincial scale-level, therefore, the concept of the double majority appears to be a very powerful demographic model for understanding conflict.

Inter-Regional Scale

Simple Hypotheses

Quantitative analysis of the geographical location of political violence at the inter-regional scale-level within Northern Ireland has been undertaken principally by Schellenberg (1977), Mitchell (1979) and Murray (1982). Each of these three authors has produced such analysis at more than one scale-level, and, though they differed in the specific measures of violence used, they all referred to the relationship between violence and the demography of ethnicity. However, the hypotheses proposed for the form of this relationship by Schellenberg and Mitchell were much simpler than those suggested by Murray. It is therefore appropriate to begin by considering the contribution of the first two writers.

Schellenberg's principal analysis was done at a scale-level involving the use of 34 regions consisting of the old County Boroughs of Belfast and Londonderry, together with 32 others formed primarily from the amalgamation of Boroughs and Urban Districts with the adjacent Rural Districts. He used correlation and regression analysis to study the relationship between the death rate and each of eleven other variables. Several of these eleven are demographic, including population size, population change, population density, and the proportion of adult males, but the variable of most interest for this chapter is the Catholic share of the total population. Schellenberg concluded that just two of the total of eleven variables could, between them, explain a very high proportion of the inter-regional variation in deaths. These were population density and the proportion Catholic, both of which were positively correlated with violence. In relation to the proportion Catholic, this positive correlation indicates that, the larger the Catholic share of the population in a region, the higher the death-rate there.

Mitchell's principal reference to the relationship between violence and ethnicity is a statement that the death-rate in areas with Catholic majorities is six times as great as in areas which are over 80 per cent Protestant and is twice as great as in areas with large Catholic minorities (Mitchell 1979, 196). The geographical framework he has used is unfortunately obscure, but the findings are consistent with those of Schellenberg on the positive correlation between violence and the Catholic share of the population.

Ethnic Origin of Violence

Neither Schellenberg nor Mitchell is strongly assertive about the reasons for this correlation. The two writers agree that support for the established regime is lowest in Catholic areas, and both suggest that the main violent challenge to established authority has come from the Catholic community (Schellenberg 1977, 77; Mitchell 1979, 182, 196). Schellenberg adds that it is within areas whose population is predominantly Catholic that such a challenge can most easily be organized, but it could be argued that, analogously to the suggestion of Spilerman (1970, 643–645) in the context of black involvement in United States riots, Catholic-dominated areas simply have more Catholics and thus more people willing to carry out the necessary violence.

The concentration of violence in predominantly Catholic areas can, in fact, be partly explained by making further use of the double majority model, introduced in the earlier discussion at the provincial scale-level. Specifically, this model can help to explain why so much of the violence originates in the Catholic ethnic group. The relevant argument suggests that, of the two groups in a double majority society, only one is likely to be a frustrated majority in the sense of having its wishes in relation to the constitutional identity of the state blocked. This is also likely to be the group which is the most frustrated in the sense of being deprived of political power. In the Northern Ireland context, this frustrated majority is, of course, the Catholic community, and its perceived majority status, especially at the island and United Kingdom scale-levels, is critical in bestowing at least a section of it with the sense both of strength and of moral righteousness to encourage it to indulge in violence to achieve passionately desired political goals which are viewed as otherwise beyond reach. For the frustrated majority, therefore, violence is legitimized.

Empirical evidence for the suggestion that the violence originates primarily in the Catholic community comes mainly from the work of the third writer listed at the start of this section, Murray (1982, 322–325). After classifying the violence into three broad categories, he estimated that, up to 1977, 53 per cent of the deaths had arisen from either the classical guerrilla war or the economic campaign, both of them fought amost exclusively by paramilitary organizations drawn from the Catholic community. The remainder was caused by sectarian conflict, in which most of the killers were Protestant. This last feature has been particularly documented by Schellenberg (1976, 15–16), whose data suggests that about 70 per cent of sectarian killers have been drawn from the Protestant community.

Much interpretation is necessarily involved in such estimates, but these figures are encouragingly consistent with those of McKeown (1977). It thus appears that about two-thirds of all killings have their ethnic origin in the Catholic community, in the sense that they are committed either by Catholics themselves or by security forces involved in a struggle with certain elements of the Catholic community.

In addition, however, the geographical variation in the ethnic origin of the violence is important in trying to understand where the killings actually occur. A re-working of Murray's data shows that, as a result of the heavy concentration in Belfast of deaths arising from sectarian conflict, the proportion of the non-Belfast deaths which have had their origin in the other type of conflict, the Catholic guerrilla and economic campaigns, is much higher than the corresponding figure for the province as a whole: this proportion is, in fact, 67 per cent. In addition, of those sectarian deaths that did occur outside Belfast, the proportion committed by Catholic killers was higher than it was in Belfast. The effect of these two factors produces an estimate that between 75 per cent and 80 per cent of all deaths attributable to the troubles outside the Belfast region have their origin in the Catholic community.

Thus, to a very large extent indeed, it is the Catholic community, rather than the Protestant, which has given rise to these deaths outside Belfast, either directly by committing them or indirectly by indulging in activities which may be said to have provoked killings by the official security forces. In view of this, it is not surprising that there is a positive correlation, as was found by Schellenberg and by Mitchell, between the Catholic share of the population and the total death rate when these two variables are studied at the inter-regional scale-level.

This is because, when Northern Ireland is divided into a large number of regions, the great majority of them outside Belfast, nearly all the inter-regional variation investigated involves regions other than Belfast. And, since killing in these regions has its origin so overwhelmingly in the Catholic community, it follows that most of the inter-regional variation occurring in the death rate is likely to be inter-regional variation in the rate of killings originating directly or indirectly in the Catholic community. In consequence, it is only to be expected that so many of the high-violence regions are regions whose population is very Catholic.

Complex Hypotheses

Murray (1982) began his discussion of the link between violence and ethnic composition by referring to the findings of Schellenberg (1977) which we reviewed earlier. Murray suggested, however, that at the much more detailed scale-level of 332 areas based on the wards of Northern Ireland, at which a large part of his own analysis was conducted, the correlation between ethnicity and violence was not at all strong. This led him to suggest two principal deviations from the tendency for a positive correlation. The first is the existence of many parts of Northern Ireland where Catholics form a majority, yet there is little political violence. This is a point to which Mitchell (1979, 196) had earlier drawn attention as an exception to the general trend he described: Catholic regions in the east of Northern Ireland, he suggested, had low levels of violence.

The second deviation suggested by Murray is, in a sense, more ambiguous. He pointed out that, if Belfast is examined as a single entity, it has a Catholic minority, yet it is a high-violence location. He added, however, that, because of intense ethnic residential segregation in this city, Catholics are a majority in certain areas and, moreover, he claims, these are the most violence-prone parts of it. Therefore, whether Belfast is an exception to the tendency for a correlation between the ethnic composition of a region and its level of violence depends entirely on the scale-level at which the investigation is conducted.

Even more important, however, Murray is here introducing the concept that the amount of violence in a region may be related not just to the over-all ethnic composition of that region, but also to the geographical distribution of ethnic groups within that region. Thus the level of violence in a region may be related to the ethnic composition existing at more than one geographical scale-level. This is a very important point to which we shall return later.

It was in order to allow for his two deviations that Murray proposed that, while a Catholic majority in an area or within easy travelling distance was a necessary condition for violence, it was not a sufficient condition. For there to be much political violence in a region, he suggested that three other conditions must be satisfied, and this inevitably generates a more complex set of hypotheses than those examined by Schellenberg and Mitchell. These three supplementary conditions were the presence of historical precedents, a high level of alienation of Catholics from Protestant society, and an environment providing both targets and security for the perpetrators of violence. Of these three further conditions, the first is not intrinsically demographic, but the other two have explicitly demographic elements which we must consider.

The alienation referred to by Murray has two main components. One is provided by opposition to partition being fostered by proximity to the Border, for, he suggested, Catholics living closest to the Border must be expected to be most aware of being in a majority in the island of Ireland because of their frequent contacts with the Republic of Ireland. The other component of alienation is stimulated by ethnic residential segregation, for, where it occurs, this will inhibit inter-ethnic contact. Thus both components of alienation have clear demographic elements. The last of Murray's necessary conditions, an environment offering both targets and security, has many non-demographic elements, but he suggested that, in towns, the large, dense population and the existence of ethnically segregated neighbourhoods provide a secure base for guerrilla activity.

It can be argued that, enshrined within these four conditions that he states are necessary for political violence to occur, Murray is introducing four refinements, compared with Schellenberg and Mitchell, into the way that he hypothesizes that the demography of ethnicity affects violence in Northern Ireland. Firstly, an assumption was made clearly by Schellenberg, and more ambiguously by Mitchell, that violence is positively correlated with the Catholic share of the population over the entire range of proportions from zero to 100. Murray, however, proposed that the difference between Catholic majority areas and Catholic minority areas is more salient in affecting the location of violence—or, more specifically, of the guerrilla warfare and the economic campaign which originate in the Catholic community. Moreover, this acknowledgment that there is another aspect of violence, the sectarian conflict, leads to a second refinement from Murray. Thus he stated that sectarian conflict is associated with Protestant majority areas, albeit in a complex way: it is greatest where there is a substantial Protestant majority, but not an overwhelming one.

The remaining two refinements introduced by Murray are, in a sense, the opposite of each other. In the first place, he suggested that a high-violence region need not itself have a Catholic majority, as long as it was within easy travelling distance of such a region. Thus, he hypothesized, it is not just the ethnic composition of the specific geographical region where the violence takes place which is relevant, for the ethnic character of adjacent areas can help to generate violence at a particular place. On the other hand, even when we are considering the ethnic structure of the region of the conflict itself, it is not just the over-all ethnic composition which is salient, for the internal geography of this composition within the region being considered may affect its over-all level of violence. This fourth refinement is the same point which was quoted in the introduction to this chapter from the suggestion of Darby, that the amount of violence in a town is influenced by the extent to which its housing is ethnically segregated.

Implications

The implication of these four refinements identified in Murray's work is that the amount and type of violence in a geographical region depends on the nature and identity of the ethnic majority in that region, on the geographical distribution of that majority within the region, and on the nature and identity of the ethnic majority in the wider territory around. The level of violence at any one location is thus dependent on the ethnic composition at a whole series of spatial scale-levels involving that location.

This inference, drawn from the work of Murray, can be used to provide some demographic reinterpretations of his material. Firstly, it can be argued that the relevance of the proximity of the Border for fostering anti-partition feeling, and thus violence, is that the Republic of Ireland is overwhelmingly Catholic, both over-all and even in most of its Border areas (C.S.O. 1977, 10–27). Therefore, regions in Northern Ireland which themselves have a Catholic majority and which are near the Border form part of a wider territory which not only has a Catholic majority over-all but which consists of a series of adjacent regions, each of which individually has a Catholic majority. The relevance of this is that, just as ethnic residential segregation fosters Catholic alienation from the Protestant community by inhibiting inter-ethnic contact, so the location of a region within a wider territory, consisting entirely of adjacent regions with a Catholic majority, will inhibit contact between ethnic groups and lead to alienation.

The second demographic reinterpretation of Murray's contribution is that, when he suggests that proximity to the Republic of Ireland facilitates violence by offering a secure base for guerrilla activity, it is the implication of such proximity for a region's location in a wider territory of adjacent regions, all with a Catholic majority, that is critical. This provides the relatively secure environment for the Catholic guerrilla in Border areas which, as Murray himself says, is ensured by ethnic residential segregation in urban areas.

These two demographic reinterpretations of the significance of the Border in affecting the location of political violence can be used to provide a demographic explanation for the remarkable concentration of such violence into a small part of the province. That such a concentration exists is made clear by Murray's inter-regional analysis, in which he identified three major violence-prone regions—Belfast, Londonderry, and a narrow, discontinuous Border region—with 59, 8 and 16 per cent respectively of deaths attributable to the Troubles in the province. Even taken together, these three regions only occupy 23 per cent of Northern Ireland's land-area, so the remaining 77 per cent of its area has only had 17 per cent of its deaths.[6]

A straightforward demographic explanation of this concentration, based only on the individual ethnic composition of the regions whose violence is being measured, is not very successful, as Murray pointed out in refuting what we have termed the 'simple hypothesis'. For example, the nine District Council Areas in which Catholics form a majority occupy, because of their low population density, no less than 55 per cent of the land-area of Northern Ireland (Compton 1978, 10–12, 80–81; N.I.G.R.O. 1975b, 2–13). This is clearly a much more extensive area than Murray's high-violence regions.

On the other hand, the hypothesis that a region must not only have a Catholic majority itself, but be part of a wider territory of adjacent localities, all with a Catholic majority, before it has much political violence, appears to go a long way towards explaining the concentration of Northern Ireland's violence into such a small portion of its area. This is because, although Catholics are in a local majority, albeit very often a small one, in rather more than half the land-area in the west of the province, as well as in certain scattered pockets in the east, the pattern of dominantly Catholic and dominantly Protestant areas in the west forms such a complex mosaic that few areas of the first type are far from an area of the second (Compton 1976, 434–435; Darby 1976, 32–33; Compton 1978, 81–83). Therefore, òf all the places in Northern Ireland, it is only those areas which have a local Catholic majority and which are close to the Border that satisfy the hypothesis proposed here.

Further support for this hypothesis is provided by the actual location of Murray's (1982, 318–319) high-violence regions. They are all within 30 kilometers of the Border, except for Belfast, and, indeed, all but Belfast and part of a County Tyrone region centred upon Dungannon and Coalisland are within 20 kilometres of the Border.

In this sub-section we have only provided empirical evidence for considering two elements of what we saw as the critical scale-level implications of Murray's complex hypotheses on the relationship between ethnic composition and the level of political violence in a region. These were the nature and identity of the ethnic majority both in that region itself and in the wider territory around. The remaining element of the scale-level implications of Murray's work is the geographical distribution of the ethnic groups within the region whose over-all level of violence is being measured. The principal aspect of this intra-regional distribution is urban residential segregation, and that is why its consideration, in the light of empirical evidence, has been deferred until the next section, dealing with the inter-urban scale-level.

Inter-Urban Scale

Shortage of Information

In addition to proposing hypotheses about the relationship between political violence and ethnic residential segregation, Murray (1982, 328–329) observed that the extent to which individual towns were subject to such violence appeared to be correlated with the intensity of their ethnic residential segregation. This apparent verification of the hypothesis of Darby, referred to in the introduction to this chapter, is not, however, supported by any empirical evidence, even of a non-quantitative nature, except for Belfast. This city, Murray states, exhibits high rates of all three of his categories of political violence because it contains both Catholic and Protestant majority areas. Darby (1976, 26) himself went a little further, for he provided a larger number of specific examples, albeit without numerical evidence, arguing that 'the worst communal violence has been concentrated in urban centres where one polarized religious bloc adjoins its rival—towns like Belfast, Derry, Lurgan and Portadown'.

The omission by these authors of any numerical data to support their contentions about the relationship between violence and urban segregation is hardly surprising in view of the remarkable dearth, until very recently, of quantitative information on ethnic residential segregation in Northern Ireland's towns (Poole 1982, 281–284). A programme of data collection to fill this information void has been reported on at the half-way stage (Poole 1982, 284–293), and this programme is now sufficiently complete to permit the measurement of segregation in 1971 for every town in the province. A section of this data, along with the list of deaths attributable to the Troubles between 1969 and 1981, will now be used in the rest of this section of the chapter to investigate the relationship between the variation of violence between towns and the urban demography of ethnicity (see table 7:3). It is hoped that this analysis will go some way towards meeting the shortage of information currently available on this aspect of the relationship between violence and ethnic demography.

The particular towns considered will be the set of 27 which had a population in excess of 5,000 within their built-up area according to the 1971 census.[7] In recording the violence and the demographic characteristics for each of these towns, it will, in fact, be the limits of the built-up area which will be taken to define the urban boundaries. The particular measure of violence employed will be the number of separate fatal incidents, which will be preferred to the more commonly-used total number of deaths because the former appears to be a better measure of the degree of risk associated with living in a place.

Urban Fatal Incidents

The total of 2,161 deaths, analysed here, between 1969 and 1981 happened in 1,715 separate fatal incidents, according to our classification. Of these, 1,260 (73.5 per cent) were urban in the sense of occurring within one of the 27 towns defined earlier. The rate of fatal incidents, expressed as a frequency per 1,000 people, is 1.29 in urban areas and 0.81 in rural areas. Political violence of this type is thus disproportionately an urban phenomenon, though not overwhelmingly so, when measured in relation to the distribution of population.

The next point to consider is whether all towns are equally prone to violence. Table 1 shows that there is, in fact, a tremendous concentration of urban violence in the two cities of Belfast and Londonderry, with 77.8 and 10.1 per cent respectively. This particular concentration has already been suggested in the work of Murray (1982, 318–319), so what is more interesting is the variation amongst the other towns, from 28 incidents in Lurgan to no incidents at all in as many as four settlements.

Table 7:1

FATAL INCIDENTS (1969–1981) AND POPULATION (1971) IN TOWNS WITH OVER 5,000 PEOPLE

Town	Fatal incidents	Population	Fatal incidents per 1,000 people
Belfast	980	554,450	1.77
Londonderry	127	66,645	1.91
Lurgan	28	27,930	1.00
Portadown	25	22,207	1.13
Armagh	21	13,606	1.54
Newry	20	20,279	0.99
Strabane	14	9,413	1.49
Dungannon	9	8,190	1.10
Bangor	5	35,260	0.14
Carrickfergus	5	16,603	0.30
Lisburn	4	31,836	0.13
Omagh	4	14,594	0.27
Ballymena	3	23,386	0.13
Larne	3	18,482	0.16
Three towns with two incidents	6	32,037	0.19
Six towns with one incident	6	56,382	0.11
Four towns with no incidents	—	23,534	—
TOTAL	1,260	974,834	1.29

Source: Fatal incidents: derived from list supplied by the R.U.C. Press Office. Population: N.I.G.R.O. (1975b, 2–13); Government of Northern Ireland (1971, 12); N.I.G.R.O., *Antrim* (1973, 3, 10), *Armagh* (1973, 2), *Belfast County Borough* (1973, 2), *Down* (1974, 2–6).

Clearly, Northern Ireland towns do vary enormously in the extent to which they have suffered political violence, but it is equally clear that there is a tendency for the larger towns to have the most incidents. Thus Belfast and Londonderry, at one extreme, are by far the two largest urban settlements in the province, while, at the other, the four towns which have suffered no incidents at all have an average population of less than 6,000. True, there is no simple correlation between violence and population-size, as the relatively small number of fatal incidents in the third and fourth largest towns in the province, Bangor and Lisburn, testifies. However, there is a sufficiently strong correlation to suggest that we shall not get much further in explaining the inter-urban variation in violence without re-expressing the number of fatal incidents as a rate per 1,000 people. When this is done, the differences between towns are reduced very substantially indeed. The range is now from a maximum of 1.91 in Londonderry to a minimum of zero in the four towns already referred to.

Table 7:2 lists the 27 towns in order according to the rate of fatal incidents per 1,000 people. This table shows that, while Belfast and Londonderry are still the top two towns on the criterion of this rate, as they were on the criterion of the absolute number of incidents, there is no longer a marked gap between these two and the rest. In fact, when towns are listed as in Table 7:2, Belfast and Londonderry are merely the top two in a set of eight high-violence towns which do not differ massively from one another in their level of violence according to this measure.

Table 7:2

FATAL INCIDENTS (1969–1981) PER 1,000 PEOPLE IN TOWNS WITH OVER 5,000 PEOPLE IN 1971

Town	Fatal incidents per 1,000 people	Town	Fatal incidents per 1,000 people
Londonderry	1.91	Larne	0.16
Belfast	1.77	Cookstown	0.14
Armagh	1.54	Bangor	0.14
Strabane	1.49	Ballymena	0.13
Portadown	1.13	Lisburn	0.13
Dungannon	1.10	Banbridge	0.13
Lurgan	1.00	Coleraine	0.12
Newry	0.99	Antrim	0.07
Limavady	0.33	Newtownards	0.06
Carrickfergus	0.30	Ballyclare	—
Omagh	0.27	Downpatrick	—
Enniskillen	0.21	Portrush	—
Comber	0.18	Portstewart	—
Ballymoney	0.18		

Sources: See Table 6:1.

What is particularly noticeable from Table 7:2, however, is the large gap between Newry, with the lowest rate of incidents per 1,000 people amongst these eight high-violence towns, and the next town in order of susceptibility to violence according to this index, Limavady. Newry has a rate of 0.99, but that of Limavady is only 0.33. In comparison with the width of this gap, there is very little variation in the rate amongst the nineteen towns below the gap—even less than there was amongst the eight towns above the gap. Therefore, there emerges a clear dichotomy in the list between the eight high-violence towns and the nineteen low-violence towns, and the attempt to relate ethnic composition to violence, which will now be made, will concentrate on discovering the extent to which ethnic variables are correlated with this dichotomy.

Ethnic Demography and Violence: Three Scale-levels

The ethnic aspect of urban demography certainly, on first examination, seems to have a potential explanatory power, for its variation from one town to another is very considerable indeed. For example, the Catholic share of the total urban population varies from the lowest value of 5.1 per cent in Comber to the highest of 83.9 per cent in Newry, with nine of the 27 towns considered having Catholic majorities and the remainder Protestant majorities. Similarly, the dissimilarity index, which measures residential segregation on a scale from zero to 100, representing minimum and maximum segregation respectively, ranges from 19.5 in Antrim to 74.0 in Armagh. In fact, only seven towns have a dissimilarity index above the mid-point of 50 and can thus be thought of as high-segregation towns, while no fewer than twenty lie below this mid-point.

The ethnic variables, whose relationship with urban violence is to be tested, can be divided into three groups according to the geographical scale-level involved. The first is a group of three variables relating to each town taken as a single entity. These are the Catholic percentage share of the population, together with the absolute size of the Catholic community and the absolute size of the Protestant community. The method of analysis used with the variables both in this group and in the later groups was the simple one of identifying the dichotomy in the ethnic variable which best predicted the dichotomy in the rate of violence. For example, for the Catholic share of the whole urban population, the best dichotomy for this purpose was a division into towns over 50 per cent Catholic and towns under 50 per cent Catholic.

Table 7:3 shows how successful this variable was in predicting the dichotomy in the rate of fatal incidents per 1,000 people. There was clearly a positive correlation between the two variables, as indeed there had been between violence and the Catholic share of the population in the inter-regional analysis examined in the last section of this chapter. The level of violence was, in fact, correctly predicted in 22 of the 27 towns considered. Not surprisingly, in view of this positive correlation, the absolute size of the Protestant community was not a good predictor of the level of violence, but Table 7:3 shows that the total number in the Catholic population was an even better predictor than the percentage Catholic share of the population. In only three towns is the level of violence incorrectly predicted by the absolute size of the Catholic community.

Table 7:3

THE ASSOCIATION BETWEEN THE RATE OF FATAL INCIDENTS PER 1,000 PEOPLE AND EACH OF EIGHT ETHNIC VARIABLES FOR THE 27 TOWNS WITH OVER 5,000 PEOPLE IN 1971

Ethnic variable	*Ethnic category*	*Rate of fatal incidents* High	Low	*Incorrectly predicted towns*
Catholic % share of population	Over 50%	6	3	5
	Under 50%	2	16	
Absolute size of Catholic community	Over 6,000	7	2	3
	Under 6,000	1	17	
Absolute size of Protestant community	Over 15,000	3	3	8
	Under 15,000	5	16	
Dissimilarity index	Over 50	6	1	3
	Under 50	2	18	
P* (Catholic)	Over 60	7	3	4
	Under 60	1	16	
Catholic population in areas over 90% Catholic	Over 500	8	1	1
	Under 500	—	18	
Distance from Border	Over 20 km.	3	18	4
	Under 20 km.	5	1	
Catholic % share of D.C.A. population	Over 40%	5	5	8
	Under 40%	3	14	

Sources: Fatal incidents: derived from list supplied by the R.U.C. Press Office. Ethnic variables: unpublished Small Area Statistics of the 1971 Northern Ireland Census of Population; Compton (1978, 80–81); unpublished clergy data on religious affiliation; electoral registers; N.I.G.R.O. (1975a, 34–36).

The second group of ethnic variables involved what, in general terms, we can refer to as the scale-level of the neighbourhood within towns. More specifically, they all involve the ethnic residential segregation identifiable on dividing each town into sub-areas containing an average of 200 households. A total of twelve different measures of segregation was correlated with violence to discover which gave the best fit, but only three are illustrated in Table 7:3. One of these, the dissimilarity index, is included because it is the most commonly-used measure of segregation in the literature on this subject (Poole and Boal 1973, 23–24; Peach 1975, 2–4), while another, P*, applied to the Catholic population, is included because there are sound theoretical reasons for supposing that this is a measure with direct consequences for inter-ethnic behaviour (Lieberson 1981, 64–70). However, it is the third of the segregation variables illustrated in the table which is the best predictor of the level of violence in a town. This is the number of Catholics living in neighbourhoods which are over 90 per cent Catholic.

In Belfast these neighbourhoods have been referred to by Boal *et al.* (1976, 99) as the 'Catholic city' in order to distinguish them from the 'Mixed city' and the 'Protestant city'. They can also be regarded as the Catholic urban ghettos, and the variable which is so successful in predicting violence can consequently be interpreted as the size of the Catholic ghetto population.[8] Table 7:3 shows that it is the towns with large Catholic ghetto populations which have the high rates of violence. Conversely, towns with very few or none of their Catholics living in this type of neighbourhood have a low level of violence. There is only one exception to this trend, and that is the County Tyrone town of Omagh, which is anomalous because it has a much lower rate of violence than would be predicted from the size of its Catholic ghetto population.

The third group of ethnic variables to be considered involves attributes of the wider territory around each town. Because of the conclusions reached at the end of the inter-regional section about the significance of location with respect to the Border, the distance from each town to the nearest part of the Irish Republic was measured. It was found to be a reasonably good predictor of violence, succeeding in 23 of the 27 towns, but this success-rate is still much lower than that achieved with the best segregation measure. The other variable relating to the wider territory around each town is the Catholic percentage share of the population of the District Council Area in which each town is located. As the final row of Table 7:3 shows, however, this is a rather poor predictor of violence.

Inter-urban and Inter-regional: A Comparison

It therefore clearly emerges that, of all the ethnic variables whose correlation with the rate of fatal incidents per 1,000 people has been examined, there is just one optimal predictor of the level of urban violence. This is the size of the Catholic ghetto population. Since this is basically a variable relating to the ethnic composition of urban neighbourhoods, rather than of the town as a whole or of the wider territory around, we are compelled to arrive at a distinctly different conclusion about the inter-urban variation in violence from that reached at the end of the preceding section on inter-regional variation. In that section, it was concluded that high-violence regions, with the exception of Belfast, were all parts of larger geographical areas composed of adjacent Catholic-dominated regions. The ethnic demography of the wider territory around the high-violence region was therefore perceived as crucial in explaining inter-regional variations in violence.

In the current section, however, it has been concluded that the ethnic demography of a town itself is the key factor in explaining inter-urban variations in violence. This would seem to imply that it is, in fact, rural violence whose location is affected by proximity to the Border. There is insufficient space to develop a full analysis of this topic, but some evidence to support this contention is the discovery that 62 per cent of the rural fatal incidents which have occurred have been concentrated into the six District Council Areas adjoining the Border, especially Newry and Mourne, Dungannon and Fermanagh. In fact, the rate of fatal incidents per 1,000 people for rural areas is 1.38 in these six Border District Council Areas, but only 0.48 elsewhere in Northern Ireland.

Though a contrast has been drawn between the inter-regional finding that distance from the Border is crucial in affecting the level of violence, except in the case of Belfast, and the inter-urban conclusion that the size of the Catholic ghetto population is critical in influencing the rate of violence, these separate discoveries have two features in common. Firstly, in neither case is the ethnic demography of the specific geographical area, whose rate of violence is being measured, of much relevance. For inter-regional variation, it is the wider territory whose ethnic composition is important, while, for inter-urban variation, it is the neighbourhood whose composition is salient. Indeed, this finding can almost certainly be extended to the one area which was exceptional in the context of inter-regional variation, Belfast, for this city is so large that it totally dominates its region. Therefore, it is probably the 'urban factor' of Catholic ghetto-size which is crucial in affecting its regional level of violence.

Secondly, it is suggested that both this urban factor of ghetto-size and the regional or rural factor of distance from the Border are relevant in affecting the rate of fatal incidents because they constitute measures of the absolute size of the Catholic population living in overwhelmingly Catholic places. This is so both in the case of the urban Catholic ghetto population and in the case of the Catholic majority regions adjacent to the massively Catholic territory of the Irish Republic.

Intra-Urban Scale

Ethnic segregation and doorstep murders

The final scale-level to be considered is the intra-urban. There is only one Northern Ireland town whose geographical pattern of political violence at this scale-level has been studied in any depth, and that is Belfast. Intra-urban studies of this city have devoted considerable attention to the relationship between violence and ethnic demography, but, almost without exception, they have evaded the topic of deaths attributable to the Troubles. Instead, they have concentrated on the location either of riots (Day et al. 1971; Easthope 1976, 436–443) or of the refugee movement investigated, as pointed out in the introduction to this chapter, as a demographic effect of intimidation and certain other forms of violence.

This virtual disregarding of Troubles-induced deaths in the research at the intra-urban level makes this scale-level similar, in this respect, to the inter-urban. However, whereas original research has been specially undertaken to fill this void at the inter-urban level, such analysis was not carried out on the location of deaths within towns. This section will, therefore, simply review the limited available literature.

Only one analysis has so far been undertaken of the geographical distribution within Belfast of deaths attributable to the troubles. This was an investigation of a very restricted, but particularly frightening, subset of these deaths, the killing of civilians in their homes, a category referred to as doorstep murders because most victims were shot on answering the door (Murray and Boal 1979, 151–153). There is a very marked concentration of these murders, especially of those carried out by Protestant killers, in north Belfast, for reasons, the authors suggest, connected with the geography of ethnic composition within this area.

The first of these reasons is the complex patchwork pattern, in much of the area, of small segregated Catholic and Protestant housing areas, which are both difficult to defend and easy to penetrate from outside by attackers who can return quickly to the security of their own neighbourhood nearby, which is often one of the larger adjacent segregated areas. The small ghettos thus provide an easy target, while the adjacent larger ghettos provide the best security. The second reason, which Murray and Boal, in fact, regard as more important than the first, is that north Belfast has been subject to much more change in its internal geography of ethnicity since 1969 than the rest of the city, especially in the form of Catholic expansion. This makes it almost unique in the city, for by far the largest part of Belfast has been characterized by a remarkable stability of ethnic composition in both its segregated and its mixed areas for at least several decades (Boal 1982, 254–257). The Catholic expansion in north Belfast, Murray and Boal claim, has made many Protestants feel threatened and resentful at their loss of territory.

It might also be hypothesized that this exodus of Protestants from those areas experiencing Catholic expansion implies that many Protestants are familiar with the lay-out of these particular Catholic areas, thus facilitating penetration to carry out a doorstep murder. This may well be a significant factor in a city where there is so little inter-ethnic contact that one community's familiarity with the territory of the other is normally very low indeed (Boal 1969, 39–47).

Murray and Boal are thus very adamant that there is a relationship between ethnic demography and the location of doorstep murders, but these killings only constituted 4 per cent of all deaths arising from the Troubles in the Belfast high-violence region in their study-period (Murray 1982, 322). They do make reference to other murders, pointing out that many take place in segregated areas, the victim usually having travelled to or through the other ethnic group's territory, but no numerical evidence is provided. In a similarly non-quantitative vein, Murray (1982, 326) claims that most violence occurs in those relatively restricted parts of Belfast where Catholics form the majority of the population: streets of this type, in fact, contain just 18 per cent of the city's households (Boal 1981, 67).

In the absence, however, of quantitative analysis of the location of any but a tiny fraction of the deaths attributable to the Troubles within either Belfast or any other Northern Ireland town, it would be premature to take such limited intra-urban observations as we have been able to make in this section and forward them to our conclusion. This final section of the chapter will therefore draw together our findings at the provincial, inter-regional and inter-urban levels, but ignore the intra-urban.

Conclusion: Scale-level and majority status

In the course of trying to examine the effect of ethnic demography on the geographical variation in the incidence of violence at a number of distinct scale-levels, it has been necessary, not surprisingly, to study the geography of ethnic composition itself at several separate scale-levels. What is much more important, however, is our finding that, at any one scale-level at which the location of violence is examined, it may be necessary to invoke the separate effects of the spatial pattern of ethnic composition at distinctly different scale-levels in order to provide an explanation. This is certainly the case for the inter-regional analysis of violence, where the ethnic composition, not only of each region identified for recording violence, but also, and more importantly, of the wider territory around and of the internal divisions of the region, had to be included in the explanation.

Similarly, the general provincial level of violence, compared with other societies elsewhere, was explained in terms of the double majority model, which involved examining the ethnic composition not only of Northern Ireland but also of the United Kingdom and of the island of Ireland. Indeed, these three scale-levels involved in the double majority model were held to play a part in explaining the ethnic group in which most of the violence originates, which, in turn, affects the location of violence at the inter-regional, inter-urban and, probably, the intra-urban scale-levels, too. There thus emerges a rather complex, multi-tiered hierarchy of geographical scale-levels, the ethnic composition at each of which is relevant in affecting the location of violence at any one scale of investigation.

The specific aspect of ethnic composition which is relevant at all these scale-levels is the identity of the ethnic group which constitutes the majority of the population. The double majority model, for example, emphasizes the paradoxes revealed by varying the scale-level in answer to Lijphart's (1975, 94–95) question, 'Majority of what?', which, he asserts, 'spells trouble for a system with boundaries that are widely questioned'. Similarly, the issue of which ethnic group has majority status is the crucial one with respect to the wider territory around a high-violence region or town, to this high-violence area itself and to the neighbourhoods into which the area may be divided.

There does seem to be a difference amongst these scale-levels, however, in the size of the majority which is important. At the level of Northern Ireland, the United Kingdom and the island of Ireland, it is the mere existence of a majority, no matter how small, which is most important, because there is a crucial difference between majority status and minority status in determining who should exercise power and determine political boundaries in a 'winner take all' democracy. There-fore, the existence of a majority, regardless of how small, provides a precondition for political violence if that majority is frustrated by having its 'democratically justified' objectives thwarted.

On the other hand, at the various smaller scale-levels, there needs to be a much larger majority before the preconditions for violence exist. This is most explicit at the level of the urban neighbourhood, where it was found that areas over 90 per cent Catholic were the most crucial ones. The situation for the wider territories around high-violence regions near the Border is more complicated, but half the wards with Catholic majorities adjoining it on the Northern Ireland side have a Catholic proportion in excess of 75 per cent of their population (Compton 1976, 435; Compton 1978, 5), while all the Rural Districts continguous with it on the Republic of Ireland side are over 75 per cent Catholic (C.S.O. 1977, 10–27).

Even in the case of these Border areas, therefore, and even more so in the case of urban neighbourhoods, it is places with large Catholic majorities, rather than with just bare majorities, which seem to provide an environment conducive to violence. Presumably, it is such overwhelmingly Catholic areas that provide the most secure base for the Catholic guerrilla and which inhibit inter-ethnic contact, and in both these ways they are conducive to political violence (Boal 1972, 167).

If there is any validity in our findings relating to the effect either of the size of the urban Catholic ghettos or of the demographic interpre-tation of proximity to the Border, then there must be clear policy implications, in terms of both desegregation and repartition, if the reduction of political violence is seen as a desirable goal. Quite apart from the issue of the practicability of these implications, it must be stressed, however, that it is not at this stage desirable to explain and evaluate them in any detail at all, because of the highly preliminary nature of our findings.

It may seem both conservative and conventional to conclude this chapter by calling for more research to confirm or refute these prelimi-nary findings, but this entire subject-area of the relationship between ethnic demography and violent conflict is one which has been so little investigated that such a call is inevitable. In particular, it is suggested that a more sophisticated methodology is required, a careful categoriz-ation of deaths is needed whenever fatal incidents form the subject of analysis, and the aspects of violence explored must be broadened and applied consistently at all scale-levels. Such a programme of analysis is surely justified by the severity of the problem of violence still engulfing Northern Ireland so many years after 1969.

Notes

1. This characterization, by Hewitt, of the Northern Ireland conflict as essentially ethnic in nature is by no means a universally agreed one, but there does appear to be strong justification for viewing ethnicity as at least a major component of the division between Protestant and Catholic in the province (Boal et al. 1976, 77–83, 114–122; Darby 1976, 169–174).

2. In one sense, the concept of ethnic composition is not a demographic one at all, for it is not so clearly a part of formal or pure demography as such other aspects of popula-tion structure as age, sex or marital status. However, there is a broader and increas-ingly used definition of demography which includes the study of ethnicity and religion, along with many other socio-economic variables, both in their own right and in relation to group differences in birth rates, death rates and migration (Kirk 1968, 342–343). It is the existence of this broader definition which justifies the use of the term 'demography' in this chapter.

3. The classification of these ethnic groups in Zanzibar and Cyprus as minorities, despite their economic and political privilege before violence occurred, indicates that, in this chapter, we are following Banton (1979, 127) in defining a minority in simple numerical terms rather than in the sense popularized by Wirth.

4. In fact, Jackson seems to have been responsible for the specific term 'double minority' rather than for the concept. For example, virtually the same set of ideas about both minority status and its behavioural consequences was expressed about the same time by Shearman (1970, 45) and by Gibson (1971, 4–5). Moreover, more than a decade earlier, Gallagher (1957, 196–224) had characterized each of Northern Ireland's two ethnic communities as a minority.

5. This 4 per cent figure is estimated from data provided by Jackson (1963, 187), Krausz (1971, 34–36) and Compton (1982, 98).

6. The data on land-area is obtained from N.I.G.R.O. (1975b, 2–13) for wards identified from a comparison of Murray's (1982, 318) map of regions with high levels of violence with the ward-location map presented by Compton (1978, 5–9).

7. The sources of this population data are described in Table 7:1. The set of 27 towns are obtained after amalgamating certain adjacent urban settlements: most import-antly, the Newtownabbey, Holywood, Castlereagh and Andersonstown–Dunmurry districts were combined with Belfast, and Brownlow was added to Lurgan.

8. The word 'ghetto' has, it must be admitted, emotive overtones, but it has a cryptic convenience. Moreover, it is commonly used in the academic literature to describe any extreme degree of ethnic residential segregation (Jones and Eyles 1977, 169–170), though a more restricted definition is preferred by some (Boal 1976, 57, 64–75).

8

From Conflict to Violence: The Re-emergence of the IRA and the Loyalist Response

Barry White

It is not only very difficult, but probably highly misleading, to try to see too much of a pattern in the violence which has been the single most consistent factor in Northern Ireland political life since 1969. A relatively small, but long-lived and experienced paramilitary organisation, the Provisional IRA, has been trying, on behalf of a minority of Northern Ireland's Nationalist minority, to bring about radical political change against the expressed wishes of the vast majority of the population, including the local and British-based security forces, supported by the British Government. In these circumstances, the methods used by the IRA—and similar Republican terrorist groups like the Irish National Liberation Army—must involve a considerable degree of violence, along a broad front, in order to try to achieve the short-term objective of intimidating the Catholic and Protestant populations, as well as presenting a credible threat to British Government rule. Of necessity, the intensity and direction of the campaign has to be varied constantly, to counter the superior numbers and firepower of the opposition, as well as to respond to political events, and this makes overall strategy confused and hard to discern. Resourcefulness is perhaps the IRA's most obvious characteristic, ensuring that, despite major setbacks, it has been able to keep up the pressure, at some level.

Broadly speaking, however, the campaign began on the streets, as a follow-up to the Civil Rights demonstrations of 1968-9, in riots and confrontations with the security forces and militant Protestants. It continued in a bombing campaign against commercial, security force and sectarian targets in the early 1970s, at first almost random, but then more selective. From time to time, there have been diversionary bombing attacks in England, or even the Continent, to make a political point or take advantage of the extra propaganda value. But since 1977, when the IRA was reorganised, to improve its resistance to effective new anti-terrorist measures, it has tended to concentrate its attacks on security personnel and military or police targets, with occasional shows of strength in border areas.

The H-Block hunger strike of 1981 provided an opportunity to popularize the IRA cause again, through martyr-like deaths, but the accompanying violence was limited and the beneficiaries were the politicians of Sinn Fein, who gained by the experience of organizing the protest, rather the militants. Out of this evolved the policy of "the Armalite in one hand and the ballot paper in the other" which was to result in the political successes of the Northern Ireland Assembly election in October 1982, when Sinn Fein captured 10.1 per cent of the first preference votes—compared to 18.8 per cent by the SDLP—in their first outing. The low-level violence continued, often reacting to increased pressure by SAS-type police units and supergrasses from within their ranks, but this did not deter young voters, in particular, swinging significantly away from the constitutional SDLP to Sinn Fein. A new phenomenon had arrived in Northern Ireland politics, a potentially powerful revolutionary party, backed by the considerable influence, in terms of physical force and money, of a well-established paramilitary organization.

Meanwhile the Protestant paramilitary organizations, who were responsible for much of the early violence, which revived the IRA, have largely been a reactive force. With their siege mentality, common to most extreme Unionists or loyalists, they regard any challenge to the status quo—even a political one—as subversive, and a cause for retaliation. This has led them not only to indulge in openly sectarian attacks, to terrorise the Catholic population, but to remind the authorities, by direct action, that they hold a veto over radical political change. So their violence can be characterized as part terror and part political, much like the IRA's. Since they are merely defending Protestant and Unionist privilege, rather than working towards a political goal, they have little ideological commitment and therefore work to a less coherent, even more confused plan of campaign. Basically, they think the only way to defeat Republicanism is by force and, although their political theorists argue for independence, there is little evidence that the rank and file has been influenced. Their role will probably continue to be to act as Unionism's strong right arm, ready to strike back at IRA violence when it threatens to overrun the conventional security forces, or to reject any imposed political solution.

Drawing up the Lines: 1965-71

The first hint that the detente in North-South relations begun by Terence O'Neill in 1965 would precipitate violence came a year later, in the Malvern Street murder, in the lower Shankill. The Catholic barman who was killed had no connection with the almost defunct IRA; he had strayed into a Loyalist pub and that was reason enough for his murder, in the over-heated atmosphere brought about by the 50th anniversary commemorations of the 1916 Easter Rising. Fears of a political sell-out had inspired the formation of small fanatical gangs in the lower Shankill, which were not centrally controlled, but became known as the Ulster Volunteer Force, after Edward Carson's original Protestant army in Home Rule days. With this murder, and another in the Falls, the UVF set a pattern for sectarian killing, which already had a long history in Belfast and was to re-establish itself as the Loyalists' primary terror weapon in the 1970s.

The murderers were duly arrested and charged—one of them saying he wished he had never heard of Ian Paisley, then an up-and-coming Protestant demagogue—but the commitment to Protestant paramilitarism survived. When the Civil Rights demonstrators took to the streets in 1968 and O'Neill's government began to surrender to their demands, a reformed UVF was ready, backed by extreme Loyalist politicians, to stage a series of devastating bomb attacks on key electricity and water installations in Spring 1969. The IRA was blamed, the Government's credibility was fatally damaged and O'Neill was forced to resign in April after an inconclusive election.

Meanwhile the civil rights protests around the province showed a degree of organization and discipline which reflected the active participation of the republican movement in this new form of politics. After the failure of the 1956-62 campaign to arouse Catholic support, the IRA turned from violence to community action, forming Republican Clubs—promptly banned in 1967—to further their socialist ambitions. Civil rights was an obvious rallying point for all Catholic dissidents, frustrated by O'Neill's ineffectiveness, but although the republican movement was heavily involved in the formation of the Northern Ireland Civil Rights Association in February 1967, it chose to stay out of the limelight. The only republican in the first executive was Kevin Agnew, a Maghera solicitor; the commanding officer of the IRA declined a nomination. As the Cameron Commission (para. 214) concluded: 'there is evidence that members of the IRA are active in the organization, there is no sign that they are in any sense dominant or in a position to control or direct policy of the CRA'.

Nevertheless, the left-wing republican element was influential in the decision to stage a march to Dungannon in August 1968, and its willingness for confrontation was demonstrated in Derry and elsewhere. By December, the NICRA moderates had called a truce, acknowledging Unionist reforms, but others were ready to test Protestant patience to destruction, culminating in the January 1969 People's Democracy march from Belfast to Derry, which was ambushed at Burntollet. Members of the 'B' Specials, the exclusively Protestant police reserve, were involved in the attack on the student marchers and this was the prelude to days and nights of rioting in Derry—and in Newry a few weeks later—which left permanent scars in both communities. With foresight, the IRA should have expected a violent Protestant backlash, but it had been thoroughly politicized, and was unprepared for what followed O'Neill's downfall.

Tension built up to a dangerous 'marching season'—period between June and August when Protestants and Catholics demonstrate their respective strenghts in marginal areas—and when a weak Government proved unable to stop the annual Apprentice Boys parade in Derry in August, Catholics rioted in resentment at this reminder of their second-class citizenship. The Battle of the Bogside followed, in which Catholics vented their rage on the RUC with bricks and petrol bombs, forcing the Government to call in the British Army for assistance, for the first time since the 1920s. Catholics in west Belfast rioted in sympathy, to divert police attention, but before the Army moved in, a day after Derry, a total of eight had died in violent confrontations, with armed Protestants taking their revenge for months of Catholic agitation in an orgy of destruction.

The arrival of the Army brought an uneasy peace, but already both communities had formed rudimentary defence committees, organized at street level, and these were to be moulded during the summer and autumn into the Provisional IRA and the Ulster Defence Association, which was finally brought together in 1971. By concentrating on leftist politics, the IRA had dropped its basic paramilitary role, as the Catholics' last defence against sectarian attack, and that was its undoing. There were no guns, or gunmen, to repel the Loyalist incursions, and community leaders resolved not to be caught defenceless again. Emissaries went South, capitalizing on the general sympathy for beleaguered Nationalist communities and, on a promise that a rival grouping would be formed to challenge the dangerously socialistic IRA, money and resources flowed North, with the blessing of the Fianna Fail Government. The result was the formation of the Provisional IRA, as rival to the Marxist Official IRA, in early 1970, headed by veterans from the 1940s, 1950s and 1960s, with traditional green Republican backgrounds.

At the same time, the Protestants were smarting from the disbandment of the 'B' Special police reserve, which had long been regarded as their most effective anti-terrorist weapon, and anger with this recommendation of the Hunt Committee in October 1969 resulted in the first police death, at loyalist hands, in the lower Shankill. The replacement was the Ulster Defence Regiment, under British Army, rather than local RUC, control and, although it began as a relatively mixed force, against all subversion, it has become almost exclusively Protestant, with a limited, but recognizable loyalist bias. UDA members are not automatically disbarred.

By the summer of 1970, the honeymoon period which marked the early stages of the Army's occupation of Catholic west Belfast was running out; the final break was achieved by the Falls curfew of July, when soldiers sealed off a large area for two days, refusing to let people leave their homes during a house-to-house search. Some arms were found, but the effect was to alienate an entire population and rally support for the Provisional IRA in a campaign that was turning increasingly against the military. Nail grenades were regularly hurled at soldiers and the bombing campaign began in earnest, with one hundred explosions during the year.

The first soldier did not die until February 1971, eighteen months after the Army's deployment on the streets, but the one hundredth victim was killed only sixteen months later, in June 1972. The IRA campaign continued its rapid escalation in 1971, with murders of off-duty soldiers, attacks on the homes of policemen and extensive use of bombs in Belfast. One of these, involving the bombing of a Protestant pub on the Shankill Road, marked the beginning of an openly sectarian campaign, and the Official IRA, which had earlier been engaged in a murderous feud with the Provisionals, denounced them as 'fiendish and sectarian bigots, whose motives are obviously to set the Protestant and Catholic working class at each other's throats'.

Internment: Reaction and Counter-reaction: 1971-72

As the security situation deteriorated on all fronts the Government finally yielded to pressure in August to introduce internment without trial, the traditional and usually effective answer to IRA militancy. But police files were out of date and instead of damping down the violence, the arrest of 300 paramilitary and political activists simply added fuel to the fire. More than 4,000 refugees fled South, where the Taoiseach, Jack Lynch, threatened not to stand idly by, but effectively did. The whole Catholic community united, temporarily, behind the militants, and the sense of grievance was added to by reports of brutal interrogation methods, finally admitted in the Compton report. Extremists exploited the situation by a return to street demonstrations and the result was the confrontation of Bloody Sunday in Derry, January 1972, when British paratroopers, believing they were under fire, shot down 13 civilians after an illegal march.

Again the effect was to unite the Catholic population against the British, providing a flood of IRA recruits and, in the international outcry which followed, the Westminster Government had little alternative but to suspend the Stormont parliament, having failed to obtain consent to a takeover of all security powers. The newly-formed UDA responded by setting up its own no-go areas, following the IRA's lead, and sniping broke out for the first time since 1969 between Protestant and Catholic areas.

Just as internment and Bloody Sunday solidified Catholic opinion, the closure of Stormont had an equally binding effect on Protestants, moderates as well as extremists, as they saw their pre-Troubles world collapse. Five days later the Official IRA declared a cease-fire, acknowledging the dangerous mood of loyalists, but the Provisionals went for the kill, until they finally declared a cease-fire in June, and won inconclusive talks in London with the Ulster Secretary, William Whitelaw.

Whatever hopes they had of British concessions were soon dashed, however, and Bloody Friday, in which 11 were killed in simultaneous bombings in Belfast, ended any thought of detente. In the shocked aftermath, the British were able to occupy the infamous no-go areas of Derry and Belfast, within which the IRA had established itself as a police and defence force, dealing out rough and sometimes fatal justice to its opponents.

The next two years were dominated by frenzied political activity, as the British Government tried to restore some measure of devolution to politicians who were increasingly polarized, like the communities they came from. Hardly a month went by without a new Government initiative, or poll, and the paramilitaries thrived in the atmosphere of uncertainty, in which the province's future appeared to be constantly in the balance. The death rate rose spectacularly, from 174 in 1971, the year of internment, to 468 in 1972, before settling down to 200-300 for the next four years.

The Loyalist Response: 1972-74

At this stage the violence turned nakedly sectarian, with Protestants reacting to the traditional Republican threat in the traditional manner—spreading terror among IRA sympathizers by gunning down innocent Catholics in the street. One of the first of these, in February 1972, was attributed to the Red Hand Commandos, one of the loosely organized gangs which had sprouted up in Protestant areas as the civil rights campaign gained momentum. These briefly centred around the Ulster Protestant Volunteers, a branch of the Rev. Ian Paisley's Ulster Constitution Defence Committee, and were active in the street defence committees of 1969. A year later, the UDA had its beginnings in the Shankill, but it was not until the post-internment chaos that the Protestant vigilante groups saw the need for an organization, distinct from the military-styled UVF, then banned. Just as the Catholic population felt let down, in 1969, by the disarmed IRA, Protestants found the Orange Order ill-equipped to deal with the new situation. 'The Orange Order was never used when the occasion arose against the IRA because its leaders didn't have the guts to turn them into soldiers', said UDA chief, Andy Tyrie, years later.

The Orange leadership was too much a part of the Unionist establishment to dirty its hands in paramilitarism, so the gap was filled by the community's tougher elements, including criminals. There was little co-ordination in the early days and vigilante groups simply affiliated to the Shankill-based UDA, while remaining virtually autonomous in their own areas. As the organization grew in size, however, a 20-man council became too unwieldy, and power struggles broke out periodically between the leading figures in west and east Belfast. Finally, after murders and shoot-outs, a durable compromise candidate emerged in Tyrie, who successfully combined the UDA's twin roles as loyalism's main paramilitary wing and fund raiser.

Many of the most terrible crimes in the early and mid-Seventies were carried out by UDA members, including the bombing of Dublin and Monaghan during the 1974 strike, but the organization managed to avoid proscription by use of a pseudonym, Ulster Freedom Fighters, when claiming credit for assassinations. The sheer size of the organization—at its height it had 15,000 members, compared to an estimated 1,500 in the UVF—made it as difficult to ban as it was easy to infiltrate and therefore the security forces were reluctant to drive it underground. While the IRA had Provisional Sinn Fein to raise funds, which were estimated at £2 million yearly in 1980, the UDA had to perform this function itself, and largely copied IRA methods, ranging from protection rackets to burglaries. But the main providers were the drinking clubs, founded after the destruction of a third of Belfast's pubs, mainly Catholic-owned.

America and the Middle East have provided fruitful sources of arms and ammunition for the IRA, but the UDA has had to rely on less reliable helpers in Canada and Scotland. The number of home-made weapons found in arms caches underlines the problems faced by loyalist groups without a convenient back-door in the Republic and it has been estimated that if Protestants had the same access to explosives as the IRA, the violence would have been even greater and more random, in Catholic areas. As it was, the Shankill-based UVF acquired a reputation for extremism, particularly after the short-lived freedom of Gusty Spence, its jailed leader, left a group of young Turks in charge. Among its more notorious episodes were the Shankill Butcher murders, nineteen killings carried out by a particularly vicious gang between 1975-7, and the 1977 trial in east Antrim, when twenty-six UVF men were given a total of 700 years' imprisonment, including eight life sentences. It also had a habit of mistakenly killing Protestants in its random attacks, unlike the UDA.

In the same way that Unionists have tended, latterly, to greater division in their ranks than Nationalists, Protestant individualism is reflected in the mass of small-scale paramilitary bodies, mainly organized on a geographical basis. In addition to the UDA, the UVF and the Red Hand Commando, regarded as the personal property of an early militant, John McKeague, there were at one time or another at least nine other loyalist groupings.

The main ones were Tara, formed in the late 1960s as 'the hard core of Protestant resistance', with strong Orange and biblical Protestant links, which was reputed to have provided guns for others; Down Orange Welfare, set up under an ex-army colonel and claimed to have 5,000 members; Orange Volunteers, mostly ex-service and reserved for a doomsday situation; Vanguard Service Corps, the military wing of the one-time Vanguard Unionist movement; the Ulster Special Constabulary Association, reserved for ex-'B' Specials.

Attempts were made, with limited success, to co-ordinate the efforts of the paramilitaries, first through the Ulster Army Council, formed in December 1973, and then through the Ulster Loyalist Central Co-ordinating Committee, which grew out of the ad hoc committee which organized the Ulster Workers' Council strike in May 1974. But experience shows that Protestant paramilitaries can only come together effectively in an emergency situation, and their extreme distrust of politicians makes them an unreliable political ally.

'An Acceptable Level of Violence': 1974-82

The interests of the Protestant and Catholic paramilitaries converged during the five months of the power-sharing executive, from January to May 1974, and the IRA's continuing violence was enough to persuade Loyalists that there were no practical benefits—and a lot of possible political disadvantages—from the coalition experiment. (Earlier, the two sides had been brought together informally in well-meaning attempts to establish better understanding of their respective beliefs, but with limited effect). The success of the UWC strike was largely due to loyalist paramilitary involvement, and represents the high point of their campaign, but their inability to capitalize on it underlines their negative rather than positive strength. In short, they proved they could terminate any political development judged to be hostile to loyalist interests, but they were unable to move Government policy in their direction.

If the strike had showed that a British Government could be influenced by loyalist violence, or threats of violence, the Feakle talks which followed it, seven months later, appeared for a time to demonstrate that IRA violence might yet get it to the bargaining table. A group of Protestant clergy and lay people made the running, with a top level IRA delegation, and the discussions were then taken up by the Government, leading to an IRA ceasefire in February 1975. Confusion still surrounds the terms, but what is clear is that the IRA thought much more was on the table than turned out to be the case and the ultimate winners were the security forces, who found it much easier to penetrate the IRA's defences in the new, relaxed atmosphere. By providing Provisional Sinn Fein with 'incident centres' for monitoring the ceasefire the Government gave it a legitimacy which has taken years to wear off, but at the same time the IRA was lulled into a false sense of security. Meanwhile the UVF proscription was lifted, to allow it to fight elections, before being re-imposed five months later. By the year's end, internment was ended, but, this apart, the IRA was no further forward, and as the ceasefire petered out, Protestant sectarian killings were met with the Whitecross massacre, near the South Armagh border, in which ten Protestant workmen were killed. The SAS was called in, the Convention which had been elected to devise a new agreed constitutional settlement ended in failure and battle commenced.

The murder of the new British ambassador to Dublin, Christopher Ewart-Biggs, in July 1976 was a reminder of the IRA's challenge, North and South, and within a month an upsurge of popular feeling against violence led to the formation of the Peace movement, out of a tragic hi-jacked car accident. Equally significant, from the point of view of containing violence, was the arrival of Roy Mason, a new breed of Secretary of State, who eschewed political solutions in favour of economic and security initiatives. Without political distractions, and with the tide of the Peace movement running high, violence fell away, and Ian Paisley badly misjudged the public mood when he led an abortive strike for tougher security measures in May 1977.

The only real effect was to sever the strained links between Paisley and the Protestant paramilitaries, particularly the UDA, who joined the strike in the belief that Paisley was serious about attempting a coup. When he backed away from confrontation with the Government, they were so disillusioned they commissioned their own political solution, which eventually turned out to be independence, with an American-style executive, but failed to get public support.

The Provisionals were also at a turning point for, despite the upsurge of violence in 1976, providing a peak of 297 deaths—second only to 1972—the combination of successful RUC interrogation methods at Castlereagh and the debilitating effect of the ceasefire led to a thorough re-think of policy. Confessions were decimating the old command structure, so the time was ripe for young Northern radicals to gain control of the seven-man Army Council and set it on a new path. Not only was the IRA to be re-organised into four or five-man cells or active service units, in order to minimise the effect of informers, but Provisional politics was to move decidedly to the left, to try to occupy the ground vacated by the Officials. In line with this new thinking, there was no more talk of 'one last heave' to get the British out of Ireland—war weariness was the prevalent mood in the Nationalist community—and instead a 'long haul' strategy was articulated by veteran Republican Jimmy Drumm at Bodenstown in 1977.

The summer was marked by an escalation in Provisional–Official tensions, as frustrated Officials left to join the more active Provisionals, taking their guns with them, and altogether four died and 25 were injured in gun battles. It was an indication of the Government's new confidence that the Queen's Jubilee visit went ahead, and the only alarm was the discovery of a new IRA delayed-action bomb at the New University of Ulster. With the re-arrest of IRA chief of staff Seamus Twomey, after four years on the run, and the interception of an arms consignment from the Middle East, the IRA campaign was at a low ebb at the end of 1977, when deaths fell by nearly two-thirds to 112, the lowest total since 1970.

This improving trend is reflected in the statistics for criminal damage payments, which reached a high of £50 million in 1976-77, but then fell away to hover around £40 million for the next three years. Nevertheless the long war strategy entailed occasional shows of strength, like a New Year blitz on hotels and clubs in 1978, to hit the tourist trade, and increased use of terror weapons like the firebomb—a petrol tin attached to an explosive device—which went disastrously wrong in the La Mon Restaurant attack, killing 12 civilians. A European dimension was added when eight bombs were exploded at BAOR bases in August, implying some German terrorist support. In November and twice in December massive bomb attacks, either in Britain or Northern Ireland, were reminders that the IRA was still in business. The first M16 machine gun, a prestige weapon that was to claim several Army casualties, was put on show in January.

Even so, the death rate fell again—to 81 in 1978—largely because of the more selective nature of the IRA campaign. Despite some spectacular attacks in 1979, resulting in the deaths of Airey Neave, killed by the INLA, a left-wing breakaway faction, in March and Lord Mountbatten in August, the most significant new factor was the increased murder rate of soldiers. Altogether 38 were killed, including 18 at Warrenpoint in August, the highest total for six years. A high proportion of these died in border areas, killed by land mines or—in the case of Warrenpoint—by radio controlled bombs. Especially in South Armagh, terrorists have virtual freedom of movement across the border and only undercover surveillance by the Army and improved cross-border co-operation has helped to minimise the IRA threat. In 1981, South Armagh managed to account for 30 out of the total of 108 murders for the year, as well as 56 attempted murders and 40 explosions.

The ability of the IRA to pick off selected targets in border areas—usually members of the security forces—and either go to ground or escape across the frontier has been a significant factor in keeping the situation on the boil. Protestants see the attacks as proof not only of the Government's ineffectiveness, but of the sectarian nature of the IRA campaign, and their paramilitaries have often reacted in kind in other areas, such as Belfast. In 1981, a series of cross-border assassinations produced the effect of mobilising Protestants behind Ian Paisley's Third Force, nominally to police border areas, as well as uniting loyalist opinion against the Dublin-London talks, equally unpopular with Unionist and Republican extremists.

Another effect of the traumatic killings of August 1979 was to accelerate the process of transferring security responsibility from the Army back to the police, which had run into difficulty since it was first enunciated by the Labour Secretary of State, Merlyn Rees, in January 1977. Relations were strained between the two forces, as the Army resisted surrendering control while its men were at risk, and the former MI6 chief, Sir Maurice Oldfield—who had earlier been an IRA target at his London home—was brought in to mediate. The steady reduction in troop levels continued, as security chiefs agreed that the Army presence in all but the worst areas for violence was merely delaying a return to normality, and locally-recruited forces took up the slack. This Ulsterisation policy saw increased recruitment to both the UDR— 7,500 members by 1982—and the RUC—12,000 part-time and full-time members—while troop levels dropped from the 1972 peak of 21,000 to 13,500 in 1978 and under 11,000 by 1982. The penalty was that the local security forces became the prime targets for the IRA, usually when they were off duty, and the police again took over a front-line role in riot situations, using potentially fatal plastic bullets, in place of CS gas.

The Limits of Violence

Nevertheless the graph of violence, by most calculations, had reached a plateau by the late 1970s which was approaching the 'acceptable level of violence' hoped for 10 years before. Deaths were down to 81 in 1978, less than a third of the 1976 total and there was a consistency about the following three years—113 (1979) 76 (1980) and 108 (1981)—suggesting that the worst was over. Even the tensions of the hunger strike, in 1981, produced nothing like the violence anticipated, although by-election results showed that political attitudes were as polarised as ever. The belief in violence, as a means of changing events, was dying, but not the alienation of which it was the expression. At the same time the quieter mood of the paramilitaries was reflected in the civilian deaths—including sectarian killings. These reached highs of 332 (122 sectarian) in 1972, 216 (144) in 1975 and 245 (121) in 1976, before dropping dramatically to 69 (42) in 1977, down to 50 (26) in 1980.

Accordingly, the numbers of persons charged with serious terrorist offences rose from 531 in 1972 to 1,414 in 1973 and stayed well above the 1,000 mark until 1978, when it fell to 843. In 1980 it was down to 540, almost on a par with 1972, and even the hunger strike year saw the figure only rise to 918. Meanwhile it is a measure of the IRA's continuing concern with internal security that the tally of kneecappings—its usual punishment—has remained high. The number dropped to 67 in 1978, but has since been in the 70-80 range.

The most detailed study of those killed, and by whom, was carried out by Michael McKeown, a Belfast lecturer, who examined the first 2,000 deaths up to January 1980. Comparing the first 500 deaths to the last 500—which brought the total to 2,000—he found that the time scale was broadly similar, 13 a month in the first cycle and 11 a month in the last. (This contrasted sharply with 23 a month during the 43 months August 1972 to April 1976, and even lower rate of 8 a month during 1980 and 1981). The most significant difference was in the groups held responsible for the deaths, showing the diminishing role of the security forces—down from 102 to 30—and the increasing involvement of the paramilitaries. Republican groups were responsible for 260 of the first 500 deaths and 330 of the last 500; Loyalists for 66 and 119.

Looking at the first 2,000 deaths, 554 (27.7 per cent) were members of the security forces, 225 (11.2 per cent) were paramilitaries or subversives, 1,163 (58.2 per cent) were civilians and only 58 (2.9 per cent) unclassified. But of the 225 subversives to die, only 88 were killed by the security forces. The IRA suffered 160 fatalities, including 63 to security forces and 77 to premature explosions. The security forces accounted for 220 deaths (11 per cent), Republicans for 1,024 (51.2 per cent) and Loyalists for 574 (28.7 per cent). But closer examination shows that only 40 per cent of the deaths caused by the security forces were proven subversives and 107 were civilians. If proof were needed that the Catholic areas suffered most from violence the tally of 1,631 deaths of natives of Northern Ireland included 916 Catholics (56.1 per cent) and 715 Protestants (43.8 per cent)—against a Catholic percentage of 35 per cent in the population at large.

Since 1977, the strategy of the IRA has been to plan for a war of attrition, aimed at demoralising the British, through destabilisation of Northern Ireland politics, and respect for their organising ability was demonstrated in a secret Army Intelligence memo, published by the IRA in 1979. The author, General James Glover, concluded that, despite pressure from the Army and the Catholic population, 'the Provisionals' campaign of violence is likely to continue while the British remain in Northern Ireland'. The 'long war' tactics have been to constantly ring the changes in targets, so that from month to month no one can feel safe, be they businessmen, off-duty UDR men, prison warders or prominent personalities, in Northern Ireland or in Britain. Bombing campaigns can be province-wide—such as co-ordinated attacks on hotels, business premises and town centres—or more selective. Discouragement of inward industrial investment has been an important short-term goal. Car bombs were an IRA innovation, now used world-wide, and other methods used to deadly effect include blast incendiaries, car booby traps, radio-controlled bombs—which accounted for 29 of the 86 killings in 1979—home-made rockets, and 'cooked' fertilizer explosives. As soon as the authorities find an effective block, IRA ingenuity finds a way around.

But there is one enemy of the IRA who cannot be eliminated—the informer. The adoption of the cell system and the emasculation of Castlereagh interrogation methods, as a result of the Bennett inquiry, helped to minimise the threat, but important defections in the winter of 1981-2 dealt a severe blow. Arms dumps were turned up on both sides of the border and arrests proliferated as leading IRA men fled to safe houses in the South. In an unprecedented move, the IRA offered an amnesty for all who confessed to informing—an admission that usually would have been suicidal. Even harder hit was the splinter group, INLA, some of whose membership overlapped with the IRA. Pressure from the Southern authorities on the IRA was stepped up after the Mountbatten murder and reached its high point under the FitzGerald coalition, with free exchange of intelligence North and South. The Republic's constitutional inability to permit extradition was a bone of contention, but alternatives continued to be sought.

The Protestant reaction to the more sophisticated IRA campaign in the late 1970s and early 1980s has been to adopt a mainly passive role, avoiding all involvement with loyalist politicians and only striking out at known republicans on rare occasions. The UDA has always claimed to be non-sectarian; 'We do not believe in sectarian violence, but we believe we are justified in making selective attacks on known Republicans and people who lead their campaign, give them orders and supply them with information', said Tyrie, in 1980. This 'terrorise the terrorists' policy has also been used against those whom it regarded as 'cheer-leaders' for the IRA, and that is the explanation for four political ass-assinations in the 1979-80 period, and an unsuccessful murder attempt on Bernadette McAliskey. But the UDA largely involved itself in its commercial activities—raising hundreds of thousands of pounds needed every year to match IRA comforts for serving prisoners— and attempts at establishing negotiated independence as an alternative allegiance for working class Protestants to pro-British Unionism. It was a fruitless exercise, against the tide of history, and demonstrated the extent to which a politically-naive leadership had lost touch with its own community.

One of the beneficial effects, however, of this more thoughtful ap-proach was the UDA's refusal to respond to IRA violence in the wake of the death of the first hunger striker, Bobby Sands, in 1981. The Catholic community was braced, by the IRA, for a loyalist onslaught which never came, not only because the UDA was satisfied with the security forces' handling of the emergency, but because it has learned from experience that mass demonstrations of force are counter-pro-ductive and win no thanks from the Protestant community.

The character of the violence and the threat posed by the para-military organisations has therefore changed considerably over the period of the Troubles, in accordance with the political situation, the Army's response and the mood of their respective communities. Both the Provisionals and the UDA have learned that there are strict limits on the support they can expect for bombings and killings, even in re-taliation, and their reaction has been to switch the emphasis from paramilitarism to politics. On the UDA side, this has met with little success—although it must have helped to save them from proscription —while on the Provisionals' side, the gains for H-Block candidates in the 1981 elections may have been the exception which proves the rule that the Irish will never abandon their gunmen, but won't vote for them. All the more so, because both sets of paramilitaries have drifted far from the traditional conservatism of their communities. This means that the IRA cannot achieve political legitimacy, and therefore will continue to use violence against schemes which exclude it, and leave a British presence. As a result, the UDA is guaranteed a continuing ex-istence as the Protestant equivalent of the IRA, in what Protestants see as their increasingly beleaguered situation, disowned by the British and out-bred by Catholics. The destructive influence of the two organisa-tions will wax and wane, according to Britain's determination to find a political solution through devolution, or an Anglo-Irish approach, but it will not disappear, and must be accounted for in any eventual settlement.

Since both sides accept that there must be limits to their paramilitary activities, or pressures from the security forces or their respective communities will become too great, the violence has never brought ordinary life to a standstill. The nearest to this was during the 1974 Ulster Workers' Council strike, which was accompanied by the threat of force rather than actual violence, and gave Protestants a confidence in their capacity to resist imposition which has been a stabilising factor. Few areas of the province, and few families, have not been touched by the conflict, either through bombing or shooting, but spread over the period since 1969, the effect has not been intense. The troubled areas are well defined, particularly in Catholic Belfast and Derry, and are strictly no-go to those who have no reason to be in them. Even the steady withdrawal of troops, undeterred by sparodic outbreaks of violence, has not altered the balance.

City centre bombing in Belfast in the mid-seventies, widened the field of combat for a time, but the establishment of a security zone, and a military presence, restored confidence. From time to time the IRA has revived its old commercial bombing campaign on the edge of the gated area, to serve as a reminder of its military potential, but the offensive is rarely sustained, and the terror effect soon wears off. Outside these areas, and towns where there is an even sectarian balance, there is a surprising degree of normality, attributable only to the achievement of an acceptable level of violence. Members of the security forces, or ex-members, are special targets, constantly in danger of attack, but retaliation has been minimal from Protestant organisations which themselves do not identify with the forces of law and order. Only two developments could alter what is virtually a stalemate situation— a radical change in the British Government's attitude to the constitution of Northern Ireland, now based on the will of the majority, or an interruption of the flow of British subsidy, up to nearly £2,000 million a year by 1983, which has helped to repair the worst effects of the violence. As long as these are avoided, and each would play into the hands of the extremists, both communities have proved they can live with, and to an extent rely on, the paramilitary organizations in their midst.

9

Reformism and Sectarianism: The State of the Union after Civil Rights

Bill Rolston

Introduction: The Need for Reform

At the base of the Civil Rights struggle of the late 1960s were certain demands. The most vocal of these concerned the need to reform housing allocation and the franchise. Less to the fore, but no less important, were reformist demands concerning public employment, education and local government. These demands were postulated on a political assessment, often meticulously documented and articulated (cf. All-Party Anti-Partition Conference 1954; Jackson 1947; Gallagher 1957; Campaign for Social Justice in Northern Ireland 1969) of the Northern Ireland state, namely, that the Unionist government had no liking for nor commitment to reforming many of the most archaic and sectarian institutions and policies in the society. Many carried that assessment forward to the political conclusion that Northern Ireland was irreformable; but even those who did not share that conclusion (for example, Barritt and Carter 1962) were willing to admit that the Unionist government was not enamoured of a social-democratic style of administration such as was beginning to typify, for example, post-war Keynesian Britain. The fact that most of these latter commentators criticised Stormont, if at all, for its lack of economic reforms (cf. Isles and Cuthbert 1957; Wilson 1965; O'Dowd 1982) does not lessen the importance of the more general conclusion that reformism was not a significant element in the workings of Stormont. In that sense, someone like Brookeborough, Northern Ireland's longest-ruling Prime Minister, was anachronistic, believing in the mid-twentieth century what early American rebels of the late eighteenth century did, that that government is best which govern least.

Given such a philosophy, much of the power in decision-making and the allocation of resources was decentralised in Northern Ireland.

Local government was the key to the daily administration of the society, with its control of health, education, welfare, housing, public employment, etc. So, it is no coincidence that much of the Civil Rights flak was directed towards local government: demands for an end to gerrymandering, for 'one man, one vote', for a fair allocation of public housing, for a fair distribution of local government jobs, for the total restructuring of local government itself.

Some of these demands were conceded by the Unionist government of Terence O'Neill, but the struggle opened a Pandora's box and O'Neill and his cautious reformism were the first victims of the 'ills' which poured out. An interesting question, but not one on which there is time to dwell here, is that of attempting to ascertain what was the main vehicle of the break-up of Unionism which followed on the civil rights campaign. Some would see the Civil Rights demands themselves as the wedge which split the Unionist tree (Devlin 1969); others give pride of place to the entry of monopoly capital and the differing responses of Unionists to that penetration (McCann 1974; Probert 1978); still others see the power struggles within the Unionist camp itself as the major factor in explaining the splintering (Bew, Gibbon and Patterson 1979). Whichever emphasis one wishes to choose, there can be no denying that the Civil Rights campaign was a major worry to Unionists. The Unionist leader who would ignore the campaign risked contributing to its escalation; yet, to concede to any of the demands was to risk one's own position of Unionist leadership. The tight-rope task facing O'Neill—and Chichester-Clark and Faulkner following him—was to get the right balance of reform and repression, keeping the Civil Rights struggle from escalating while not antagonizing Unionists. None of the three Prime Ministers discovered the secret of that correct balance.

One element in their frustration was the increasing intervention of first the Labour government (cf. Callaghan 1973), and later the Tories, in Northern Ireland's affairs. British politicians saw nothing wrong with Northern Ireland that could not be cured by a good strong dose of the same social-democratic reformism that had emerged in post-War Britain. Reforms were 'imported' faster than any Unionist leader could or would have implemented them if the only pressure to reform-ism had been internal to the society. Ultimately this jeapordised the chances of any Unionist leader remaining in a leadership position, a fact which convinced the British to intervene even more decisively through Direct Rule in 1972.

From the British point of view it could be said that a unitary logic infused its enthusiastic commitment to the initial flurry of reform in Northern Ireland. Where administration was dogged by sectarian practices, the priority was to remove administration from that domain and ground it instead in rational British practice. The eradication of sectarianism was thus paramount, not only in the restructuring of old institutions which administered housing, education, etc., but also, and more obviously perhaps, in some new institutions, such as the Community Relations Commission (CRC) inaugurated to confront directly sectarian practices. Given that, the fact that a second and more substantial logic existed in the reform process was not initially apparent. This latter logic consisted of the importation into Northern Ireland administration of the newest prevailing management ideology and techniques already well on the way to being established in Britain itself. Throughout the 1960s local government management in Britain was transformed. Managers 'geared up to govern', as Cockburn (1977) puts it, changing their techniques to match the needs of late twentieth century capitalism. Now, the reforming of Northern Ireland may have meant the relative hobbling of local government, but there was no reason, according to this 'progressive' logic, why similar principles should not infuse the practices of whatever institutions took over those tasks in Northern Ireland which were carried out by local government in Britain. The rise of this new managerialism meant the demise of the initial reformist logic. Reforms were seen as necessary and efficient in themselves, rather than instituted in order to eradicate sectarianism. Of course, the technocratic logic as applied to Northern Ireland did rest on an assessment of sectarianism. Technocracy by definition is rational and therefore non-sectarian. The new managerialism was seen as linked in a see-saw manner with sectarian administration: the rise of one was the inevitable fall of the other. Of course, institutions would be necessary in the transition period to mop up the residual elements of sectarian practice, but in the long run technocracy needed no reformist institutions directly geared towards eradicating sectarianism.

So because of a number of factors—the persistence of the Civil Rights activists, the splintering of Unionism and the pressures exerted by the British—the years between 1968 and 1972 saw a number of major changes in Northern Ireland. Many of these were in the realms of emergency laws, and the growth of security personnel, technology and training (cf. *Belfast Bulletin* 1982)—what I will collectively call 're-pression'. But the 'reforming of repression' (cf. Tomlinson 1980a) will not be the concern of this chapter. (For a critical look at analyses of the growth of state power in Ireland, north and south, see Rolston and Tomlinson 1982). Instead, the concentration will be on those changes which can more easily be termed 'reforms'. In short, within the four years mentioned, the major demands of the Civil Rights struggle were conceded. Yet, by 1972 it was also apparent that such concessions had not served to lessen the escalation of violence. This has led some observers to declare with retrospective exasperation that the civil rights activists got what they wanted: what more can they want? Why did the violence increase? An obvious, but incomplete, reply would be that the reforms were too little, too late; such an answer does not of itself explain why the violence has continued for well over a decade; it postulates too direct a relationship between the original demands and violence. It also presumes that all the violence emanates from one source, namely, from Civil Rights activists and their successors. That presumption comes to the fore in some of the pieces of 'historical revisionism' now beginning to emerge which will be examined later in this chapter.

A more valuable starting point is not to ask why the violence did not stop once the reforms were instituted, but to seriously examine what it was that was 'won' in terms of reforms. What has been the substance in the establishment of the Northern Ireland Housing Executive, the institution of the CRC and the Fair Employment Agency, the reforming of local government, the establishment of non-elected Health and Social Services and Education and Library Boards? More fundamentally, in what way is Northern Ireland in 1983 a 'normal' social democratic reformist state? If it is such, does this mean that sectarianism has been eradicated? In short, how successful has been the union between contemporary capitalist reformism and traditional sectarian division in Northern Ireland?

At most some of these reforms have dealt with symptoms only and did not come near to touching the fundamental causes. Or, to use a geographical rather than a medical metaphor, they have operated at the level of the epicentres of trouble, but have been unable to penetrate to the structural faults underneath. Reformism and sectarianism can happily coexist; they are not mutually antagonistic. This means that not only have the reforms not necessarily eradicated sectarian division, but they have often reconstituted that division in new and often more pervasive ways than before. Reforms do not occur in the abstract. The process and consequences of introducing reforms in a social democracy are not the same as those which emerge when the same reforms are instituted in a society where sectarian class relations prevail.

Assessing the Reforms

In a sense, everything that has been written about Northern Ireland since Civil Rights days has touched in one way or another, inadvertently or otherwise, on the questions of reform and sectarianism. Yet, paradoxically, remarkably little has been written which directly tackles the relationship between reformism and sectarianism in the last decade.

In an attempt to establish some order out of the copious literature, it is perhaps useful to arrange what has been written into four categories, as follows:

1. Description

Description has been by far the most common approach to the recent past in Northern Ireland. Some pieces in this genre have been superficial, even opportunistic. At the other extreme have been substantial pieces of work. The rapid changes in politics, the decline of the economy, the social conditions and the policies of the state all require careful charting if any valid analysis is to be undertaken. Hence the value of many of the descriptive accounts.

Within this category, journalists' accounts predominate—from the daily copy of local journalists and those doing tours of duty on behalf of British media, through semi-autobiographical considerations of the problem of being a journalist in Northern Ireland (cf. Bell 1972; Hoggart 1973; Winchester 1974; Holland 1981) to substantive pieces of research which are indispensible in drawing an accurate picture of post-Civil Rights Northern Ireland. In the last category have been such books as the Sunday Times Insight Team's (1972) investigation of the origins of the Troubles and Robert Fisk's (1975) incisive account of the Ulster Workers' Council strike in 1974.

Some journalists have attempted to use their knowledge through a different medium, the novel, with varying degrees of success. The most critically acclaimed has been Kevin Dowling's *Interface Ireland* (1979). Even the least successful novel allows journalists to reveal in slightly disguised fiction what they could not otherwise state in factual reporting. There are limits to such revelations, however. Dowling's novel was withdrawn from circulation after a threatened suit from a politician less than enchanted by his fictional other self.

To an even greater degree than journalists, participants in the events of Northern Ireland during Civil Rights and after are in a unique position to give the 'inside story'. On the other hand, there are many obstacles preventing them going into print. Public figures, for example, may be constrained by law or protocol from revealing all. Moreover, the task of writing requires one to stand back at least momentarily from events, a feat for which not every participant has time or ability. Consequently, participants' accounts cover a wide spectrum as regards quality and accuracy. This has not prevented a substantial number of participants from taking the plunge, however. Civil Rights activists have written of their involvement, notably McCann (1974), Devlin (1969) and Farrell and McCullough (1974). Others have used their experience to more academic ends, such as Arthur (1974) in his account of People's Democracy. In contrast to the reticence of earlier politicians, recent politicians in Northern Ireland have been prepared to write either memoirs (O'Neill 1972; Faulkner 1978), or accounts of key events in their experience (Devlin 1975). The earlier reticence may have derived from an unwillingness to reveal the mechanisms of patronage in Northern Ireland. Those who would see a new-found willingness of politicians to write books as a sign of the death of patronage would do well to recall that there is much that remains unsaid, despite these autobiographical meanderings.

If that is true of politicians' accounts, it is even more so of civil servants' autobiographies. Sworn to secrecy all their working lives, civil servants in retirement are unable to reveal much about anything except themselves. Their accounts thus become perhaps the most idiosyncratic of all participants' accounts. The prime example here is the tale of the ex-head of the Civil Service at Stormont, John Oliver (1978). More useful, if not for titbits of government secrets, at least about the psychology of a Catholic top civil servant at Stormont, is Paddy Shea's (1981) story.

Some participants have heard the same siren call as some journalists, and been drawn onto the rocks of fiction, with perhaps even more disastrous results. Notable here is the novel of ex-Stormont Minister of Commerce Roy Bradford (1981), with its mixture of partial fact, fiction and sheer fantasy.

Like journalists and participants, many academic researchers have turned their attention to description. To categorise their work thus is not to belittle it, but is to stress that their over-riding task has been to describe accurately the present nature of Northern Ireland society, with fundamental theoretical analysis a secondary, even minor, element in their work. Much of this work has been crucial in unravelling the mysteries of present social policy (cf., for example, Birrell and Murie 1972 and 1980; Morrissey and Ditch 1979), and specifically of housing (Kennedy and Birrell 1978; Birrell, Hillyard, Murie and Roche 1971), poverty (Evason 1978 and 1980; Ditch and McWilliams 1982; Black *et al.* 1980), and others. To the best of my knowledge, no academic researcher has as yet turned to the novel form!

2. Fiction

The Troubles in Northern Ireland have provided the subject matter for a number of television plays, to take just one form of fiction, among them Stewart Parker's *Catch Penny Twist* (December 1977), Colin Welland's *Your Man From Six Counties* (BBC 1, October 1976), Caryl Churchill's *Willie: the Legion Hall Bombing* (BBC 1, August 1978; the script was based on the transcript of an actual trial), and Jennifer Johnston's *Shadows on Our Skin* (March 1980; originally a novel). In addition, the Troubles have found their way to varying degrees into television series, notably *Spearhead* and *The Professionals.* In some cases the violence of Northern Ireland has been the background (for example, in Graham Reid's *Too Late to Talk to Billy*), though in most cases it has been central. Such centrality seems to require most of the authors to distance themselves quickly from the violence and present a moral judgment through drama. In as far as the public nature of their art requires them to choose in the struggle between 'good' and 'evil', in this case between 'terrorism' and 'democracy', it could thus be suspected that these authors' opposition to violence is simultaneously an acceptance of reform in Northern Ireland. Be that as it may, reform and its institutions have not been a direct subject for any dramatic author.

The same conclusion may be drawn from a consideration of live drama within Northern Ireland that deals with the Troubles. Plays such as John Boyd's *The Flats,* Martin Lynch's *The Interrogation of Ambrose Fogarty,* etc., have concentrated on the violence of Northern Ireland, not the question of reformism. This is not to say, however, that the concern of many playwrights in Northern Ireland, in as far as they set out to condemn violence, is at base a reformist one.

Elliot, Murdock and Schlesinger (1981) point out that, despite a powerful constraint towards upholding dominant definitions in drama, fictional television allows some scope for 'oppositional' definitions.

As one example they cite David Leland's *Psy-Warriors* (BBC 1, May 1981), a play with very direct and critical conclusions about army inter-rogation techniques in Northern Ireland. Beyond that one example, it is possible to find a good deal of evidence to support their general con-clusion in television drama as a form of fiction. However, another form of fiction, the novel, would appear to be much more monolithic in its approach. Elsewhere I have noted that a spate of novels for teenagers about the Troubles focus on their heroes' need to escape from Belfast (Rolston 1978). In their inability to come to terms with violence, these heroes display qualities and moral conclusions more fitting to the novelist as outsider than to the insider in Northern Ireland. A remarkably similar conclusion has been reached by McMinn (1981) in his consideration of adult novels. Compared to the dramas, the opposi-tional assessment seems to have even less outlet in novels. The novels thus, even more emphatically than drama, confirm the superiority of 'good', and consequently can be seen as being on the side of reform in Northern Ireland, even though never directly taking up the question.

3. Analysis: Reformability versus Irreformability

Those who go beyond description usually divide quickly and clearly into two camps—those who argue that the Northern Ireland state is irreformable and those who argue the converse.

The first position is in many ways a logical successor to much of the civil rights literature. Some activists who held in the 1960s that Northern Ireland needed reforms also hoped that those reforms could be delivered. However, their delivery as part of a package which also included increased repression convinced many that the reforms were a sham. It was a relatively short step from this to the belief that even the sincerest reformer would have little chance in Northern Ireland, and the conclusion that Northern Ireland is irreformable. Other Civil Rights activists believed from the beginning that the state was beyond reforming and have found no reason to question that conclusion in the intervening years. Given these two roads to the same point, the irreformability thesis has been evident not only from an early stage in the Troubles (De Paor 1970), but also in most nationalist and repub-lican and some socialist literature since (McCann 1974; O'Hearn 1981; Revolutionary Communist Group 1978; Revolutionary Communist Tendency 1978). The strongest and most coherent statement of this position is in the work of Farrell (1976).

Similarly, there are old-guard and newly-arrived protagonists of reformability. There were those who held at the time when O'Neill was cautiously wooing sections of the Catholic bourgeoisie through reforms that Civil Rights demands were part of a republican plot against Ulster. (This conclusion was well caught by the few researchers who examined Protestant consciousness in the first half of the 1970s; cf. Nelson 1975 and 1979; Wright 1973). Recently, a second and more sophisticated variant of the position has appeared. The past need for reforms is conceded, but it is argued that these reforms have been established and Northern Ireland is to all intents and purposes a proper bourgeois democracy. If the reforms are not operating as fully or successfully as they might, that is due in large part to the continuing irredentist claims of reactionary nationalists and the Left republicans who tail-end them (Bew, Gibbon and Patterson 1979 and 1980; Morgan 1980). What is needed is to forget such 'side issues' (Devlin 1981) as the supposed 'outstanding national question' (as well as, for some, the supposed repression that is rife in Northern Ireland; cf. Byrne 1980, 43) and get on with the task of 'proper class politics' in Northern Ireland (Devlin 1981; Gibbon 1977).

It should be obvious that specific sets of politics follow from these contrary analytical positions. Without exploring the intricacies of each position, it is possible to typify them. The irreformability thesis has lead at various times to tactics such as armed struggle, mass action and abstentionism. The goal of socialist supporters of this position, as much as republicans, is the dissolution of the Northern Ireland state. The reformability thesis has at various points espoused trade union activity, community action and the provision of a 'viable socialist alternative' to voters. The socialist variant of the position may be summed up by stating that sections of the Left in Northern Ireland have taken to heart the admonition of Boserup (1972, 27):

> It needs to be recognised that the destruction of the Orange system and its replacement by the 'welfare state' of managerial capitalism is historically necessary and historically progressive.

4. Analysis: The Reproduction of Sectarian Class Relations

It is possible—and, as I have argued elsewhere with others (cf. O'Dowd, Rolston and Tomlinson 1980), necessary—to begin with neither of the above two positions. There are practical reasons for this, not least the fact that pro-reformists and anti-reformists can often spend much of their time pirouetting in a sort of moral pas-de-deux. In short, abandoning *a priori* positionalism is a necessary first step on the path to analysis. However, it is not of itself sufficient. It is also necessary to examine in close detail the actual effects of the operations of the British state in Northern Ireland in order to accurately answer the questions: How far are reforms merely superimposed on a society that remains basically as sectarian as ever? Have reforms meant a substantial dismantling of sectarianism?

One preliminary piece of definition is necessary. The word 'sectarianism' is not used in a narrow sense to connote merely a set of attitudes. It refers to a material reality, reconstructed and hence perpetuated in everyday life. If 'sectarianism' is taken in the narrow sense of a set of attitudes only, then it can refer to the attitudes of both the dominating and the dominated. But in a structural sense of the word, it can only be fully applied to the activities of the dominating. This approach to the analysis of sectarianism has respectable links with analyses of other ideologies, for example, racism (Downing 1981) and sexism (Barrett 1980). By analogy, if racism exists only at the level of attitudes, then blacks who hate whites can be said to be as racist as whites who hate blacks. Many state policies to supposedly counteract racism are built on that assessment. But, if racism is a phenomenon at the structural level, then it is only institutions and policies designed and managed by powerful whites that can properly be said to be racist in as far as they perpetuate the domination of blacks. In this sense, even those institutions and policies designed to counteract racist attitudes can themselves be racist.

Our analysis of the operations of the British state in Northern Ireland led us to conclude that there were many ways in which changes had occurred in Northern Ireland, especially since Direct Rule. Policies have changed, technocracy predominates, the rhetoric of fairness and impartiality prevails at governmental level, many laws have been updated, repression has been refined, and traditional class alignments have been disjointed to the point where, ten years after the imposition of Direct Rule, concrete and lasting realignments have not as yet emerged. In fact, it can be said that the last few years of Direct Rule have seen the struggle between, on the one hand, British politicians intent on a new class alliance of centre bourgeois parties on a non-sectarian basis, and on the other, Paisley of the Democratic Unionist Party and Molyneaux of the Official Unionist Party locked in what John Hume of the Social Democratic and Labour Party once neatly titled a 'virility contest' to determine who will be patriarch of 'the Unionist family'. In short, many things have changed in Northern Ireland.

However, the basic structures of Northern Ireland's inequality remain remarkably undented despite these changes. Not only does sectarianism remain—a phenomenon which could be explained in terms of past legacies, or residue—but also the combined actions of capital and the British state in Northern Ireland serve to reconstitute sectarianism in new ways. We have shown how this process operates as regards regional policy, housing, trade unions, community politics, local councils and repression. Hence the conclusion that 'the UK state is not "above" the NI problem, it is an integral part of that problem' (O'Dowd, Rolston and Tomlinson 1980, 208).

Some may partially accept that statement, seeing the state as being partly benign and partly malign. British repression may thus be seen as part of the problem, but British reformism as part of the solution. However, it must be stressed that both are actions of the same state, and, despite contradictions and anomalies within that state, must be seen as having an underlying unity of effect. Repression and reformism can happily coexist as twin elements of British technocracy in Northern Ireland.

Similarly, reformism and sectarianism can coexist. More, technocracy can reproduce sectarian division. To give two examples: one may devise the most rational procedures in which to guarantee the hiring of the best skilled manual person for a job, thus eradicating traditional forms of patronage. But, in a society where that skilled manual person is more likely to be Protestant, such rational procedures contribute to the perpetuation of inequality. Furthermore, capital has a tendency to go where capital is established, for reasons of proven profitability, existing infrastructure, etc. In Northern Ireland such areas are in the predominantly Protestant East of the Bann area. Thus, even in the absence of sectarian intentions or traditional patronage, the influx of capital can easily perpetuate sectarian division. Capitalism in Northern Ireland has simultaneously class and sectarian biases.

To be 'fair' in the midst of inequality is not enough. Politically, then, it is logical to argue for policies of reverse discrimination. This, however, is not an acceptable official logic within Northern Ireland. Technocracy is seen to be fair and non-sectarian by definition. Sectarianism is consequently seen as residual, requiring a 'mopping up' exercise by a few quite low-level institutions. It is on those institutions that I will focus in what follows. The assumption that technocracy reproduces sectarianism is taken as given, and the task at hand is to examine the successes and failures of these institutions in the light of that assumption.

Reforming Sectarianism

In 1969 the Community Relations Commission (CRC) was established to bring Catholics and Protestants together. Modelled on the similar CRC in Britain it was, however, placed under the wing of a completely new Ministry, the Ministry of Community Relations. The British CRC was under the Home Office, but placing the Northern Ireland CRC under the equivalent Ministry of Home Affairs would not have been politically wise. The CRC was put forward as a response to civil rights demands, although the establishment of such a body had never been mooted in civil rights circles. It would have been impossible to put it forward in such a manner if it had been placed in the same Ministry with that other area of responsibility which was under close scrutiny as a result of civil rights pressure, that is, the police. Other than overseeing the CRC, the Ministry of Community Relations' only reason for existence initially was the administration of Social Needs legislation, whereby money was distributed to areas of special social need.

The CRC instituted a community development programme, arguing that the surest way to bring about a deep-rooted meeting of the Catholic and Protestant working class was to encourage both to organise independently on issues of immediate local concern, such as redevelopment and motorways. The argument was that both would then see that the solution to such issues could not be at the local level alone and would come together to organise jointly on issues of common concern (Hayes 1971). Eventually this argument led the Commission's community development team to demand much greater autonomy and resources, a demand which the Ministry did not concede. Instead the Ministry built up its responsibilities and staff over time, until the point where Ivan Cooper, SDLP Minister of Community Relations in the 1974 power-sharing Executive, abolished the CRC, arguing that now the Catholic community, through the SDLP, had a stake in power, there was no need for an independent community relations body (cf. Rolston 1976 and 1978). The demise of the CRC resulted not merely from the empire-building moves of the Ministry and the consequent confrontation between it and the Commission, as Griffiths (1974) argues, but from the establishment of technocratic administration in Northern Ireland and the consequent British withdrawal from policies directly seeking to eradicate sectarianism (Rolston 1980). Only such an assessment can make sense of the fact that when Direct Rule was re-established later in 1974, the British not only confirmed the closure of the CRC, but disbanded the Ministry of Community Relations as well.

A similar retreat from the initial enthusiasm regarding direct attacks on sectarianism can be seen in the case of the Prevention of Incitement to Hatred Act (1970). Again modelled on similar British practice (the Race Relations Act 1965, from which Northern Ireland had initially been excluded at the request of the Stormont government), the law in Northern Ireland allowed for the prosecution of people for stirring up sectarian emotions. But such legislation operates in a most nebulous legal area. There are problems of assessing intentionality, of judging the effects of a statement or publication, of making links between causes and effects—all of which had led to extreme caution. Only one prosecution has ever occurred under the legislation, that of the late John McKeague and two other men for the publication of a book of Orange Loyalist Songs in 1971, and specifically for a song titled 'I was Born Under a Union Jack'. Sung to the tune of 'I Was Born Under a Wandering Star', the lyrics included the aphorism that the only good Catholic was one with a bullet in his back. The three men were acquitted. Those who have concluded in the years since that there have been many—including notable politicians—who might equally deservedly be charged under the Act might take consolation from the anomaly of British practice where an Act ostensibly to protect blacks from the racism of dominant white Britain has been used more often against black people than white (Dickey 1972).

One other institution which emerged from the early days of reform and which was initially inspired by the then dominant logic of eradicating sectarian administration was the Ombudsman. Initially there were two Ombudsmen, the Northern Ireland Commissioner for Complaints and the Parliamentary Commissioner for Administration (cf. Benn 1973). But for some years both posts have been held by the same person, who has thus had overall responsibility for investigating individual complaints of maladministration by local government, central government departments and public bodies. Although originally the Ombudsman saw his brief as subsuming complaints of religious discrimination, a more recent practice is to pass on most of these complaints to the Fair Employment Agency (FEA). The Ombudsman's task has been then the more mundane one of handling complaints of what might be termed non-sectarian maladministration, for example, where a person disagrees with the outcome of a planning decision of the Department of the Environment, or with the Department of Health and Social Services regarding social security payments. Of the 149 complaints against government departments received in 1980, 108 (72 per cent) concerned the above mentioned Departments. 109 cases were rejected as being outside the Ombudsman's jurisdiction, 4 were discontinued after partial investigation and 22 were still in progress at the end of the year. In short, investigations were completed in only 34 cases. In most of these cases no finding of maladministration was made. A less severe attrition rate emerged as regards complaints against local government and public bodies. In 1980 there were 593 complaints, the vast majority of which were against the Northern Ireland Housing Executive. 452 cases were investigated, but of these a judgment of maladministration was made in only 23 cases. (5 per cent). All in all, the Ombudsman's task is seen as that of safety net. The number of complaints each year is few, and the number of findings of maladministration miniscule. The Ombudsman's Annual Reports therefore bear testimony to the belief that technocracy is working rationally and efficiently.

Finally, mention needs to be made of the Standing Advisory Commission on Human Rights. Superficially this statutory body, set up in 1973 as a result of the Northern Ireland Constitution Act, seems to fit into the logic of a direct attack on sectarianism. In fact its *raison d'etre* is entirely different. The Commission's relevance from the British state's point of view is not internal to Northern Ireland. Its primary purpose is not that of pressure group to force the British government to be more concerned about human rights in Northern Ireland, no matter how much the commissioners themselves should judge that to be their task. Thus, the Commission's agonised deliberations on emergency legislation, its advice to government on divorce and gay rights legislation and its commitment to a Bill of Rights (cf. Standing Advisory Commission on Human Rights 1976; Campbell 1980) are of little immediate concern to British politicians and administrators. The value of the Commission is external. Faced with international concern and even opposition over its management of the Northern Ireland problem, especially in the midst of the H-Blocks crisis of 1981, and of its continual derogation from the European Convention for the Protection of Human Rights and Fundamental Freedoms (of which it is a signatory) in order to continually implement emergency legislation in Northern Ireland, Britain can point to the Commission as proof of its concern about human rights in Northern Ireland. The Commission's function becomes that of show-piece, or shield to deflect some international flak. As to the Commission's space to be a vital pressure group, Secretary of State Humphrey Atkins put the matter clearly in perspective at the annual renewal of the Emergency Provisions Act in Parliament in 1979; commenting on arguments such as those sometimes put forward by the Commission, he said:

> I am well aware that there is a contrary view: that, in fact, the temporary powers are an irritant rather than an emollient, tending to enhance the opposition to the forces of law and order, and to encourage disrespect for the law. I recognise that this is no frivolous argument . . . But the hard fact is that the powers which I asked the House to renew need to be available (NI Information Service, Press Release, 11.12.79).

The Possibilities of Reforming Sectarianism: the Case of the Fair Employment Agency

The FEA is the major reformist body in existence in 1983 whose task is to specifically counter sectarianism. It was established as a result of the Fair Employment (NI) Act 1976

> to promote equality of opportunity in employment and occupations between people of different religious beliefs . . . and to work for the elimination of religious and political discrimination in employment and occupations.

It was envisaged that the FEA's tasks would include the investigation of individual complaints of discrimination, the investigation of the practices of specific employers and organisations, the carrying out of research, and a cluster of tasks (such as holding conferences, running training courses) which might collectively be termed 'education'. In assessing the success of the FEA, it is essential to examine each of these functions.

Section 24 of the Act empowers the FEA to investigate individual allegations of discrimination. However, there are a number of problems involved in this task. Much as many crimes are not 'known to the police', many cases of discrimination never reach the point of beginning the perilous path through the legislative labyrinth, a fact which the FEA itself acknowledges (FEA 1979, 19). Furthermore, many individual complaints are not investigated, either because they fall outside the FEA's jurisdiction, or because there is not enough evidence to warrant investigation. If a *prima facie* case is thought to exist, evidence is collected by conciliation officers (documentary evidence, or verbal evidence, the latter taken under oath) in order that the officers can make a report to a sub-committee of the FEA. It is the whole Agency itself which finally judges whether a case of 'unlawful discrimination' has occurred.

The sheer quantity of hurdles involved means that many complaints do not last the course. In addition are qualitative problems: how is one to judge whether discrimination has occurred or not, or if there was a religious or political motive in the victimisation of the complainant? It would seem that, on the basis of experience, the FEA has come up with a number of rules of thumb. For example, if the person actually appointed was of the same religion as the complainant, it is unlikely that a finding of discrimination will be made (cf. case number 8; FEA 1979, 47). On the other hand, the non-appointment of a candidate for possibly unfair, but not discriminatory (as defined), reasons is not judged as discrimination (cf. case number 3; FEA 1979, 39). Lastly, even the initial declaration of the employer that the reason for not hiring the candidate was his/her religion will not necessarily lead to a judgment of discrimination if the employer later claims that this was an excuse to cover up more funda-mental reasons for not hiring the candidate (cf. case number 10; FEA 1979, 52).

While conceding the difficulty of ascertaining intentional bias in such cases, McCrudden (1982) in his confidential examination of the FEA, is severely critical of such rules of thumb.

> I recommend there should be increasing reliance on making infer-ences of discrimination on the basis of 'harder' evidence of this (statistical) type, and a decreasing reliance on intuitive judgment based on the 'feel' of a case (McCrudden 1982, 20).

The overall effect of relying on such rules of thumb seems to be that the benefit of doubt is given to the respondent rather than the complainant. This may be due in great part to the backgrounds of the Agency mem-bers themselves, middle-of-the-road political types, businessmen, trade unionists, etc., all of them government-appointed, and most of them appointed on the basis of their respectibility . Such people are undoubtedly inclined to move in the same ideological and political (not to mention social) space as many of the respondents with whom they deal. There is thus an inbuilt tendency for them to behave in a rational manner with the respondents, seeking to solve difficulties in a 'gentlemanly' manner, rather than to use the might of their quasi-legal muscle on behalf of the complainants. (For allegations of one notable case of caution and pro-respondent bias, cf. McConnell 1978).

As a result of these quantitative and qualitative factors, very few findings of 'unlawful discrimination' have been made by the FEA, as table 9:1 shows.

Table 9:1

COMPLAINTS ON WHICH DECISIONS HAVE BEEN TAKEN BY THE FEA, 1 APRIL 1977 TO 31 MARCH 1982

(Source FEA Annual Reports)

	Discrimination	*No Discrimination*
Government Departments	0	24
Local Authorities	6	9
Education and Library Boards	0	16
Health and Social Services Board	2	15
Other Public Bodies	0	14
Food, Drink and Tobacco Industry	1	12
Chemical and Allied Industries	0	2
Engineering Industries	0	13
Textiles and Clothing	1	8
Manufacturing Industries	1	6
Construction Industry	2	6
Transport	0	2
Distributive Trades	0	9
Other businesses	0	8
Total	13	144

Even a finding of discrimination is not the end of the matter. The FEA's finding has the force of law, requiring the respondent to compensate the complainant. An appeal against a finding of discrimination thus goes through the Courts. In the Courts, four of the FEA's first six findings of discrimination were overturned. Disagreeing with their very first finding of discrimination against the Northern Ireland Civil Service Commission, Judge Topping concluded that the FEA,

> probably convinced that this attitude was expected of it, appears to have gone to considerable lengths to reach a finding that unlawful discrimination had taken place (FEA 1979, 35-5).

Furthermore, although respondents found 'guilty' of discrimination may be required to pay compensation, they frequently do not, thus requiring the FEA to bring *them* to court for the money. As a result, only one of the cases where a finding of discrimination has been upheld has to date led to compensation in the complainant's hand.

In short, the investigation of individual complaints is a costly task in terms of both time involved and in finances. Only a Department of Manpower Services concession whereby legal costs above and beyond the FEA's budget are met by the Department prevents the FEA reaching the point already reached by the Equal Opportunities Commission of finding that the cost of considering individual complaints has left little by way of finances to engage in other tasks.

Section 12 of the Act empowers the FEA to investigate specific employers or industries to ascertain the religious composition of their workforces. This task can be thwarted by employers' reluctance to co-operate, often justified in quite plausible terms. The most notorious case of a formal investigation being blocked is that of the Civil Service investigation, where opposition to FEA 'snooping' reached to the highest level, to Ministers of State themselves (cf. Moloney 1979). It is telling that, faced with such lofty opposition, the Agency did not use its full legal weight to win the compliance of a Department of a government supposedly committed to supporting equality of opportunity unreservedly, but sought to smooth matters over in a conciliatory manner.

Even if an investigation is completed, further criticisms can be made. Some of the more publicly contentious investigations have been noted, even summarized, in FEA Annual Reports (for example, the Civil Service investigations in FEA 1981, and Cookstown and part of the Engineering investigation in FEA 1982). But six years into the life of the Agency, only one of the investigations has been published, that into the Northern Ireland Electricity Service (FEA 1982b). But, for detailed information about Cookstown and Civil Service investigations, one has had to rely on well-informed press coverage. The same holds true for the cluster of individual investigations which comprise the FEA's formal investigation of the engineering industry: Ford Motor Co., Davidson & Co. (Sirocco), James Mackie, Short Brothers, Harland & Wolff, Standard Telephone and Cables, Hughes Tool Co., Hugh J. Scott and Co., Tilley Lamp Co., Grundig and Strathearn Audio. It is of paramount important to note the findings of these investigations, for they constitute the little evidence there is (outside of the FEA's own research reports) to enable one to judge whether sectarian division in employment persists. In the case of the Northern Ireland Electricity Service, the evidence is damning:

> It is evident that the numbers of management staff who could be classified as Roman Catholic were very small both at the highest level and perhaps more surprisingly at the next most important levels . . .

(This) coupled with a promotion policy which gives first preference to in-house candidates must result in a very slow rate of change in the higher echelons of management from a pattern which may have initially been influenced by prejudice. (NI Electricity Service investigation, paragraphs 6.1 and 6.4).

Similarly, in the case of the engineering industry:

In all the companies visited the predominance of Protestants in the craftsmen engineering trades confirmed the census figures. In two companies it was not disputed that the skilled fitters and similar tradesmen (in both cases, workforces of three figure strength were involved) employed almost certainly did not include a Catholic. If there were any Catholics, one employer told the Agency, they would be 'sleepers'. (Engineering Investigation and Report, 3).

Given these conclusions and the FEA's reluctance to publish them, it is evident that the potential for public debate on the question of continuing discrimination in employment in Northern Ireland is lessened by the self-imposed secrecy of the FEA.

What is the purpose of these formal investigations in the view of the FEA? It would seem that they are regarded as an element in their task of gently pressuring employers to mend their ways. In other words, they are not seen in the first place as a contribution to public debate. Their target audience is not the public, but the employers investigated, and the investigations thus become part of the refined and 'gentlemanly' discourse between employers and Agency members. They could be much more than that. Just as they sometimes grow out of individual complaints against the firm or sector investigated, a further link could be made between investigation and research. However, that link is not made, leaving the FEA's researchers to rely on already published statistics, such information as may be made available by government departments, and information gathered by the researchers, for example, through questionnaires. The non-publication of formal investigation findings is thus one factor contributing to a strong tendency towards narrow empiricism and a frequent lack of imagination as regards both the scope and the methods of the research conducted. At the same time some of the reports (cf. FEA 1978a; Miller 1978; Osborne and Murray 1978; Miller 1979; Cormack, Osborne and Thompson 1980; Murray and Darby 1980) have helped to lift the debate on discrimination above the most simple level of direct one-to-one intentional bias to that of structures within employment, and by extension education, which reproduce sectarian division.

The difficulty, however, is imagining what the FEA might do to operationalize this latter understanding of inequality in its daily work. There is, in short, a major disjunction between the logic of the Research Reports and the exigencies of the FEA's daily casework task, the latter looking for evidence of direct one-to-one bias. This is a point to which I will return in the final section of this chapter.

The only other major task pursued by the FEA is that of having employers sign a Declaration of Principle and Intent, thus supposedly committing themselves to the pursuit of fair employment. But signing the Declaration does not necessarily mean one is actually or even potentially a fair employer. In the absence of any link between the Declaration and any of the Agency's other tasks, especially its right to conduct formal investigations, the Declaration becomes innocuous. No candidate seeking to sign is subject to investigation to see if the firm does in fact practice fair employment. Conversely, Shorts for years refused to sign. When the firm eventually got around to signing, the FEA permitted it to do so, even though its own formal investigation of the firm revealed a massive inbuilt sectarian imbalance in the firm's workforce. Only a total failure to link the various elements of its strategy could account for the fact that when it came to acquiring a printer to print their *Guide to Manpower Policy and Practice,* they did not choose a firm which was a signatory to their Declaration of Principle and Intent! Recently the FEA has made much of a government policy change which the Agency has been advocating for some time. From 1982

> the government have decided that tenders for government contracts will not normally be accepted from firms . . . unless they hold an equal opportunity employer certificate issued by the Fair Employment Agency following the signing of the statutory declaration of principle and intent (Mr John Patten, House of Commons, 10.12.81.)

One can confidently expect a rush of firms to sign the Declaration, including firms which have consistently refused to do so in the past. But, will such a rush prove that these firms are in fact any less discriminatory, or that their workforces are likely to be any more balanced than at present?

Instead of linking tactics the FEA has been content to pursue the more nebulous strategy of 'educating' employers. It has compiled (as instructed under the Act, Section 5), a *Guide to Manpower Policy and Practice;* but few employers have gone out of their way to implement the recommendations of the Guide (cf. FEA 1981, 7). The FEA has increasingly involved itself in advice services and training sessions for employers.

But these are puny weapons indeed with which to fight structural inequality. They all exist in the grey area of cajolery and appeals to employers' consciences. In addition, it is not improbable that increased dialogue with employers will enhance the chances of Agency members also being 'educated' into 'seeing the employers's point of view' and 'not stepping on the toes' of someone providing precious jobs.

It is often said of organizations such as the FEA that they lack teeth. But this is not true of the FEA. As a quasi-legal body with the force of law to back it up, it has some potentially formidable weapons. That it does not use them, or use them enough, is at least partially its fault. Unable to deal with structural inequality, it concentrates on individual grievances. Unwilling to force, it is reduced to cajolery and gentlemanly persuasion. Knowing that changing attitudes is not enough, it does not pursue any other consistent strategy than attempting to change attitudes. As McCrudden (1982, 36) concludes:

> The experience of the legal enforcement of the Fair Employment Act, thus far, is a depressing picture of a massive task, of the possibility of change, but of an Agency which failed to meet that challenge. A complete overhauling of the FEA is necessary . . . It is by no means certain that the Act will then prove successful. What *is* clear, however, is that without such changes the ideals which the Act was meant to achieve stand little chance of success.

The Politics of Reform

> The FEA is a baby which should have been strangled at birth. (Mrs. Dorothy Dunlop, Belfast City Council; cited in *Belfast Telegraph,* 26.4.77).

> The sooner they are Thatcherized, the better. (Mr. Paddy Newell, Belfast businessman; cited in *Belfast Telegraph* 16.12.80).

The FEA, no less than the other reformist institutions which have existed to directly counter sectarianism, does not exist in a vacuum. It is not possible to comment on its potential or actual success in isolation from the fact that there is a politics of reform in Northern Ireland. Within that politics the FEA has few adamant supporters. Reformists have tended to accept the dominant characterization of the task of such bodies as the FEA as residual, namely, mopping up the remaining vestiges of sectarianism. Given that, they have concentrated their support (sometimes critical, sometimes not) on the supposedly non-sectarian technocratic bodies such as the Northern Ireland Housing

Executive. On the other hand, the FEA has had its opponents. For example, the Northern Ireland Chamber of Commerce and Industry opposes the FEA from a base of local bourgeois conservatism; in an oddly non-sectarian sort of way they are opposed to *all* reformist bodies.

> In our view the Equal Opportunities Commission and the FEA have not had a useful effect on industrial relations. The EOC has experienced internal dissension; its existence has stimulated female workers to take action against their employers, while the FEA is considered by many to have operated to the detriment of business. (Memorandum to Adam Butler, Minister of State, February 1981).

But the most vocal of the FEA's opponents have been loyalists of various shades. Loyalist councillors in 1977 led a sustained attack on the FEA's Declaration of Principle and Intent. As a result few of Northern Ireland's 26 District Councils signed. Various reasons were voiced for this refusal: Councillor Jack McKee of Larne, having publicly torn up the Declaration, stated the most commonly articulated objection to signing.

> To sign the Act would only give credence to the old republican propaganda cries about '50 years of misrule' which are proven unfounded (cited in *East Antrim Times,* 4.2.77).

The opposition, in short, is to the very existence of the FEA itself. That existence is seen as a

> capitulation by the British government to a minority of people in Northern Ireland who have clamoured for certain things to put them in a place of privilege above the majority (Councillor George Willey of Craigavon Council, 8.2.77).

The policy that follows is therefore one of non-cooperation and a call for the disbandment of the Agency altogether.

Inconsistently, loyalist politicians seem to have at times sought the best of both worlds, dismissing the FEA while demanding that it also investigate discrimination against Protestants. For example, Martin Smyth, head of the Orange Order and MP for South Belfast, called for the FEA's disbandment on the ground that it has been kept busy doing virtually nothing at enormous cost (cited in *Belfast Telegraph,* 16.2.80). Later in the same speech he went on to demand that the FEA investigate recruitment to the health service, where, he alleged, discrimination against Protestants was rife.

Loyalist opposition to the FEA, and indeed any similar reformist body, has from time to time received a fillip from an apparently unusual source, namely, from academics. In 1980 Paul Compton singled out the FEA's research reports for criticism. They had all failed, he claimed, to include one vital factor in their quantification of inequality, the relationship between religion and fertility. The persistence of Catholic disadvantage therefore should not be attributed to discrimination (as is argued by the FEA), but 'in considerable part to the structure of the Roman Catholic community itself' (Compton 1980; cf. also his elaboration of these arguments in Compton 1981; cf. also the reply to the original piece by Osborne and Miller 1980). There is much in this argument that is reminiscent of traditional loyalist disclaimers of discrimination, and indeed of a standard right-wing dismissal of the poor. More specifically, the approach rightly rejects a concentration solely on 'discrimination', but equally narrowly judges the Catholic community apart from all the other elements in Northern Irish society. Compton sees a 'structural' approach as a counter to the inadequacy of relying on the concept of 'discrimination', but reduces his concept to refer to certain demographic characteristics of the Catholic community. A truly structural approach must see the interconnection of many factors in the reproduction of sectarianism, of which sectarian intentions and Catholic behaviour patterns are but two.

Similar criticisms of reductionism and narrowness of definition can be made of what might be described as the recent historical revisionist approach to the civil rights struggle. Although the academics here do not consider the FEA as such, their conclusions have repercussions for an assessment of contemporary reformism in general and institutions formed to combat sectarianism in particular. Hewitt has concluded as follows:

> Supposedly the civil rights demonstrators wanted reforms. Yet the violence was not reduced in the slightest by a 'one man one vote' franchise, the redrawing of local council boundaries, a massive housebuilding programme and an allocation system for housing that favoured Catholics. There are two reasons for this: first since the old system was not particularly inequitable, reforms could not have much impact, second the nationalists who predominated in the movement were not really interested in reforms (Hewitt 1981, 377).

Despite its concentration on history, Hewitt's piece is really a statement about the present, as the above quotation reveals. Yet he produces no evidence for his conclusions about the present effectiveness and impartiality of reforms. His evidence for the supposed absence of discrimination in the past is presented, but it is weak. For example, he argues that many Protestants were disenfranchised by the lack of 'one man, one vote', and that gerrymandering was less widespread than civil rights activists maintained. In short, democracy was more alive and well than 'nationalist mythology' would have it. But, in concluding that he fails to investigate the ways in which democracy—that is, majority rule—in a sectarian setting has sectarian effects and leads to the perpetuation of sectarian division in ways not captured by quantification.

In fact, it is to the most dubious of statistical methods that he turns in order to prove his corollary conclusion, that Catholics were not interested in reform. For example, one piece of 'evidence' is that Catholics in the 1960s consistently voted 'nationalist', a category which is obtained only by subsuming every party for which Catholics could reasonably vote, with the exception of the Northern Ireland Labour Party, under one undifferentiated label. Similar reductionism is required in his pursuit of an 'objective' measure of the relationship between 'nationalism' and violence.

Much more sophisticted, but no less revisionist, is Whyte's reassessment of the civil rights campaign with the benefits of hindsight. He examines allegations of discrimination in six areas under the Unionist government. His conclusion is that those allegations have differing degrees of merit, allowing him to rank the levels of discrimination in descending order as follows: electoral practices, public employment, security, private employment, public housing and regional policy (Whyte 1981, 40). But even the amount of discrimination in the area of electoral practice is less than is normally suggested. Hence,

> the most serious charge against the Unionist government is not that it was directly guilty of widespread discrimination, but that it failed to restrain a portion of its followers who were. By that failure, it provoked the reaction which eventually brought the whole Unionist regime crashing down (Whyte 1981, 41).

The argument is clear, but its major flaw is in the narrowness of the definition of 'discrimination'. It is a concept most often used in an intentional sense; that was how it was used by Civil Rights activists. Taking that same usage, Whyte concludes that there was less 'discrimination' than was believed at the time.

In the light of arguments put forward earlier in this chapter, it can be said briefly that the major flaw in Whyte's analysis is in his unarticulated, but operational, definition of the concept 'discrimination'. He defines it in intentional, even conscious, terms, thus not only ignoring the ways in which apparently non-sectarian actions can have sectarian effects, but also failing to move beyond the level of interaction to a consideration of structural inequality and disadvantage. For example, he concludes at one point that 'the Housing Trust has generally been exonerated of all *conscious desire* to discriminate' (Whyte 1981, 26; my italics.) Yet it is entirely possible to prove that at least two 'rational' policies of the Housing Trust—that is, allocating houses to more 'responsible' tenants, and building estates near new factories for skilled workers—had, given the sectarian balance of skill and wealth in Northern Ireland, markedly sectarian consequences, even in the absence of intentional bias (cf. Tomlinson 1980b, 123-131).

To return to the FEA, academic arguments such as the above indirectly and in some cases inadvertently add fuel to opposition to the Agency. However, it must be stressed that the FEA's greatest antagonists need no such rational arguments to assure them that the Agency should not exist. In the face of all this opposition, then, it should not be surprising that FEA members are easily tempted to proceed with caution. Their fears are real, not imaginary. The problem is, however, that their caution lends support to their opponents. In short, by hobbling themselves FEA members play into the hands of those who seek to hobble it. One example will perhaps portray the weakness of the FEA's response to criticism. The Reverend Martin Smyth, in the speech already cited, called for the FEA's dissolution on financial grounds; the Agency cost £80,000 per annum to run, he said, with next to nothing to show in terms of results. In reply Bob Cooper, Chairperson of the FEA, could have pointed out that the task of delivering equal opportunity for Catholics and Protestants in Northern Ireland could not be fulfilled at the mere cost of £80,000 per annum. Instead he argued that the original estimates for the FEA were for 40 staff and a budget of £280,000. He went on:

> In fact, the FEA is now costing £80,000 a year and has a staff of 12. I challenge Mr. Smyth to name any organisation which costs such a small fraction of the cost ancitipated. (cited in *Belfast Telegraph,* 16.2.80).

But surely this is winning a battle only to lose the war. In effect the Chairperson is boasting about the FEA's weakness, and in doing so is giving credence to Smyth's claim that the Agency has no real purpose.

Compare this to the comments of Christopher McCrudden to the effect that if the FEA is to being to be serious about its task it must at very least use its original budget to the full (McCrudden 1982, 16). For

McCrudden the FEA's failure to do so is one sign of its overall failure to work at full capacity. Hence he urges a commitment on the FEA's part to 'affirmative action' for fair employment. He hastens to add (McCrudden 1982, 29) that he is not advocating 'positive discrimination'. In stating this, he is recognising the fact that the FEA is bound, not only specifically by the Act, but also, apparently, by the ideology of the Department of Manpower Services-appointed Agency members themselves, to a position of staunch opposition to any notion of 'positive', 'reverse', or 'benign discrimination'—that is, it will not countenance the countering of structural inequality by a policy of hiring people on the basis of their religious background. In fact, one of the successful FEA findings of unlawful discrimination was in the case of Newry and Mourne District Council, which hired a Protestant for its sports staff because it had no Protestants thus employed. Finding for the Catholic refused a job, the FEA concluded that 'it is wrong that an individual should suffer because of possible prejudice in favour of his or her section of the community in the past' (FEA 1980, 61). It is true that Bob Cooper did at one point seem to come close to arguing for a form of positive discrimination, namely, a system of quotas in employment. Although there are 'substantial moral objections' to such an approach, he said, 'if we are unable to deal with this major social problem, then the argument for quotas will surface very strongly indeed' (Cooper 1979, 6). But as he does not seem to have returned to the suggestion publicly at any later date, it would seem that he was doing no more than flying a kite briefly. Those with experience of attempts at positive discrimination as regards black people and women in the U.S. would surely argue that such a strategy is by no means an instant panacea. The point regarding Northern Ireland is that it is a strategy ruled out in advance.

The paradox is that McCrudden's notion of 'affirmative action' sounds remarkably close to a policy of positive discrimination. He argues that the FEA must work towards the point that in the future employment patterns in Northern Ireland more or less reflect the sectarian balance in the wider society. Such a policy would require taking on, not only those who have a conscious stake in continued sectarian imbalance, but also the technocratic institutions themselves. It is imperative to spell out what 'taking on technocracy' in the pursuit of fair employment would in fact mean. The problem is not just that technocrats are not amenable to formal democratic influence. This is an argument with which even the Right can easily agree. In doing so they can even appropriate the rhetoric of their political rivals, as when loyalist councillor Esmond Thompson of Maghera claimed that the present powerless local councils were merely a facade for British colonial rule in Northern Ireland (cited in *Belfast Bulletin* 1981, 33).

Nor does the problem of technocracy derive only from the fact that technocracy is not amenable to popular pressure, for all that this is probably true. O'Dowd and Tomlinson (1980) have illustrated the confrontation between popular pressure groups and planners on the issues of housing and urban motorways in Belfast (as regards motorways, cf. also Community Groups Action Committee 1980), and have shown that, despite the verbal commitment to democracy through the medium of public inquiries, the processes whereby technocrats arrive at their decisions are remarkably impervious to popular pressure. More studies of this sort are required, not least because they illustrate that for all their opposition to technocrats on the grounds of formal democracy, the Right is often in no doubt as to where it stands when the choice must be made between supporting technocratic versus popular control of decision-making.

'Taking on technocracy' must rest on the realization that technocracy enables the reconstitution of sectarian imbalance in Northern Ireland. Given that, the task of the FEA is far from residual, but entails a full-frontal attack on the structures within Northern Ireland. 'Affirmative action' in practice requires confronting not only loyalist patronage, but also the logic of technocracy. Three predictions can be made about such a strategy: Firstly, on the basis of the past practice of Agency members, there is no possibility of such a militant strategy being pursued by the FEA. Secondly, this strategy would lead to an incredible amount of opposition from both loyalists and technocrats, such as would make the FEA's previous encounters with Martin Smyth and Ministers of State pale into insignificance. On the positive side, it should be added that as the FEA is going to experience opposition anyway, it might as well do something to earn that opposition. Thirdly, while it is highly unlikely that such a strategy would be pursued, or, if pursued, be successful, any success could be expected to contribute to destabilisation, for it would practically call into question the whole logic at the basis of British management of Northern Ireland in the past decade. Whether the British state could weather such a criticism of its management, in other words, the extent to which such a policy of positive discrimination would in fact be destabilizing, is, if not a hypothetical question, at least one too massive to be answered here.

Reformism is not the counter to sectarianism. A real strategy for elimination of sectarianism would quickly lead to a confrontation with reformism. For this reason it is far-fetched to imagine the British state sponsoring such a strategy. It has not even been able to sponsor such a strategy as regards racism on its home front. Peter Newsam, Chairperson of the Commission for Racial Equality in Britain, recognized this fact, and was thus implicitly criticizing his employer, the state, when he said, 'the real problem, after all, is with the white community. If it wasn't, we wouldn't have a problem' (cited in *Guardian* 17.1.82.). The relationship between the FEA and the British state in Northern Ireland, between reformism and the elimination of sectarianism, is perhaps illustrated in no better way than imagining the unlikely: what would be the consequences of an equivalent statement emanating from the Chairperson of Northern Ireland's FEA?

10

The Logistics of Enquiry: A Guide for Researchers

John Darby

There has never been a shortage of myths about the Irish conflict, and the renewed demand for information since 1969 has added to the total. Some of them are based on an element of truth. During the early 1970s, for example, the evening cluster of visiting reporters in the bar of the Europa hotel in Belfast did lend some support to the popular view that its bar provided a more frequent source of news stories than the dangerous streets outside; since then, of course, this picture has been embroidered by apocryphal stories of gullible reporters and mickey-taking Irishmen. Gullibility was also a characteristic of some academics. Few locally-based researchers in Northern Ireland during the early 1970s can have avoided meeting carpetbagging American researchers, in transit to Cyprus, the Lebanon or other troubled spots, who were visiting Ulster for a fortnight to collect data for a comparative analysis of community conflict. Most departed, disappointed.

The research scene has changed considerably since those heady days when Northern Ireland, for a brief and unaccustomed few years, was academically fashionable for conflict research. While the rate of publications may have diminished slightly, their substance has improved. A body of theory, as distinct from polemic, has emerged; more empirical studies have been carried out, and more time has been spent on them; the province's academic institutions have become more concerned with the problems, and better equipped to tackle them. At every level, from undergraduate dissertation to major research project, a more serious approach has been adopted to the conflict.

At all these levels remains the problem of where a research investigation might be started. In this chapter, despite the risks in providing a tourists' guide to the Northern Irish conflict, the more modest aim is to consider what information is available to serious researchers, whether undergraduates or established academics, and to suggest possible starting points for their inquiries.

Basic References: Registers, Bibliographies and Chronologies

The preliminary information required by social scientists varies little between different settings. What research is being carried out, and by whom? Has it been published, and when? Is it possible to establish reliably when particular events took place? Until the early 1970s these questions could not be answered without considerable inconvenience. However, as the amount of social research increases, so do the research tools required to carry it out.

Two registers of research dealing exclusively with the Irish conflict have been published since the current violence began in 1969 (Darby 1972; Darby, Dodge and Hepburn 1981). Apart from providing information about individual researchers and their projects, they allow comparison between the strengths and weaknesses of conflict research at the two dates. Registers of a more general nature are produced by public bodies north and south of the Irish border—by the Policy, Planning and Research Unit at the Department of Finance in Northern Ireland, and by the Economic and Social Research Institute in Dublin; both deal with social and economic research, and the latter includes details of research being conducted in all Irish institutions. At a more specialized level, four registers of research on educational themes have been published by the Northern Ireland Council for Educational Research, which are unusual in that they include undergraduate dissertations. Equally specialised is the register of 71 projects into mental illness (Roche and Williamson 1977). However, most specialised projects are also described in the *Register of Social and Economic Research on Northern Ireland* sponsored by the SSRC (Darby *et al* 1983).

Research registers are primarily concerned with the present and the future, and are designed to inform researchers or other scholars working in similar fields. To find out what books, pamphlets, articles and ephemera have been printed in the past, one must go to the numerous bibliographies on the conflict. These are essentially parasitic publications, each one absorbing its predecessors, so some earlier bibliographies now have only limited value (Rose 1972; Deutsch 1975; Darby 1976). The two most comprehensive bibliographies of Irish materials have been published by the Library Association in London, and both contain many references to the conflict: Eager's *Guide to Irish Bibliographical Material* contains more than 9,000 entries, and Shannon's *Modern Ireland* has more than 5,000 (Eager 1980; Shannon 1982). Rather more accessible, if less complete, is *A Bibliography of the United Kingdom* (Pollock and McAllister 1980). The difficult task of collating all social and economic references to Northern Ireland since 1945, and making them available in computer readable form, is being attempted by a group of social scientists in Belfast, but its completion date is uncertain.

Most bibliographers include details of some unpublished theses, and the few conflict-related ones written before 1968 are detailed in *Theses Related to Ireland* (Institute of Irish Studies 1968). Undergraduate dissertations are more difficult to track down, and require visits to individual departments; this is occasionally worth the journey.

The review pages of all Irish newspapers are characterized by instinct rather than method, and they are uncertain guides to new publications. Two specialist publications are more thorough: *Irish Booklore* which is printed irregularly in Belfast, and *Books Ireland,* a monthly review printed in Dublin since 1976.

Chronologies, especially of events since 1969, are included in many of the more general books on the conflict. Most of these may be waived by serious students in favour of more detailed chronologies. In particular, the three volumes of *Northern Ireland: A Chronology of Events* (Deutsch and Magowan 1973-5) cover the period 1968 to 1974 on a daily basis. These are carefully researched, have excellent indices and appendices, and are indispensible for more modern investigations. For events during the previous half century, Richard Mansbach's 1973 chronology may be consulted. The post-1974 period causes greater difficulties, but the most useful references are the annual chronologies printed in *Hibernia* until its closure in 1980, and in the *Irish Times;* these are produced at the turn of each year. *Northern Ireland: A Political Directory 1968-79* also contains a chronology for the period, as well as useful reference material (Flackes 1980), and at least three general books on terrorism include chronological references to Northern Ireland (Sobel 1979, Vols. 1 and 2; Micholus 1980).

Official Publications

The quantity of information published by official bodies often seems to have an inverse relationship to its usefulness. Certainly there is no shortage of government publications. A cyclostyled paper compiled by the Policy, Planning and Research Unit at the Department of Finance, *Northern Ireland Sources for Social and Economic Research* (PPRU 1981) details 58 separate themes, each with up to sixteen references. Guidance is needed through this mountain of paper, and some is supplied by the Stationery Office catalogues (HMSO Occasional) and by a useful breviate of Northern Ireland government publications (Maltby 1974).

Some of the more general publications contain sufficient information to provide a statistical backcloth. The *Ulster Year Book* and *Facts at Your Fingertips* are general descriptions of broad social and economic trends, and may be supplemented by other regular publications such as *Social and Economic Trends in Northern Ireland,* the *Annual Abstract of Statistics (Northern Ireland)* and the *Digest of Statistics (Northern Ireland).* Command papers published by both Westminster and Stormont are usually more analytical examinations of specific issues, and a number of them are directly concerned with the conflict. The Northern Ireland *Census of Population* is also published every decade, but only in the form of secondary analyses by counties, religion, etc.; for more interpretive examinations it is necessary to look to academic researchers, and the 1971 census, for example, has been broken down by geographical distribution (Compton 1976) and by occupations (Aunger 1975). The Registrar-General, at his discretion, may provide more detailed tables.

Many government departments also issue their own publications. The Department of Education, for example, issues annually two volumes of *Northern Ireland Education Statistics,* which contain information on many aspects of the school population, with the notable and characteristic omission of their religions. The monthly analysis of unemployment statistics produced by the Department of Manpower Services also has interest for social scientists. Social and economic research conducted from within the civil service is mainly the responsibility of the Policy, Planning and Research unit at the Department of Finance, and from 1983 it began the publication of some of its own—mainly internal—research papers. It welcomes visits by serious researchers.

Annual reports from a number of public bodies contain relevant material. These include the Royal Ulster Constabulary, the Northern Ireland Housing Trust and, later, Housing Executive, the Community Relations Commission (until 1974), the Fair Employment Agency, the Northern Ireland Commissioner for Complaints and Parliamentary Commissioner, and the Standing Commission on Human Rights.

Local government is less well served by published reports. Financial returns are printed, and minutes of meetings of the 26 District councils are available for consultation. So are annual reports of the Health and Social Services Boards, and the Education and Library Boards, which took over some of the main functions of local authorities in 1973. However, apart from a chapter in the annual financial report of the

Department of the Environment, no synthesis of local government data is provided officially. Birrell has examined, by means of a survey, how councillors and their work were effected by the 1973 reorganization (Birrell 1981), and McAllister has carried out a study of councillors belonging to the Alliance party (McAllister 1977). Beyond these, very little is available.

History

For the Irish, according to ATQ Stewart, 'all history is applied history' (Stewart 1977, 16), unconsciously underlining the importance of its study for social scientists. The marked increase in the number of general histories since the 1960s, however, has not made it any easier to prepare a selective bibliography for the general reader. The specialist, on the other hand, has a number of historiographies as convenient starting points. J. Carty's two earlier *Bibliographies of Irish History* (1936 and 1940) deal with the period 1870-1921, while E. Johnston's *Bibliography of Irish History* (1969) includes more modern references. Joseph Lee's *Irish Historiography 1970-79* (1981) is a sequel to *Irish Historiography 1936-70* (Moody 1971); and an annual bibliography entitled 'Writings on Irish History', previously printed in *Irish Historical Studies,* is now available on microfiche by the Irish Committee of Historical Sciences. Closer to ground level is a checklist of books and articles on local history in Northern Ireland (City of Belfast Public Libraries 1972).

These may be augmented by general books of historical reference. Hickey and Doherty's *Dictionary of Irish History since 1800* (1980) is a substantial research aid, and the *Atlas of Irish History* (R. Dudley Edwards 1981) adds a geographical perspective. Recently, too, collections of historical documents have become more accessible: the Northern Ireland Public Record Office, for example, have published a series of Educational Facsimiles—collections of documents on such themes as the 1798 Rebellion and the Famine, with brief introductions—which have an obvious educational function. The violence in Northern Ireland during the 1970s has also led to the publication of extracts from conflict-related papers. Hepburn's *Conflict of Nationality in Modern Ireland* (1980) and Magee's *Northern Ireland: Crisis and Conflict* (1974) both help to place the violence within an historical context, while a collection of documents on the Ulster Troubles by Carlton (1977) was printed in the United States. European interest in the conflict is affirmed by the publication of no less than three separate collections of documents in German (Vogt 1972; Schilling 1972; Hermle 1976).

Any advice for the general reader is inevitably more subjective. Books by Beckett (1952 and 1966) and Lyons (1971) are standard references, and the Gill series on Irish history maintains a good standard. On the more detailed history of Northern Ireland, a wide range of interpretations have recently become available: Buckland (1979) and Stewart (1977) adopt traditional forms of historical analysis, while Farrell (1976) and Bew, Gibbon and Patterson (1979) approach the issue from different Marxist interpretations. Shearman has written one of the few histories which is strongly sympathetic to the Unionist administrations in Stormont (1971).

Access to primary data is obviously more difficult for the historian. Depending on the subject under study, a visit to the Public Record Offices in Belfast or Dublin will almost certainly be necessary. Under the 1867 Public Record (Ireland) Act, the holdings in many Irish repositories were centralised in Dublin, and annual reports were printed between 1869 and 1921. On June 30 1922 the main record repository in the Four Courts building was destroyed by bomb and fire as the Irish Civil war began. Fortunately indexes and catalogues were saved, and many records have subsequently been copied and are now available for consultation in Dublin.

The Public Record Office of Northern Ireland (PRONI) was set up in 1924, and attempted to replace some of the materials relating to Northern Ireland which had been destroyed in the fire. For many years PRONI's most valuable holdings were the private collections which it obtained through purchase or donation. Since the early 1970s, however, records of many of the old local authorities have been deposited, and the Office has become responsible for the records of the Northern Ireland Government, which were previously unavailable. Access to the latter is restricted to files which are more than 30 years old, although some earlier government material is also withheld from public scrutiny. In some cases this amounts to a serious obstruction to research. PRONI is generally well-regarded by researchers, and has excellent facilities and staff in Belfast.

Newspapers and Periodicals,

Newspapers and periodicals are the starting point for most social reporters, and for some the complete race. It is appropriate, therefore, to consider the value of the media for researchers. To some extent this depends upon whether they are interested in the events reported in the newspapers, or in the way the media report them. There has been a growing research interest in the treatment of Northern Ireland by the British press, and one major analysis of newspaper coverage (Elliott 1977). Those wishing to look at the coverage of the violence by Northern Ireland's three daily newspapers will find a terrain which has been largely uncharted. However readership figures are available for all the main publications read in the province (Research Services Limited 1970), and some interesting subjective descriptions of the local press have been written (see, for example, Firth 1971 and Winchester 1974).

The use of newspapers as a source of information on events in Northern Ireland since 1969 is complicated by their variety. Within the province, the *Belfast Telegraph,* which crosses the sectarian barriers, has a larger readership than that of the two daily morning newspapers, which do not; for purposes of record it is the most useful local newspaper. All three Dublin morning newspapers have offices in Belfast, but only the *Irish Times* has consistently devoted much space to events in Northern Ireland, and some of its reporting has been excellent. British media coverage has been very inconsistent: the interest of the popular press declined as the violence became repetitious, leaving the field to more serious newspapers. The *Observer* and *Times* have taken a close interest in the issue, and the *Sunday Times* has conducted useful, if occasionally flashy, investigations. The most consistent and reliable British coverage has undoubtedly been supplied by the *Guardian.*

Periodicals in Ireland have always struggled to keep their heads above the ground financially, but two are essential references for researchers. *Fortnight,* produced regularly in Belfast between 1970 and 1976, and thereafter with a fitfulness which belies its name, provides an important commentary on events, adopting a liberal stance. The Dublin magazine *Hibernia,* if more unreliable on details, performed a similar function from a republican perspective until its closure in 1980. Occasionally major investigations concerning Northern Ireland have been carried out by *Magill,* which is produced in Dublin.

A strangely underused, and very valuable, source of information are the underground and political newspapers which flourished especially in the early 1970s. These were produced by a wide variety of loyalist, republican, socialist and community organisations in an almost equally wide variety of formats. Some lasted only for a few issues; others have been published regularly for decades—notably the *United Irishman* since 1931; a few transmogrified with bewildering rapidity, closing down to reemerge under another name and format. Fortunately tracks through this complicated minefield have been charted by a number of librarians: the Northern Ireland branch of the Library Association published a catalogue of *Northern Ireland Newspapers 1737-1979* (Adams 1980), with details of where copies can be located. Small-format political papers are not included in this catalogue, but some of the more important of these have been described elsewhere (Gracey and Howard 1971; Howard 1972; *Sunday News* 1981). The most useful guide to alternative newspapers and periodicals, with brief descriptions, was compiled by the Belfast Workers Research group (*Belfast Bulletin* Spring 1979).

It is not possible to consult all these newspapers and periodicals under a single roof. Belfast's Central Library has the fullest collection, but other libraries also have some, and a small number of libraries also have partial collections of political newspapers. Nowhere in Northern Ireland is it possible to examine the back files of British popular newspapers, even in the Belfast offices of these newspapers; for this thankless task it is necessary to visit the British Library newspaper archives at Colindale in London. There are also microfilm copies of, among others, the *Irish Times, Belfast Newsletter, Guardian, Sunday Times, Observer* and London *Times*. Most important, the Linenhall Library in Belfast has produced microfiche copies of political newspapers for the years 1973-75, under the general categories of republican press, loyalist press and socialist press. These include some of the most extreme political expressions to be found in any newspapers, and are a valuable research tool.

Ephemeral and Audio-visual Materials

The production of political newspapers is not the only literary accompaniment to periods of violence and instability. Pamphlets, broadsheets, campaign buttons, posters, graffiti, songs and poetry—these are the ephemera of unrest. They share the qualities of being essential for anyone interested in political and social attitudes, and extraordinarily elusive. By their very nature ephemeral materials are intended to have an immediate impact, and have a short life. Retrospective collection is notoriously difficult, so there is a particular debt to those institutions which had sufficient prescience to build up contemporary collections.

By far the most important of these is the Linenhall Library, which has been operating in some form since 1792. Its Irish collection of historical publications is excellent, and many of these were the ephemera of earlier periods of violence. It was natural, therefore, for the Linenhall to begin a new collection during the Civil Rights campaigns of the mid-1960s. The real strength naturally lies in its Northern Irish ephemera, although Southern material is also well represented. Unfortunately the library's endemic financial problems has prevented the cataloguing of most of the material.

There are other ephemeral collections within Northern Ireland's libraries, although none to compare with the Linenhall's. The Central Library in Belfast started its ephemeral collection in 1977, relying on purchasing existing materials, and is particularly strong on papers relating to the People's Democracy. Its holdings, described in the Library's own *Guide to the Irish and Local Studies department* (1976), include 88 indexed cuttings books from local newspapers since the turn of the century, and an expanding photographic archive. There is also a small uncatalogued collection in the Ulster Museum. Outside Belfast, the New University of Ulster begn assembling ephemera in 1980, and purchased an important collection for 1968 to 1974, which has subsequently been augmented by other purchases and donations; an Archive committee, jointly initiated by the Centre for the Study of Conflict and the University Library, is beginning to build on these holdings. There is also a small, recently catalogued, collection of materials, mainly relating to Londonderry, at NUU's Magee University College campus. The Library of Queen's University Belfast also has a well catalogued collection, which includes a number of foreign items.

In the Irish Republic the largest archive is housed in Trinity College Dublin which, as a copyright deposit library, includes much of the relevant material printed in Britain. Its holdings of Dublin-produced ephemera are also good, although its collection of materials produced north of the border is less comprehensive. The National Library in Dublin also holds some relevant publications.

An increasing demand for audio-visual materials has been largely unsatisfied. Propaganda films aimed at public opinion in Europe and North America have been produced both by the Provisional IRA and by the British government. Television and radio, however, constitute the great bulk of material. On television alone, and not counting news broadcasts, 162 programmes wholly or primarily devoted to Northern Ireland have been identified between 1968 and 1978 (*Belfast Bulletin* 1979). It is not easy to secure access to these programmes. BBC news bulletins on national television, which include items on Northern Ireland, may be consulted in the British Film Archive in London, but programmes produced in Northern Ireland are not normally available to researchers. Nevertheless, exceptions have been made in the past. Apart from these sources, the History Film and Sound Archive at the New University of Ulster includes some valuable sound and visual records.

Politics and Religion

Two of Northern Ireland's political parties—the Official Unionists and the Social Democratic and Labour Party—have been the subjects of books (Harbinson 1973; McAllister 1977); the others await their Boswells. In the meantime, the most useful introductions to the issues and personalities in Northern Irish politics are W. D. Flackes' *Political Directory* (1980) and Rose and McAllister's *United Kingdom Facts* (1982), and there are biographical notes in Farrell (1976) and Harbinson (1973).

The mutations which most Northern Irish political parties have undergone since 1969 are reflected most clearly in the literature which they produce themselves. Curiously, until recently neither of the main unionist parties—the Official Unionist and Democratic Unionist parties—had a regular publication, relying respectively on duplicated local newsheets and on the *Protestant Telegraph* (circulation 7,000), which in fact closely reflected DUP political views; In 1982 both launched new newspapers, the Official Unionist *Unionist '82* (10,000 monthly) and the DUP *Voice of Ulster* (10,000), which replaced the *Protestant Telegraph*. Other parties became conscious of the need for publicity earlier. The Ulster Defence Association has had a monthly magazine since 1972, and recent issues of *Ulster* (13,000) make it possible to examine the process by which the UDA decided to become involved in elections. The largest of the political newspapers, *An Phoblacht* (circulation 44,000) is produced weekly by Sinn Fein and circulates widely outside Northern Ireland. However the Social Democratic and Labour Party has had a much more unsettled history: the *Social Democrat* was printed for a time in the 1970s but by 1982 had been replaced by the twice yearly *SDLP News* (13,000). Straddling the sectarian fence is *Alliance* (formerly *Alliance Bulletin*) which has been produced since the Alliance party was formed in 1971; in 1982 7,000 copies were printed each month.

In addition to these regular publications, most of the parties produce other literature, especially during election campaigns. More to the point, it is now at least theoretically possible to contact most party offices by telephone, an improvement since 1969.

A number of other bodies with a direct concern about the prevalence of violence also produce publications. The Peace People produce *Peace by Peace* (2,000 monthly), and publications have also been issued by Protestant and Catholic Encounter (*Pace Journal*), the Quakers and the Corrymeela Community. *Dawn* (2,000), an Irish journal of non-violence, is produced in Belfast, and issue 38-39 has a description of Irish peace groups since the 1930s.

Clearly the churches also have an interest here, but have published little. *Violence in Ireland* was written by a joint group on social questions, which was appointed by the Catholic hierarchy and the Irish Council of Churches in an attempt to find a cross-confessional approach to community violence. Apart from this, the Catholic church has been responsible for very few publications, though some papers, especially on peace education, have been issued by the Irish Council of Churches. The best guide to publications by the main churches may be found in the bibliography of *Christians in Ulster* (Gallagher and Worrall 1982).

Public Opinion: Elections and Surveys

With three tiers of elected bodies for most of its existence—Westminster, Stormont, and local councils—Northern Ireland is potentially a psephologist's paradise. The reality is different. While it is relatively easy to find the election returns for the twelve Westminster seats, it has been necessary until recently to assemble the results from other elections from unreliable newspaper reports. This problem has been partly resolved by the publication of *Northern Ireland Parliamentary Election Results* (Elliott 1973), a meticulous summary of election results for the Stormont parliament from 1921 until its prorogation in March 1972.

The political controversies of the 1970s rekindled academic and political interest in elections, and some of the more significant elections during this period have been the subject of specific studies: the 1969 Stormont election which saw the eclipse of the old Nationalist party and the emergence of Paisleyism was examined by Boal and Buchanan (1969) for its demographic implications; the 1973 Assembly elections were analysed by both Knight (1974) and Lawrence *et al* (1975), while Knight (1975) and McAllister (1975) published papers on the elections to the 1975 Constitutional Convention. Northern Ireland's first elections to the European parliament, when the entire province comprised the constituency, were described in a book by Elliott (1980). Nor has the activity been confined to academics. The Ulster Unionist party published two papers in 1975, on the 1973 Assembly elections and the 1974 Westminster elections, and on the 1975 Convention elections. The poverty of election studies of the 1960s has been replaced by almost an embarrassment of riches.

Local election returns pose the greatest problems of all, although Elliott has monitored the elections of 1977 and 1981. In most other cases researchers must go to the newspapers for the raw material on local elections.

It is equally difficult to secure access to the raw data from academic and private public opinion surveys, or even to their published results. In only a few cases have findings been published in sufficient detail to allow a proper assessment of methodology, or permit replication. Of these the most important is Rose's 1969 survey (1971), which has also been the basis for follow-up research by Moxon–Browne and others. Other academic surveys have never been fully analysed, and some not even published. A similarly unsatisfactory situation applies to the surveys and polls which have been conducted for the *Belfast Telegraph, Fortnight* and other newspapers.

There is no central depository for such data in Northern Ireland, although the Centre for the Study of Public Policy in Strathclyde keeps a file of public opinion data. John Coakley has built up an archive at the National Institute for Higher Education in Limerick but, with the exception of the Eurobarometer surveys, the survey data there relates exclusively to the Irish Republic. The Social Science Research Council archive at the University of Essex contains relevant materials, but it is necessary to examine its periodic Bulletins to find them. Clearly expense is the main obstacle to establishing and maintaining a data archive for Northern Ireland, which would include both academic research data and the raw material from commercial surveys. Its absence is a major problem which is only likely to be resolved by co-operation between funding bodies and all the institutions of higher education in the province.

Quantifying the Violence

The level of violence since 1969 is undoubtedly the main reason for the subsequent avalanche of research and publications on Northern Ireland, so there has been a constant demand for reliable information on its effects. Such information as is available comes from a variety of primary and secondary sources, but virtually none of them has been accepted universally as indisputable.

Most basic information on the course of the violence comes from the Royal Ulster Constabulary. The Chief Constable's report, published annually since 1970, has an appendix on terrorist crimes, which records, among other statistics, the number of murders, explosions and security incidents. For a more detailed breakdown it is necessary to consult the security statistics which are issued each month by the RUC Press Office.

Beyond these published data, the RUC Press Office occasionally provides additional facilities to what it describes as 'the serious academic researcher who is pursuing a reasonably "benign" thesis'.* Each request is judged on an *ad hoc* basis.

The closeness of the 'information' and 'propaganda' roles implied in this quotation is inevitable during periods of violence, and is equally evident in the activities of the Army Information Office. The importance of this office as a course of information to the press is well illustrated in the observation of Simon Hoggart from the *Guardian*:

> When the British press prints an account of an incident as if it were an established fact, and it is clear that the reporter himself is not on the spot, it is a 99 per cent certainty that it is the army's version that is being given. (Hoggart 1973).

Although security statistics are available from the Army Information Office, they are regarded as 'principally for the use of the press'.* This may help explain why so little of the information has been used by researchers. One exception, however, perhaps explained by the 'benign thesis' assessment, are the four volumes on the British army in Ulster by David Barzilay (1973-81).

A major limitation in the official data is their lack of detail. Although the RUC statistics identify general categories of victims, for example, they do not discriminate between different groups of civilian casualties. Consequently it is not possible from the statistics to analyse the 2,000 plus deaths since 1969 on the basis of religion, or to discover which groups of individuals were responsible for them. Analyses of this sort have been carried out, however, mainly from newspaper files and personal research: Dillon and Lehane tried to explain the patterns of violence and the reasons behind them by classifying the deaths caused by the IRA, Protestant paramilitaries and the British army (Dillon and Lehane 1974). McKeown also examined the groups responsible for fatalities, and the backgrounds of the victims themselves—discovering, for example, that 62 per cent of the casualties who could be classified accurately were 'civilian noncombatants'; he also provides interesting insights into the problems involved in this type of research (McKeown 1977).

The wide variations in the incidence of violence between different regions of Northern Ireland are often underestimated by commentators and researchers. Darby and Williamson (1978) attempted to demon-

* Correspondence with the author, April 27 and April 15 1982.

strate the special distribution of different types of violence by extracting all recorded incidents during an arbitrary sample period for each year from 1969 to 1975; during these periods 72 per cent of deaths and 91 per cent of injuries resulting from civil disorder took place in Belfast or Londonderry. A more systematic study of Schellenberg (1977) further substantiated the uneven pattern of violence in the province.

Some bases for comparing the violence of the 1970s with earlier outbreaks is possible from official reports. A number of Parliamentary papers published since 1969 include data on the civil disturbances. The Cameron report (1969), for example, considered evidence of the long-term and immediate causes of the violence, and the published reports of the Scarman (1972) and Widgery (1972) Tribunals are also important. Transcripts of the evidence taken by the Scarman Tribunal are also available in the Province's two university libraries. These reports, and the newspaper debates accompanying them, provide some basis for comparison with earlier riot reports, notably those into the 1857 and 1866 Belfast riots. The nineteenth century reports include evidence on intimidation and enforced population movement, subjects which have been examined in closer detail during the more recent disturbances (Darby and Morris 1974; Boal, Murray and Poole 1976).

No previous riots have lasted as long as the post-1969 violence. One effect of this is that the violence itself, and its effects, has become a subject for study while still going on. The economic cost of such sustained destruction, a highly difficult research task, has been attempted by Davies and McGurnaghan (1975) and by Rowthorn (1981). The effects of violence on Northern Ireland's social institutions—education, health and social welfare services, policing, housing and community action—was the subject of a book by Darby and Williamson (1978). The papers in the book illustrate the extent to which private research was necessary to fill the gaps left by official statistics, and how many gaps still remain.

Centres for Conflict Study in Ireland

Study of the Irish conflict has been greatly boosted by recent developments within Northern Ireland's two universities. The Centre for the Study of Conflict at the New University of Ulster in Coleraine was formed in 1977, and became a formal part of the university's structure in 1980. Its activities include the development and maintenance of a resource collection on the conflict, the publication of research papers, conferences and seminars. It also provides facilities for visiting researchers, who may apply for honorary fellowships at the Centre. The Centre's emphasis is on comparative and cross-disciplinary research, and there are regular meetings within the university of those involved in conflict studies.

The Institute of Irish Studies at Queen's University Belfast has been in operation since 1970, and offers fellowships to visiting academics. Its interests include Irish literature, languge, history and other branches of Irish studies, including conflict studies.

In the Irish Republic, the School of Irish Studies in Dublin was formed in 1969. While it provides courses in Irish literature, history and culture for students from abroad, it functions mainly at undergraduate and graduate levels, and is not primarily concerned with conflict studies.

Outside Ireland

There has been an extensive, if fluctuating, interest in the Northern Irish conflict outside Ireland—educationalists interested in its segregated school system, churchmen in the apparently denominational basis of the conflict, students of violence and its effects, medical researchers examining the emergency procedures and surgical techniques in its hospitals. Of 151 research projects on the conflict detailed in 1981 (Darby, Dodge and Hepburn), 23 per cent were being carried out in Britain, and 7 per cent outside the British Isles. The findings of many of these researchers are often unknown or ignored in Ireland.

In Britain there are recognisable centres of interest in the conflict, sometimes encouraged by the work of individual researchers. The School of Peace Studies at Bradford University has long had Irish connections, and published *Contemporary Irish Studies* in 1983. Many of the *Studies in Public Policy,* produced from the Centre for the Study of Public Policy at the University of Strathclyde, reflect Richard Rose's interest in Northern Ireland and its politics; the Centre itself maintains a bibliography of United Kingdom politics and a life of machine-readable surveys about public opinion in Northern Ireland. The Centre for Mass Communications Research in Leicester has also initiated research into the media and the conflict (Elliott 1977).

North American interest in Irish matters is more traditional. The American Committee for Irish Studies produces a regular newsheet for its members which contains book reviews, and has also commissioned an important *Guide to Irish Studies in the United States* (Murphy 1978). Its annual conference, and that of the Canadian Committee for Irish

Studies, often includes papers on Northern Ireland, but really demonstrate that the predominant American interest in Ireland is literary or historical. *Eire-Ireland,* the quarterly publication of the Irish American Cultural Institute in St. Paul Minnesota, also has a literary bias, but has published papers on the conflict. A substantial number of American colleges and universities have developed links with Irish universities, and some have built up collections of Irish materials. Most of these are on the east coast, but there is also an interest in Ulster-Scots studies in the Carolinas, and Stanford University in California has an Irish collection. As a general observation, there is no recognisable centre on the conflict in North America, but quite a substantial amount of individual research.

Outside North America, most foreign research on Northern Ireland has come from Europe. The level of interest in Germany between 1969 and 1976 is reflected in the publication of three collections of documents in German, and in the devotion of an entire issue of *Das Parlament,* the German parliamentary paper, to the theme (August 11, 1973). The Dutch churches have supported research into the conflict, and this concern has been maintained. In France, the Centre d'etudes et de recherches irlandaises at the University of Lille is an important centre of study and, though its main focus is literary, there have been articles on the conflict by Richard Deutsch and Pierre Joannon in its journal *Etudes Irlandaises.* Other centres of interest are Rennes and Caen. The Centre d'etudes irlandaises at the Sorbonne has become increasingly concerned with Northern Ireland, and publishes papers on this and related themes. Indeed French academic interest in the conflict shows distinct signs of revival in the 1980s.

Problems of Co-ordination

If the two published Registers of Research into the Irish conflict are accurate reflections of research activity, they record an increase in the number of projects from 92 in 1972 to 153 in 1981. During that decade basic data have become more readily available to researchers; a body of reference has been built up; the growth of interest both inside Northern Ireland and elsewhere is reflected in a variety of associations, centres, study groups and other forms of research collaboration; more subjectively, the depth of scholarship has also improved. These improvements have brought with them both challenges and opportunities. In effect a relatively simple set of primary problems has been replaced by more complex and potentially more serious ones. In 1969 the key obstacle to the pursuit of research was shortage of information; by 1983 the obstacles had become those of co-ordination.

1. Co-ordination of Data

One of the most encouraging changes in conflict research during the 1970s has been the growing recognition of how important it is to collect ephemeral materials at the time of their production, and make them available to researchers. The lone furrow ploughed by the Linenhall library for so many years has become the model for other institutions, some of them developing particular specialisms. For political and social scientists, however, the difficulty of securing access to public opinion data is a continuing frustration. Sidney Elliott's work on election results and the Strathclyde collection of survey data have improved matters, but the need for a data archive to include material from commercial and academic surveys becomes greater as the number of surveys increases. The two major obstacles to the establishment of such an archive are lack of finance, and inter-disciplinary and inter-institutional suspicion. These can only be overcome by an initiative which co-ordinates the interests of the institutions of higher education, libraries and other interested bodies, to establish and maintain a depository for public opinion materials, and to make them readily accessible to researchers. It is an initiative which could only be introduced by a major funding body or, better still, a combination of funding bodies.

2. Co-ordination of Researchers

The passage of time has also underlined the need for more effective co-ordination between researchers in Northern Ireland and those from outside the province. The latter group constituted 38 per cent of the research projects described in the 1981 Register, and there are signs of a growing schism between them and local researchers. The effects of the low level of co-ordination are different for the two parties: for those outside Northern Ireland who are interested in its conflict, the main difficulties are finding out who is doing related research, and how to get access to data; local researchers, on the other hand, are often ignorant of the extent and nature of foreign study. The point may be illustrated by comparing the references in articles and books on the two sides of the Atlantic: publications in Northern Ireland are usually dominated by local references, while in American publications references typically include the more standard Irish references, but also lean heavily on the American literature. Indeed the chauvinism is multilateral rather than bilateral. Apart from the core sources, French researchers rely as exclusively on French references as the American ones do on their own. The danger, therefore, is that a series of independent reference islands will continue to drift apart, each sharing the same agreed set of central references, but ignoring the more specialist work in the other islands. This issue has become more serious as interest in the conflict has grown outside Northern Ireland. Co-ordination between the different parties can only be organised effectively by the institutions within Northern Ireland itself, and the time appears to be right for such an initiative.

3. Co-ordination between Research and Policy

Mutual suspicion between policy-makers and independent researchers is both inevitable and healthy. It is rooted in the intrinsic secrecy of the former and the intrinsic scepticism of the latter. Whatever the justification, the effect has been an unwillingness by policy-makers to trust external research, and a relative failure by researchers to provide decision makers with directions for their policy. Of course this is too sweeping a judgment, but it has more than a grain of truth in relation to conflict research. Equally true, however, is the fact that some researchers, whatever their ideological view of the conflict and the value they place on their own independence, have an important contribution to make in the field of policy. One example is the research which has been carried out into the enforced population movements during the early years of the Troubles, which has important implications for housing and educational planning, as well as monitoring the major demographic changes in some parts of the province. Another is the research into segregated schooling: whatever their views on the issue of integration, almost every serious researcher in the field has reached the conclusion that it is not realisable in the short term; if this is accepted, the question of how relationships between the two separate school systems might be improved then becomes a researchable issue, and one where policy-makers and researchers might usefully find some degree of common ground. Many similar examples might be cited. For them to materialise, some avenue between research and policy-making must be constructed. Of the three forms of co-ordination detailed in this conclusion, this is likely to be the most difficult.

I would like to record my gratitude to the individuals and organizations who provided information about their resources and activities. My particular thanks are due to Stephen Gregory, Tony Hepburn and John Whyte for their advice and suggestions.

Bibliography

Ackroyd, C., Margolis, K., Rosenhead, J. and Shallice, T., *The Technology of Political Control*, London, Penguin, 1977.

Adams, J. R. R., *Northern Ireland Newspapers*, Library Association, N.I. Branch, N.D.

Akenson, D. H., *Education and Enmity: The Control of Schooling in Northern Ireland 1920–50*, London, David & Charles, 1973.

Alcorn, D., 'Who Plans Belfast?' *Scope*, 52, 4–6, 1982.

All Party Anti-Partition Conference, *Discrimination: A Study in Injustice to a Minority*, Dublin, 1954.

Amnesty International, *Report of an Amnesty International Mission to Northern Ireland*, London, Amnesty International, 1978.

Amnesty International, *Report of an Inquiry into Allegations of Ill-treatment in Northern Ireland.* London, Amnesty International, 1975.

Amnesty International, *Report on Torture.* London, Duckworth, 1975.

Annual Abstract of Statistics, London, H.M.S.O.

Arthur, P., *The People's Democracy*, Belfast, Blackstaff, 1974.

Arthur, P., *The Government and Politics of Northern Ireland*, London, Longman, 1980.

Association for Legal Justice, *Torture—The Record of British Brutality in Ireland*, Belfast, ALJ, 1971.

Aunger, E. A., 'Religion and Occupational Class in Northern Ireland', *Economic and Social Review*, 7, 1, 1975.

Baker, S. E., 'Orange and Green: Belfast, 1832–1912' in Dyos, H. J. and Wolff, M., (eds.), *The Victorian city: images and realities*, London, Routledge and Kegan Paul, 1973, 789–814.

Banton, M. P., 'Minority', in G. D. Mitchell (ed.), *A New Dictionary of Sociology*, Routledge and Kegan Paul, London, 1979.

Barrett, M. *Women's Oppression Today*, London, Verso, 1980.

Barritt, D. P. and Carter, C. F., *The Northern Ireland Problem: A Study in Community Relations*, Oxford, Oxford University Press, 1962.

Barrow, J., *Tour Round Ireland*, London, John Murray, 1836.

Barzilay, D., *The British Army in Ulster* (4 Volumes), Belfast, Century Services, 1973–81.

Bax, Mart, *Harpstrings and Confessions*, Assen, Netherlands. Van Gorcum, 1976.

Beckett, J. C. and Glasscock, R. (eds.), *Belfast: The Origin and Growth of an Industrial City*, London, BBC, 1967.

Beckett, J. C., *A Short History of Ireland*, London, 1952.

Beckett, J. C., *The Making of Modern Ireland*, London, Faber, 1966.

Beckett, J. C., *The Ulster Debate*, London, The Bodley Head, 1972.

Belfast Bulletin, 9, 'Still Crazy After all These Years: A Look at the Unionist Local Councils', Belfast, Workers' Research Unit, 1981, 24–33.

Belfast Bulletin, 10, 'Rough Justice: The Law in Northern Ireland', Belfast Workers' Research Unit, 1982.

Belfast Central Library, *Guide to Irish & Local Studies Department*, B.C.L., 1970.

Bell, J., 'Relations of Mutual Aid Between Ulster Farmers', *Ulster Folklike*, 24, 1978, 48–58.

Bell, M., 'Views', *The Listener*, 6 January 1972.

Benn, J. *A Commissioner's Complaint*, New University of Ulster, Coleraine, 1973.

Bennett Committee, *Report of the Committee of Inquiry into Police Interrogation Procedures in Northern Ireland*, Cmnd. 7497, London, HMSO, 1979.

Bew, P. and Norton C., 'The Unionist State and the Outdoor Relief Riots of 1932', *Economic and Social Review*, 10, 3, 1979, 255–65.

Bew, P., Gibbon, P. and Patterson, H., *The State in Northern Ireland*, Manchester, Manchester University Press, 1979.

Bew, P., Gibbon, P. and Patterson, H., 'Some Aspects of Nationalism and Socialism in Ireland, 1968–1978', in Morgan, A. and Purdie, B. (eds.) 1980, 152–171.

Birrell, W. D., Hillyard, P. A. R., Murie, A. S. and Roche, D. J. D., *Housing in Northern Ireland*, London, Centre for Environmental Studies, 1971.

Birrell, W. D. and Murie, A. S., 'Social Policy in Northern Ireland', in Jones, K., (ed.), *The Year Book of Social Policy in Britain*, London, Routledge and Kegan Paul, 1972, 134–155.

Birrell, W. D. and Murie, A. S., *Policy and Government in Northern Ireland: Lessons of Devolution*, Dublin, Gill and Macmillan, 1980.

Black Committee, *Report of the Working Party for Northern Ireland: The Handling of Complaints against the Police*, Cmnd. 6475, Belfast, HMSO, 1976.

Black Review Group, *Report of the Children and Young Persons Review Group*, Belfast, HMSO, 1979.

Black, B., Ditch, J., Morrissey, M. and Steele, R., *Low Pay in Northern Ireland*, London, Low Pay Unit, 1980.

Black, R., 'Flight in Belfast', *Community Forum*, 2.1, 1972, 9–12.

Black, R., Pinter, F. and Ovary, B., Flight: *A Report on Population Movement in Belfast during August 1971*, Northern Ireland Community Relations Commission, Belfast, 1971.

Blacking, J. A. R., and Holy, L., *Situational Determinants of Recruitment in Four Northern Irish Communities*, Report to SSRC; retained by British Library Lending Division, 1978.

Boal, F. W., and Buchanan, R., 'The 1969 Northern Ireland Election', *Irish Geography*, 6, 1, 1969, 22–29.

Boal, F. W., 'Territoriality on the Shankill–Falls Divide in Belfast', *Irish Geography*, 6, 1, 1969, 30–50.

Boal, F. W., 'Social Space in the Belfast Urban Area', N. Stephens and R. E. Glasscock, (eds.), *Irish Geographical Studies*, Belfast, Queen's University, Belfast, 1970.

Boal, F. W., 'Territory and Class: A Study of Two Residential Areas in Belfast', *Irish Geography*, 6, 1973, 229–248.

Boal, F. W., 'The Urban Residential Sub-community: A conflict Interpretation', *Area*, 4, 1972, 164–168.

Boal, F. W., 'Ethnic Residential Segregation', in Herbert, D. T., and Johnston, R. J., (eds.), *Social Areas in Cities, 1. Spatial Processes and Form*, Chichester, John Wiley, 1976, 41–79.

Boal, F. W., 'Residential segregation and mixing in a situation of ethnic and national conflict: Belfast', in Compton, P. A., (ed.), *The contemporary population of Northern Ireland and population-related issues*, Institute of Irish Studies, Queen's University of Belfast, 1981, 58–84.

Boal, F. W., 'Segregation and mixing: space and residence in Belfast', in Boal, F. W., and Douglas, J. N. H., (eds.), *Integration and division: geographical perspectives on the Northern Ireland problem*, London, Academic Press, 1982, 249–280.

Boal, F. W., Murray, R. C., and Poole, M. A., 'Belfast: the urban encapsulation of a national conflict', in Clarke, S. E., and Obler, J. L., (eds.), *Urban ethnic conflict: a comparative perspective*, Institute for Research in Social Science, University of North Carolina, Chapel Hill, 1976, 77–131.

Boehringer, G. H., 'Beyond Hunt: A Policing Policy for Northern Ireland', *Social Studies*, 2, 4, 1973.

Bonnet, Gerald, *The Orange Order*, Paris, unpublished University of Paris III Ph.D. thesis, 1972.

Boserup, A., *Who is the Principal Enemy?* London, Independent Labour Party, 1972.

Bowyer Bell, J., *The Secret Army*, London, Sphere, 1972.

Boyd, A., *Holy War in Belfast*, Tralee, Anvil, 1969.

Boyle, John W., 'The Belfast Protestant Association and the Independent Orange Order, 1901–10', *Irish Historical Studies*, 13, 1962, 113–52.

Boyle, K., 'The 'Minimum Sentences' Act', *Northern Ireland Legal Quarterly*, 21, 4, 1970, 425–441.

Boyle, K., Chesney, R. and Hadden, T., 'Who are the Terrorists?', *New Society*, 36, 1976, 709.

Boyle, K., Hadden, T. and Hillyard, P., *Law and State: The Case of Northern Ireland*, London, Martin Robertson, 1975.

Boyle, K., Hadden, T. and Hillyard, P., *Ten Years on in Northern Ireland: The Legal Control of Political Violence*, London, Cobden Trust, 1980.

Boyle, K. and Hannum, H., 'Ireland in Strasbourg', *Irish Jurist*, 7, New Series, 1972, 329–348.

Bradford, R., *The Last Ditch*, Belfast, Blackstaff, 1981.

Brady, B., Faul, D. and Murray, R., *Corruption of Law: Memorandum to the Gardiner Committee*, Dungannon, 1974.

Brady, B., Faul, D. and Murray, R., *British Army Murder: Leo Norney (17 Years)*, Dungannon, 1975.

Brady, B., Faul, D. and Murray, R., *British Army Terror Tactics, West Belfast, September–October 1976*, Dungannon, 1977.

Browne, V., 'H-Block Crisis: Courage, Lies and Confusion', *Magill*, August 1981.

Buckland, Patrick, *Ulster Unionism and the Origins of Northern Ireland, 1886–1922*, Dublin, Gill and Macmillan, 1973.

Buckland, Patrick, 'The Unity of Ulster Unionism, 1886–1939', *History*, 60, 1975, 211–23.

Buckland, Patrick, *The Factory of Grievances: Devolved Government in Northern Ireland 1921–1939*, Dublin, Gill and Macmillan, 1979.

Buckland, Patrick, *A History of Northern Ireland*, Dublin, Gill and Macmillan. 1981.

Buckley, A. D., *The Gentle People: A Study of a Peaceful Community in Ulster*, Ulster Folk Museum, 1982.

Bunyan, T., *Political Police in Britain*, London, Quartet Books, 1977.

Burton, F., *The Politics of Legitimacy: Struggles in a Belfast Community*, London, Routledge and Kegan Paul, 1978.

Burton, F., 'Ideological Social Relations in Northern Ireland', *British Journal of Sociology*, 30, 1974, 61–80.

Burton, F. and Carlen, P., *Official Discourse: On discourse analysis, government publications, ideology and the state*, London, Routledge and Kegan Paul, 1978.

Byrne, D., *Theorising Northern Ireland*, Unpublished Paper, Department of Sociology and Social Administration, University of Durham, 1980.

Cairncross Review, *Review of Economic and Social Development in Northern Ireland*, Cmd. 564, 1971.

Callaghan, J. *A House Divided*, London, Collins, 1973.

Calvert, H., 'Special Powers Extraordinary', *Northern Ireland Legal Quarterly*, 20, 1, 1969, 1–18.

Cameron Commission, *Disturbances in Northern Ireland*, Cmd. 532, Belfast, HMSO, 1969.

Campaign for Social Justice in Northern Ireland, *The Mailed Fist*, C.S.J., Dungannon, 1971.

Campaign for Social Justice in Northern Ireland, *Northern Ireland: The Plain Truth*, C.S.J., Dungannon, 1969.

Campbell, C. M., *Do We Need a Bill of Rights?*, London, Maurice Temple Smith, 1980.

Campbell, J. J., *Catholic Schools: A Survey of a Northern Ireland Problem*, Dublin, Fallons, 1964.

Carlton, Charles (Ed.), *Bigotry and Blood: Documents on the Ulster Troubles*, Chicago, Nelson-Hall, 1977.

Carroll, W. D. 'Search for Justice in Northern Ireland', New York, *University Journal of International Law and Politics*, 6, 28, 1973, 28–56.

Carty, J., Bibliography of Irish History 1911–1921, Dublin, 1936.

Carty, J., Bibliography of Irish History 1870–1911, Dublin, 1940.

Central Citizens Defence Committee, *Black Paper: The Story of the Police*, Belfast, CCDC, 1973.

Central Statistics Office, *Census of Population of Ireland 1971*, Vol. 9, Religion Stationery Office, Dublin, 1977.

Cockburn, C., *The Local State*, London, Pluto, 1977.

Community Groups Action Committee, *Roads to Destruction*, Belfast, 1980.

Compton Committee, *Report of the Enquiry into Allegations against the Security Forces of Physical Brutality in Northern Ireland arising out of Events on the 9th August, 1971*, CMND. 4823, London, HMSO, 1971.

Compton, P. A., 'Religious Affiliation and Demographic Variability in Northern Ireland', *Transactions of the Institute of British Geographers*, 1, 1976, 433–452.

Compton, P. A., *Northern Ireland: A Census Atlas,* Dublin, Gill and Macmillan, 1978.

Compton, P. A., 'The Other Crucial Factors Why Catholics don't get more Jobs', *Belfast Telegraph*, 28th October, 1980.

Compton, P. A., *The Contemporary Population of Northern Ireland and Population-related Issues*, Institute of Irish Studies, Queen's University of Belfast, 1981.

Compton, P. A., 'The demographic dimension of integration and division in Northern Ireland', in Boal, F. W., and Douglas, J. N. H., (ed.), *Integration and division: geographical perspectives on the Northern Ireland problem*, London, Academic Press, 1982, 75–104.

Compton, P. A., and Boal, F. W., 'Aspects of the Intercommunity Population Balance in Northern Ireland', *Economic and Social Review*, 1, 4, July 1970, 455–476.

Conway, Cardinal William, *Catholic Schools*, Dublin, Catholic Communications Institute of Ireland, 1971.

Coogan, T. P., *Ireland Since the Rising*, London, Pall Mall, 1966.

Coogan, T. P., *On the Blanket: The H-Block Story*, Dublin, Ward River Press, 1980.

Cooper, B., 'Responsibility is the Key to Success', *Fair Employment in Action*, 2, Fair Employment Agency, Belfast, 1979.

Cormack, R., Osborne, R. and Thompson, W., *Into Work? Young School Leavers and the Structure of Opportunity in Belfast,* Belfast, Fair Employment Agency, Research Paper 5, 1980.

Crawford, C., *Long Kesh: An Alternative Perspective*, M.Sc. Degree Thesis, Cranfield Institute of Technology, 1979.

Criminal Law Revision Committee, *Eleventh Report*, Cmnd. 4991, London, HMSO, 1972.

Darby, J., *Register of Research into the Irish Conflict*, Northern Ireland Community Relations Commission Research Paper, Belfast, 1972.

Darby, J., 'History in the School', *Community Forum, 4, 2, 1974.*

Darby, J. and Morris, G., *Intimidation in Housing,* Northern Ireland Community Relations Commission, Belfast, 1974.

Darby, J., *Conflict in Northern Ireland: The Development of a Polarised Community*, Dublin, Gill and Macmillan, 1976.

Darby, J., et al, *Education and Community in Northern Ireland: Schools Apart?,* New University of Ulster, Coleraine, 1977.

Darby, J., 'Northern Ireland: Bonds and Breaks in Education', *British Journal of Educational Studies*, XXVI, 3, 1978, 215–223.

Darby, J. and Williamson, A., (eds.), *Violence and the Social Services in Northern Ireland*, London, Heinemann, 1978.

Dash, S., *Justice Denied: A Challenge to Lord Widgery's Report on Bloody Sunday*, London, NCCL, 1972.

Davies, R. and McGurnaghan, M., 'Northern Ireland, The Economics of Adversity', *National Westminster Bank Review*, May 1975.

Day, M. C., Poole, M. A. and Boal, E. W., 'The Spatial Distribution of Disturbances in Belfast, 1969–71', Paper read at the Conference of Irish Geographers in Coleraine, May 1971 (summarised in Poole, M. A. and Boal, F. W., 'Religious Residential segregation in Belfast in mid-1969: a Multi-Level Analysis', in Clark, B. D. and Gleave, M. B. (eds.), *Social Patterns in Cities*, London, Institute of British Geographers, 1973, 1–40).

Dent, G. I., *The Law of Education in Northern Ireland and the influence of English Law*, Unpublished Ph.D. thesis, University of London, 1965.

De Paor, L., *Divided Ulster*, Middlesex, Penguin, 1970.

Deutsch, R., *Northern Ireland 1921–1974. A Select Bibliography*, Garland, 1975.

Deutsch, R. and Magowan, V., *Northern Ireland: Chronology of Events* (3 Volumes) Belfast, Blackstaff, 1973–75.

Devlin, B., *The Price of my Soul*, London, Pan, 1969.

Devlin, P., *The Fall of the Executive*, Belfast, Author, 1975.

Devlin, P., 'The Politics of Class', *Left Perspectives*, 1, 3, 1981, 20–23.

Dickey, A., 'Anti-Incitement Legislation in Britain and Northern Ireland', *New Community*, 1, 2, 1972, 133–128.

Digest of Statistics, Belfast, H.M.S.O., Annual.

Dillon, M. and Lehane, D., *Political Murder in Northern Ireland*, London, Penguin, 1973.

Diplock Commission, *Report of the Commission to consider Legal Procedures to deal with Terrorist Activities in Northern Ireland*, CMND. 5185, London, HMSO, 1972.

Ditch, J. and Morrissey, M., 'Recent Developments in Northern Ireland's Social Policy', in Brown, M., Baldwin, S. (eds.) *The Year Book of Social Policy in Britain 1979*, London, Routledge and Kegan Paul, 1979.

Ditch, J. and McWilliams, M., *The Supplementary Benefits System in Northern Ireland, 1980–1981*, Belfast, Northern Ireland Consumer Council, 1982.

Douglas, J. N. H. and Boal, F. W., 'The Northern Ireland Problem', in Boal, F. W. and Douglas, J. N. H., (eds.), *Integration and Division: Geographical Perspectives on the Northern Ireland Problem*, London, Academic Press, 1982, 1–18.

Dowling, K., *Interface Ireland*, London, Barrie and Jenkins, 1979.

Downing, J., *The Media Machine*, London, Pluto, 1980.

Dudley Edwards, R., *An Atlas of Irish History*, London, Methuen, 1973.

Eager, A. R., *A Guide to Irish Bibliographical Material*, London, Library Association, 1980.

Easthope, G., 'Religious War in Northern Ireland', *Sociology*, 10, 1976, 427–450.

Economic and Social Research Institute, *Register of Current Social Science Research in Ireland*, Dublin, E.S.R.I., Occasional.

Egan, B. and McCormack, V., *Burntollet*, London, LRS Publishers, 1969.

Elliott, P., 'Reporting Northern Ireland' in O'Halloran, J. et al., (eds.), *Ethnicity and the Media*, Paris, UNESCO, 1977.

Elliott, P., Murdock, G. and Schlesinger, P., *The State and 'Terrorism' on British Television*, Paper delivered to Festival Dei Popoli, Florence, Italy, 1981.

Elliott, Sydney, *Northern Ireland Parliamentary Election Results, 1921–72*, Chichester, Political Reference Publications, 1973.

Elliott, Sydney and Smith, F. J., *The Northern Ireland Local Election Results of 1977,* Belfast, Queen's University of Belfast, 1977.

Elliott, Sydney, *The Northern Ireland local government elections 1981*, Queen's University Belfast, 1981.

European Commission of Human Rights, *Ireland against the United Kingdom, Application No. 5310/71, Report of the Commission* (Adopted 25 January, 1976) Strasbourg, 1976.

European Commission of Human Rights, *McFeeley v United Kingdom, Application No. 8317/78*, (Partial Decision, adopted 15 May 1980), Strasbourg, 1980.

Evason, E., *Family Poverty in Northern Ireland*, London, Child Poverty Action Group, 1978.

Evason, E., *Ends That Won't Meet*, London, Child Poverty Action Group, 1980.

Fabian Society, *Emergency Powers: A Fresh Start*, London, Fabian Society, 1972.

Fahy, P. A., 'Some Political Behaviour Patterns and Attitudes of Roman Catholic Priests in a Rural Part of Northern Ireland', *Economic and Social Review*, 3, 1, 1971, 1–24.

Fair Employment Agency, *First Report of the FEA for Northern Ireland, 1 September 1976–31 March 1977*, Belfast, FEA, 1978a.

Fair Employment Agency, *An Industrial and Occupational Profile of the Two Sections of the Population in Northern Ireland*, Belfast, FEA, Research Paper 1, 1978b.

Fair Employment Agency, *Second Report of the FEA for Northern Ireland, 1 April 1977–31 March 1978*, Belfast, FEA, 1979.

Fair Employment Agency, *Third Report of the FEA for Northern Ireland, 1 April 1978–31 March 1979*, Belfast, FEA, 1980.

Fair Employment Agency, *Fourth Report of the FEA for Northern Ireland, 1 April 1979–31 March 1980*, Belfast, FEA, 1981.

Fair Employment Agency, *Sixth Report of the FEA for Northern Ireland, 1 April 1981–31 March 1982*, Belfast, FEA, 1982a.

Fair Employment Agency, *A Final Report of the Fair Employment Agency for Northern Ireland into the Employment Practices of the Northern Ireland Electricity Service*, Belfast, FEA, 1982b.

Fair Employment Agency, *Engineering Investigation and Report*, Unpublished, Belfast, FEA, n.d.

Farrell, M., *Northern Ireland: the Orange State*, London, Pluto, 1976.

Farrell, M. and McCullough, P., *Behind the Wire*, Belfast, People's Democracy, 1974.

Farrell, Michael, *Arms Outside the Law: Problems of the Ulster Special Constabulary 1920–22*, Glasgow, Unpublished University of Strathclyde Msc. dissertation, 1978.

Farrell, M., 'The Establishment of the Ulster Constabulary', in Morgan, A. and Purdie, B., *Ireland: Divided Nation Divided Class*, London, Irish Links, 1980.

Faul, D. and Murray, R., *British Army and Special Branch RUC Brutalities, December 1971–72*, Cavan, 1972.

Faul, D. and Murray, R., *Whitelaw's Tribunals: Long Kesh Internment Camp, November 1972–January 1973*, Dungannon, 1973.

Faul, D. and Murray, R., *Flames of Long Kesh*, Belfast, 1974.

Faul, D. and Murray, R., *Castlereagh File*, Belfast, 1978.

Faul, D. and Murray, R., *The British Dimension: Brutality, Murder and Legal Publicity in Northern Ireland*, Dungannon, 1980.

Faulkner, B. *Memoirs of a Statesman*, London, Weidenfeld and Nicolson, 1978.

Firth, G., 'Polar Press', *Fortnight*, 14 May 1971.

Fisk, R., *The Point of No Return: The Strike which broke the British in Ulster*, London, Deutsch, 1975.

Flackes, W. F., *Northern Ireland: A Political Directory*, Dublin, Gill & Macmillan, 1980.

Foy, Michael, *The Ancient Order of Hibernians: An Irish Political-Religious Pressure Group, 1884–1976*, Belfast, Unpublished Queen's University MA Thesis, 1976.

Gallagher, E, and Worrall, F., *Christians in Ulster 1968–1980*, Oxford, 1982.

Gallagher, F., *The Indivisible Island*, London, Gollancz, 1957.

Gardiner Committee, *Report of a Committee to consider, in the Context of Civil Liberties and Human Rights, Measures to Deal with Terrorism in Northern Ireland*, CMND. 5847, London, 1975.

Geraghty, T., *Who Dares Wins: The Story of the SAS 1950–1980*, London, Fontana, 1980.

Gibbon, P., 'Some Basic Problems of the Contemporary Situation', in Miliband, R. and Saville, J. (eds.), *The Socialist Register*, London, Merlin, 1977, 81–87.

Gibson, N. (Ed.), *Economic and Social Implications of the Political Alternatives that my be Open to Northern Ireland*, Coleraine, New University of Ulster, 1974.

Gibson, N., 'The Northern Problem: Religious or Economic or What?', *Community Forum*, 1, 1, 1971, 2–5.

Government of Northern Ireland, *Census of Population 1971*, Preliminary Report, Belfast, HMSO., 1971.

Government of Northern Ireland: Department of Commerce, *Facts and Figures on the Northern Ireland Economy*, Survey Prepared for the Department of Commerce, October 1980.

Government of Northern Ireland: Department of Education, *Northern Ireland Education Statistics,* Annual.

Government of Northern Ireiand: Department of Finance, *Northern Ireland Sources of Social and Economic Research*, Policy, Planning and Research Unit, No Date.

Government of Northern Ireland: Department of Finance, *Register of Research*, Policy, Planning and Research Unit, 1973.

Government of Northern Ireland: Department of Manpower Services, *Northern Ireland Unemployment Figures*, D.M.S., Monthly.

Government of Northern Ireland, *Proposals for Further Discussion*, Cmd. 7950, London, HMSO., July 1980.

Gracey, J. and Howard, P., 'Northern Ireland Political Literature: 1968–70', *Irish Booklore*, 1, 1, 1971.

Graham, John, *The Consensus Forming Strategy of the Northern*

Ireland Party, 1949–68, Belfast, Unpublished Queen's University MSSc Thesis, 1972.

Greer, D., 'The Admissibility of Confessions Under the Northern Ireland (Emergency Provisions) Act', *Northern Legal Quarterly*, 31, 3, 1980, 205–238.

Greer, J., *A Questioning Generation*, Belfast, Church of Ireland Board of Education, 1972.

Griffiths, H., *Community Development in Northern Ireland: A Case Study in Agency Conflict*, Coleraine, New University of Ulster, 1974.

Griffiths, H., 'Community Reaction and Voluntary Involvement', In Darby, J. and Williamson, A. (eds.), *Violence and the Social Services in Northern Ireland*, London, Heinemann, 1978, 165–194.

Hadden, T. and Hillyard, P., *Justice in Northern Ireland: A Study in Social Confidence*, London, Cobden Trust, 1973.

Hall Report, *Report of the Joint Working Party on the Economy of Northern Ireland*, Cmnd. 1835, 1962.

Harbinson, John F., *A History of the Northern Ireland Labour Party, 1884–1949*, Belfast, Unpublished Queen's University MSc. Thesis, 1966.

Harbinson, John F., *The Ulster Unionist Party*, 1882–1972, Belfast, Blackstaff, 1973.

Harbinson, R., *No Surrender*, London, Faber & Faber, 1960.

Harris, R., *Social Relations and Attitudes in a Northern Ireland Rural Area: Ballybeg*, University of London, Unpublished M.A. thesis, 1954.

Harris, R., 'The Selection of Leaders in Ballybeg, Northern Ireland', *Sociological Review (N.S.)*, 8, 1961, 137–149.

Harris, R., *Prejudice and Tolerance in Ulster: A Study of Neighbours and 'Strangers' in a Border Community*, Manchester, Manchester University Press, 1972.

Harris, R., 'Religious Change on Rathlin Island', *Pace*, 6, 1974, 11–16.

Harris, R., 'Community Relationships in Northern and Sourthern Ireland: A Comparison and a Paradox', *Sociological Review*, 27, 1979, 41–53.

Harris, R., 'Myth and Reality in Northern Ireland: An Anthropological View', in McWhirter, L. and Trew, K., (Eds.) *The Northern Ireland Conflict: Myth and Reality; Social and Political Perspectives*, Ormskirk, Planned Publication Date 1983.

Harvey, R., *Diplock and the Assault on Civil Liberties*, London, Haldane Society, 1981.

Hayes, M., *Community Relations and the Role of the Community Relations Commission in Northern Ireland*, London, Runnymede Trust, 1971.

Hepburn, A. C., (ed.) *The Conflict of Nationality in Modern Ireland*, 1980.

Hermle, R., (ed.), *Konflikt und Gewalt: Texte Zur Lage in Nordirland, 1972–74*, Munich, Kaiser, 1976.

Hewitt, C., 'Majorities and Minorities: A Comparative Survey of Ethnic Violence', *Annals of the American Academy of Political and Social Science*, 433, September 1977, 150–160.

Hewitt, C., 'Catholic Grievances, Catholic Nationalism and Violence in Northern Ireland During the Civil Rights Period: A Reconsideration', *British Journal of Sociology*, 32, 3, 1981, 362–380.

Hezlet, B., *Fermanagh 'B' Specials*, London, Tom Stacey, 1972.

Hickey, D. J. and Doherty, J. E., *A Dictionary of Irish History Since 1800*, Dublin, Gill & Macmillan, 1980.

Hillyard, P., 'From Belfast to Britain: The Royal Commission on Criminal Procedure', in *Law, Politics and Justice*, London, Routledge and Kegan Paul, 1981.

Hillyard, P., *The Media Coverage of Crime and Justice in Northern Ireland*, Cropwood Conference Paper, 1982.

Hoggart, S., 'The Army PR Men in Northern Ireland', *New Society*, 11 Actober, 1973.

Holland, J., *Too Long a Sacrifice: Life and Death in Northern Ireland Since 1969*, N.Y., Dodd, Mead and Co., 1981.

Howard, P., 'The Paper War', (Three Articles), *Fortnight*, 11 January, 25 January, 8 February 1974.

Howard, R., *The Movement of Manufacturing Industry in the United Kingdom, 1945–65*, HMSO, 1968.

Hunt Committee, *Report of the Advisory Committee on Police in Northern Ireland*, Cmd. 535, Belfast, HMSO, 1969.

Hull, R. H., *The Irish Triangle: Conflict in Northern Ireland*, Princeton, N.J., Princeton University Press, 1976.

Information on Ireland, *The British Media and Ireland*, London, Information on Ireland, 1980.

Institute of Irish Studies, *Theses Related to Ireland*, Belfast, Institute of Irish Studies, Queen's University Belfast, 1968.

Irish Council of Churches, *Violence in Ireland*, Dublin, Christian Journals Ltd., 1976.

Irish Historical Studies, *Writings on Irish History*, Microfiche, 1983.

Isles, K. S. and Cuthbert, N., *Economic Survey of Northern Ireland*, Cmd. 475, Belfast, HMSO, 1957.

Jackson, H., *The Two Irelands: A Dual Study of Inter-group Tensions*, London, Minority Rights Group, London, 1971.

Jackson, J. A., *The Irish in Britain*, London, Routledge and Kegan Paul, 1963.

Jackson, T. A., *Ireland Her Own*, London, Lawrence and Wishart, 1947.

Jenkins, R., 'Doing a Double', *New Society*, 44, 1978, 121.

Jenkins, R., 'Thinking and Doing: Towards a Model of Cognitive Practice', in Holy, L. and Stuchlik, M., (eds.), *The Structure of Folk Models*, London, Academic Press, 1981a.

Jenkins, R., *Young People, Education and Work in a Belfast Housing Estate*, Cambridge University, Ph.D. Thesis, 1981b.

Johnston, E., *Irish History: A Selected Bibliography*, Historical Association Pamphlet, 73, 1969.

Jones, E., 'The Distribution and Segregation of Roman Catholics in Belfast', *Sociological Review*, 4, 1956, 167–189.

Jones, E. and Eyles, J., *An Introduction to Social Geography*, Oxford, Oxford University Press, 1977.

Kennedy, S. and Birrell, W. D., 'Housing', in Darby, J. and Williamson, A. (eds.), *Violence and the Social Services in Northern Ireland*, London, Heinemann, 1978, 98–116.

Kirk, D., 'The Field of Demography', in Sills, D. L. (ed.), *International Encyclopaedia of the Social Sciences*, 12, Macmillan, 1968, 342–349.

Kirk, T., *The Religious Distribution in Lurgan*, Queen's University Belfast, Unpublished M.A. Thesis, 1967.

Kitson, F., *Low Intensity Operations: Subversion, Insurgency and Peace-keeping*, London, Faber and Faber, 1971.

Knight, J., *Northern Ireland: The Elections of 1973*, London, Arthur McDougall Fund, 1974.

Knight, J., *Northern Ireland: The Election of the Constitutional Assembly*, London, Arthur McDougall Fund, 1975.

Krausz, E., *Ethnic Minorities in Britain*, London, MacGibbon and Kee, 1971.

Laver, Michael, (1976), *The Theory and Practice of Party Competition: Ulster, 1973–75*, London, Sage Contemporary Political Sociology Series 06–014, 1976.

Law Enforcement Commission, *Report to the Minister for Justice of Ireland and the Secretary of State for Northern Ireland*, Prl. 3832, Dublin, Stationery Office, 1974.

Law Officers' Department, (1974), *Prosecutions in Northern Ireland: A Study of Facts*, London, HMSO, 1974.

Lawrence, R. J. et al, *The Northern Ireland General Election of 1973*, London, HMSO, 1975.

Lee, J., *Irish Historiography 1970–1979*, Cork, Cork University Press, 1981.

Leyton, E., 'Conscious Models and Dispute Regulation in an Ulster Village', *Man* (N.S.), 1, 1966, 534–542.

Leyton, E., 'Spheres of Inheritance in Aughnaboy', *American Anthropologist*, 72, 1970a, 1378–1388.

Leyton, E., 'Death and Authority in the Fishing Authority', *Resurgence, 3, 1970b, 12*–13.

Leyton, E., 'Opposition and Integration in Ulster', *Man* (N.S.), 9, 1974a, 185–198.

Leyton, E., 'Irish Friends and 'Friends': the Nexus of Friendship, Kinship and Class in Aughnaboy', in Leyton, E. (ed.), *The Compact: Selected Dimensions of Friendship*, St. John's Newfoundland, Institute of Social and Economic Research, Memorial University, 1974b.

Leyton, E., *The One Blood: Kinship and Class in an Irish Village*, St. John's Newfoundland, Institute of Social and Economic Research, Memorial University, Newfoundland Social and Economic Studies, 15, 1975.

Leyton, E., 'Studies in Irish Social Organisation: the State of the Art', Dublin, *Social Studies*, 6, 1977.

Lieberson, S., 'An Asymmetrical Approach to Segregation', in Peach, C., Robinson, V. and Smith, S. (eds.), *Ethnic Segregation in Cities*, London, Croom Helm, 1981, 61–82.

Lijphart, A., 'The Northern Ireland Problem: Cases, Theories, and Solutions', *British Journal of Political Science*, 5, 1975, 83–106.

Lindsay, K., *The British Intelligence Service in Action*, Dundalk, Dundrod, 1980.

Linenhall Library, *Northern Ireland Political Literature* 1973–74 (2 vols), 1975 (1 vol), Irish Microform, ND.

Lowry, D. R., 'Legislation in a Social Vacuum: the Failure of the Fair Employment (Northern Ireland) Act 1976 and Alternative Solutions', *New York University Journal of International Law and Politics*, 9, 3, 1977, 345–388.

Lyons, F. S. L., *Ireland Since the Famine*, London, Weidenfeld & Nicholson, 1971.

McAllister, Ian, *The 1975 Northern Ireland Convention Election*, Glasgow, Survey Research Centre Occasional Paper No. 14, 1975a.

McAllister, Ian, 'Political Opposition in Northern Ireland: The National Democratic Party, 1965–70', *Economic and Social Review*, 6, 3, 1975b, 353–66.

McAllister, Ian, *The Northern Ireland Social Democratic and Labour Party*, London, Macmillan, 1977.

McAllister, Ian and Wilson, Brian, 'Bi-confessionalism in a Confessional Party System: The Northern Ireland Alliance Party', *Economic and Social Review*, 9, 3, 1978, 207–25.

McAllister, Ian and Nelson, Sarah, 'The Modern Development of the Northern Ireland Party System', *Parliamentary Affairs*, 32, 3, 1979, 279–316.

McCafferty, N., *The Armagh Women*, Dublin, Co-op Books, 1981.

McCann, E., *War and an Irish Town*, Middlesex, Penguin, 1974.

McConnell, J., 'The Michael Farrell Case: Discrimination in Belfast's College of Technology', *Hibernia*, 21 December, 1978.

McCracken, J. L., 'The Political Scene in Northern Ireland, 1926–37' in McManus, F. (ed.), *The Years of the Great Test, 1926–39*, Dublin, Mercier, 1967.

McCrudden, C., *A Report to the Fair Employment Agency*, unpublished, February 1982.

McElligott, T., *Intermediate Education and the Work of the Commissioners 1870–1922*, Trinity College Dublin, Unpublished M.Litt. Thesis, 1969.

McFarlane, W. G., *Gossip and Social Relations in a Northern Irish Village*, Queen's University, Belfast, Unpublished Ph.D., Thesis, 1978.

McFarlane, W. G., ''Mixed' Marriages in Ballycuan, Northern Ireland', *Journal of Comparative Family Studies*, 10, 1979, 191–205.

McFarlane, W. G., 'Social Life in Northern Ireland', *Social Science Research Council Newsletter*, 42, 1980, 12–13.

McKeown, M., *The First Five Hundred*, Belfast, Irish News Ltd., 1972.

McKeown, M., 'Considerations on the Statistics of Violence', *Fortnight*, 151, July 1977, 4–5.

McGuffin, J., *The Guineapigs*, Middlesex, Penguin, 1974.

McGuffin, J., *Internment*, Tralee, Anvil Press, 1973.

McMahon, B. M. E., 'The Impaired Asset: A Legal Commentary on the Report of the Widgery Tribunal', *The Human Context*, VI, 3, 1974, 681–699.

McMinn, J., 'Contemporary Novels on the 'Troubles'', *Etudes Irlandaises*, 5, 1980.

Magee, J., 'The Teaching of Irish History in Irish Schools', Belfast, *The Northern Teacher*, 10, 1, 1970.

Magee, J., *Northern Ireland, Crisis & Conflict*, London, Routledge and Kegan Paul, 1974.

Maltby, A. *The Government of Northern Ireland*, Shannon, Irish University Press, 1974.

Mansbach, R. (ed.) *Northern Ireland: Half a Century of Partition*, New York, Facts on File, 1973.

Marquand, J., *Measuring the Effects and Costs of Regional Incentives*, London, Government Economic Service Working Paper 32, 1980.

Matthew Report, *Belfast Regional Survey and Plan*, Cmd. 451, Belfast, HMSO., 1963.

Micholas, E., *International Terrorism: A Chronology of Events, 1968–1979*, London, Aldwych, 1980.

Miller, David W., *Queen's Rebels*, Dublin, Gill and Macmillan, 1978.

Miller, R., *Attitudes to Work in Northern Ireland*, Belfast, Fair Employment Agency, Research Paper 2, 1978.

Miller, R., *Occupational Mobility of Protestants and Roman Catholics in Northern Ireland*, Belfast, Fair Employment Agency, Research Paper 4, 1979.

Mitchell, J. K., 'Social Violence in Northern Ireland', *Geographical Review*, 69, 1979, 179–201.

Mogey, J. McF., *Rural Life in Northern Ireland: Five Regional Studies made for the Northern Ireland Council of Social Services*, London, Oxford University Press, 1947.

Mogey, J. McF., 'The Community in Northern Ireland', *Man*, 48, 1948, 85–87.

Moloney, E., 'Dirty Tricks in the North's Fair Employment Agency', Dublin, *Hibernia*, 26 July 1979.

Monaghan, C. M., *Coping with Mixed Marriage among a Group of Professional People in Belfast*, Queen's University Belfast, Unpublished B.A. dissertation, 1980.

Moody, T. W. (ed.) *Irish Historiography 1936–70*, Dublin, Irish Committee of Historical Studies, 1971.

Morgan, A., 'Socialism in Ireland: Red, Green and Orange', in Morgan, A. and Purdie, B. (eds.), 1980, 172–225.

Morgan, A. and Purdie, B. (eds.), *Ireland: Divided Nation, Divided Class*, London, Ink Links, 1980.

Morrisey, M. and Ditch, J., 'Social Policy Implications of Emergency Legislation in Northern Ireland', *Critical Social Policy*, 1, 3, 1982, 19–39.

Moxon-Browne, E., 'The Water and the Fish: Public Opinion and the Provisional IRA in Northern Ireland', in Wilkinson, P. (ed.), *British Perspectives on Terrorism*, London, George Allen and Unwin, 1981.

Moxon-Browne, E., 'Terrorism in Northern Ireland: The Case of the Provisional IRA', in Lodge, J. (ed.), *Terrorism: A Challenge to the State*, London, Martin Robertson, 1981.

Murphy, M., *Irish Studies in the United States*, ACIS, 1979.

Murray Inquiry, *Report into Proposed Compulsory Acquisition of Land at Maghaberry for Prison Accommodation*, Belfast, HMSO, 1975.

Murray, D. and Darby, J., *The Vocational Aspirations and Expectations of School Leavers in Londonderry and Strabane*, Belfast, Fair Employment Agency, Research Paper 6, 1980.

Murray, D., *The Character and Culture of Protestant and Catholic Primary Schools in Northern Ireland*, New University of Ulster, Unpublished Ph.D. Dissertation, 1983.

Murray, R., 'Political Violence in Northern Ireland 1969–1977', in Boal, F. W. and Douglas, J. N. H. (ed.), *Integration and Division: Geographical Perspectives on the Northern Ireland Problem*, London, Academic Press, 1982, 309–331.

Murray, R., and Boal, F. W., 'The Social Ecology of Urban Violence', in Herbert, D. T. and Smith, D. M. (eds.), *Social Problems and the City: Geographical Perspectives*, Oxford, Oxford University Press, 1979, 139–157.

Murray, R. C. and Boal, F. W., 'Forced Residential Mobility in Belfast 1969–1972', in Harbison, J. and Harbison, J. (Eds.), *A Society under Stress: Children and Young People in Northern Ireland*, Somerset, Open Books, 1980, 25–30.

Murray, R., Boal, F. W. and Poole, M. A., 'Psychology and the Threatening Environment', *Architectural Psychology Newsletter*, 5, 4, December 1975, 30–34.

Nairn, T., *The Break-up of Britain: Crisis and Neo-Nationalism*, London, New Left Books, 1977.

National Council for Civil Liberty, *The RUC: A Report on Complaints Procedure*, London, NCCL, 1975.

National Council for Civil Liberty, *The Special Powers Act of Northern Ireland*, (First Edition, 1935), London, NCCL, 1972.

Nelson, S., 'Discrimination in Northern Ireland: The Protestant Response', in Veenhoven, W. A. (ed.), *Case Studies on Human Rights and Fundamental Freedoms: A World Survey*, The Hague, Martinus Nijhoff, 1976a, 404–429.

Nelson, S., 'Developments in Protestant Working Class Politics', Dublin, *Social Studies*, 5, 1976b, 202–224.

Nelson, S., *Ulster's Uncertain Defenders: A Study of Protestant Politics, 1969–75*, University of Strathclyde, Ph.D. Thesis, 1980.

Northern Ireland Council for Educational Research, *Register of Research in Education*, Belfast, NICER, Occasional.

Northern Ireland Development Programme 1970–75, Report of the three Consultants, Professor T. Wilson, Professor J. Parkinson and Professor Sir Robert Matthew, HMSO, 1970.

Northern Ireland Development Programme, 1970–75, Government Statement, Cmd. 547, Belfast, HMSO, 1970.

Northern Ireland Police Authority, *The First Three Years, 1970–73*, Belfast, NIPA, 1973.

Northern Ireland General Register Office, *Census of Population 1971: Religion Tables*, Belfast, HMSO, 1975a.

Northern Ireland General Register Office, *Census of Population 1971: Summary Tables*, Belfast, HMSO, 1975b.

Northern Ireland General Register Office, *Census of Population 1971: County Reports*, Belfast, HMSO, 1973–4.

Northern Ireland Housing Executive, *Seventh Annual Report: 1st April 1977 to 31st March 1978*, Belfast, NIHE, 1978.

Northern Ireland Information Service, *Facts at Your Fingertips*, Belfast, NIIS, Irregular.

O'Boyle, M. P., 'Torture and Emergency Powers under the European Convention on Human Rights', *American Journal of International Law*, 71, 4, 1977.

O'Donnell, E. F., *Northern Irish Stereotypes*, Dublin, College of Industrial Relations, 1977.

O'Dowd, L. and Tomlinson, M., 'Urban Politics in Belfast: Two Case Studies', *International Journal of Urban and Regional Research*, 4, 1, 1980, 72–95.

O'Dowd, L., Rolston, B. and Tomlinson, B., *Northern Ireland Between Civil Rights and Civil War*, London, CSE Books, 1980.

O'Dowd, L., *Intellectuals on the Road to Modernity: Aspects of Social Ideology in the 1950s*, Paper delivered to Sociology Association of Ireland Annual Conference, Ballyvaughan, Co. Clare, April 1982.

O'Fearghail, S., *Law (?) and Orders: The Belfast Curfew of 3rd–5th July, 1970*, Belfast, Central Citizens' Defence Committee, 1970.

O'Hearn, D., 'Accumulation and the Irish Crisis', *Monthly Review*, 32, 10, 1981, 31–44.

Oliver, J., *Working at Stormont*, Dublin, Institute of Public Administration, 1978.

O'Neill, T., *Ulster at the Crossroads*, London, Faber, 1969.

O'Neill, T., *Autobiography*, London, Hart-Davis, 1972.

Osborne, R. and Murray, R., *Educational Qualifications and Religious Affiliation in Northern Ireland*, Belfast, Fair Employment Agency, Research Paper 3, 1978.

Osborne, R. and Miller, R., 'Why Catholics Don't Get More Jobs—A Reply', *Belfast Telegraph*, 14 November 1980.

Osborne, R., 'Fair Employment in Northern Ireland', *New Community*, 8, 1–2, 1980, 129–137.

Osborne, R., 'Voting Behaviour in Northern Ireland 1921–1977', in Boal, F. W., Douglas, J. N. H., (ed.), *Integration and Division: Geographical Pespectives on the Northern Ireland Problem*, London, Academic Press, 1982, 137–166.

Palley, C., 'Evolution, Disintegration and Possible Reconstruction of the Northern Ireland Constitution', *Anglo–American Law Review*, 1, 1972.

Park, A. T., 'An Analysis of Human Fertility in Northern Ireland', *Journal of Statistical and Social Inquiry Society of Ireland*, 21, 1, 1962–63, 1–13.

Parker Committee, *Report of the Committee of Privy Counsellors Appointed to consider Authorised Procedures for the Interrogation of Persons Suspected of Terrorism*, Cmnd. 4901, HMSO, 1972.

Patterson, H., 'Review of Burton 1978', *Sociological Review*, 27, 1979, 582–583.

Paxton, J. (ed.), *The Stateman's Yearbook: Statistical and Historical Annual of the States of the World for the Year 1981–1982*, London, Macmillan, 1981.

Peach, C., '*Introduction: The Spatial Analysis of Ethnicity and Class*', in Peach, C. (ed.), *Urban Social Segregation*, London, Longman, 1975, 1–17.

Pollack, A., 'Overhaul of Northern Ireland Job Agency Urged', *Irish Times*, 29 March, 1982.

Pollock, Laurence and McAllister, Ian, *A Bibliography of United Kingdom Politics: Scotland, Wales and Northern Ireland*, Glasgow, University of Strathclyde Studies in Public Policy, III, 1980.

Poole, M. A., 'Riot Displacement in 1969', *Fortnight*, 22, 6–31 August 1971.

Poole, M. A., 'Religious Residential Segregation in Urban Northern

Ireland', in Boal, F. W. and Douglas, J. N. H., (eds.), *Integration and Division: Geographical Perspectives on the Northern Ireland Problem*, London, Academic Press, 1982, 281-308.

Poole, M. A. and Boal, F. W., 'Religious Residential Segregation in Belfast in mid-1969: A Multi-level Analysis', in Clarke, B. D. and Gleave, M. B. (eds.), *Social Patterns in Cities*, London, Institute of British Geographers, 1973, 1-40.

Poulantzas, N., *State, Power and Socialism*, London, NLB, 1978.

Pounce, R. J., *Industrial Movement in the United Kingdom, 1966-75*, London, HMSO, 1981.

Probert, B., *Beyond Orange and Green: The Political Economy of the Northern Ireland Crisis*, London, Zed Press, 1978.

Quigley Review Team, *Economic and Industrial Strategy for Northern Ireland, Report by Review Team*, Belfast, HMSO, 1976.

Radzinowicz, L. and Hood, R., 'The Status of Political Prisoners in England: The Struggle for Recognition', *Virginia Law Review Association*, 65, 8, 1979, 1421-1481.

Rauche, E., 'The Compatability of the Detention of Terrorists Order', *New York Journal of Internal Law and Politics*, 6, 1, 1979.

Red Cross, *Report on the Visits Carried out by Delegates from the international Committee of the Red Cross to Places of Detention in Northern Ireland, July 1973*, Geneve, Comite International de la Croix-Rouge, 1973.

Regional Physical Development Strategy 1975-1995, Discussion Paper, London, HMSO, 1975.

Research Services Limited, *Readership Survey of Northern Ireland*, London, RSL, 1970.

Revolutionary Communist Group, 'Ireland: Imperialism in Crisis, 1968-1978', *Revolutionary Communist*, 8, 1978, 5-33.

Revolutionary Communist Tendency, 'British Imperialism and the Irish Crisis', *Revolutionary Communist Papers*, 2, 1978, 3-20.

Roberts, David, A., 'The Orange Order in Ireland: A Religious Institution?', *British Journal of Sociology*, 22, 3, 1971, 269-282.

Robinson, A., *A Social Geography of Londonderry*, Queen's University Belfast, M.A. Thesis, 1967.

Robinson, A., 'Education and Sectarian Conflict in Northern Ireland', *New Era*, 52, 1, January 1971.

Roche, D. and Williamson, A., *Register of Recent Research into Mental Illness and Handicap in Ireland*, Coleraine, N.U.U., 1977.

Rolston, B., 'Reforming the Orange State: Problems of the Northern

Ireland Community Relations Commission', in Downing, J., Smyth, J. and Rolston, B., *Northern Ireland*, Thames Papers in Social Analysis, Series 1, Thames Polytechnic, London, 1976, 56–85.

Rolston, B., *Community Development and the Capitalist State: The Case of the Northern Ireland Community Relations Commission*, Queen's University Belfast, Ph.D. Thesis, 1978.

Rolston, B., 'Escaping from Belfast: Class, Ideology and Literature in Northern Ireland', *Race and Class*, 20, 1, 1978, 41–62.

Rolston, B., 'Community Politics', in O'Dowd, L. Rolston, B. and Tomlinson, M., 1980, 148–177.

Rose, Richard, 'The Dynamics of a Divided Regime', *Government and Opposition*, 5, 2, 1970, 166–92.

Rose, Richard, *Governing Without Consensus*, London, Faber, 1971.

Rose, Richard, 'Discord in Ulster', *New Community*, 1, 2, 1972, 122–27.

Rose, Richard, *Northern Ireland: A Time of Choice*, London, Macmillan, 1976.

Rose, Richard, 'Is the United Kingdom a State? Northern Ireland as a Test Case', in Madgewick, P. and Rose, R. (eds.), *The Territorial Dimension in United Kingdom Politics*, London, Macmillan, 1982.

Rose, R., McAllister, I. and Mair, P., *Is There a Concurring Majority about Northern Ireland?*, Centre for the Study of Public Policy, University of Strathclyde, 1978.

Rose, R, and McAllister, Ian, *United Kingdom Facts*, London, Macmillan, 1982.

Rowthorn, W., 'Northern Ireland: An Economy in Crisis', *Cambridge Review of Economics*, 1981, 5.

Royal Ulster Constabulary, *Chief Constable's Report*, Belfast, R.U.C., Annual.

Royal Commission on Criminal Procedure, *Report*, Cmnd. 8092, London, HMSO, 1976.

Rumpf, E. and Hepburn, A. C., *Nationalism and Socialism in Twentieth Century Ireland*, Liverpool, Liverpool University Press, 1977.

Rutan, Gerard, F., 'The Labour Party in Ulster: Opposition by Cartel', *Review of Politics*, 29, 4, 1969, 326–35.

Russell, J., *Some Aspects of the Civic Education of Secondary School-boys in Northern Ireland*, Belfast, Northern Ireland Community Relations Commission, 1972.

Sacks, Paul, *The Donegal Mafia*, New Haven, Conn., Yale University Press, 1977.

Savage, D. C., 'The Origins of the Ulster Unionist Party, 1885–1886', *Irish Historical Studies*, 12, 1961, 185–208.

Scarman Tribunal, *Report of Tribunal of Inquiry into Violence and Civil Disturbances in Northern Ireland, 1969*, Vol. 1 and 2, Cmd. 566, Belfast, HMSO, 1972.

Schellenberg, J. A., 'Violence in Northern Ireland, 1965–1975', *International Journal of Group Tension*, 6, 1976, 6–21.

Schellenberg, J. A., 'Area Variations of Violence in Northern Ireland', *Sociological Focus*, 10, 1977, 69–78.

Schilling, F. C. (ed.), *Lokaltermin in Belfast: Die Kirchen im Nordirischen Konflikt*, Eckart (GFR), 1972.

Schools Cultural Studies Project, *The (1982) Director's Report*, Coleraine, New University of Ulster, 1982.

Scorer, C. and Hewitt, P., *The Prevention of Terrorism Act: The Case for Repeal*, London, NCCL, 1981.

Shallice, T., 'The Ulster Depth Interrogation Techniques', *Cognition*, 1, 4, 1973.

Shannon, M. O., *Modern Ireland: A Bibliography for Research, Planning and Development*, London, Library Association, 1982.

Shea, P., *Voices and the Sound of Drums,* Belfast, Blackstaff, 1981.

Shearman, H., *Northern Ireland 1921–1971*, Belfast, HMSO, 1971.

Shearman, H., 'Conflict in Northern Ireland', *Year Book of World Affairs*, 24, 1970, 40–53.

Sheehy, M., *Divided We Stand*, London, Faber and Faber, 1955.

Simpson, J., 'The Finances of the Public Sector in Northern Ireland, 1968–78', *Journal of the Statistical and Social Inquiry Society of Ireland, 1981.*

Smith, P., *Emergency Legislation: The Prevention of Terrorism Acts*, European Group for the Study of Deviance and Social Control, Working Paper No. 3, 1982.

Sobel, L. (ed.), *Political Terrorism*, Oxford, Clio Press, Two Volumes, 1979.

Spense, W., *The Growth and Development of the Secondary Intermediate School in Northern Ireland Since the Education Act of 1947*, Queen's University Belfast, M.A. Thesis, 1959.

Spilerman, S., 'The Causes of Racial Disturbances: A Comparison of alternative explanations', *American Sociological Review.* 35, 1970, 627–649.

Spjut, R., 'Executive Detention in Northern Ireland: The Gardiner Report and the Northern Ireland (Emergency Provisions) (Amendment) Act 1975', *Irish Jurist*, 10, 1975, 272–299.

Spjut, R., 'Torture under the European Convention' *American Journal of International Law*, 73, 2, 1979.

Standing Advisory Commission on Human Rights, *Bill of Rights: A Discussion Paper*, Belfast, 1976.

Starling, S., *The Sociology of Voluntary Organisations in Belfast*, Queen's University Belfast, Unpublished Dissertation, 1971.

Stewart, A. T. Q., *The Narrow Ground: Aspects of Ulster, 1609–1969*, London, Faber and Faber, 1977.

Sunday News, Belfast, 16 August 1980.

Sunday Times Insight Team, *Ulster*, London, Penguin, 1972.

Taylor, D., *Power and Prayer: A Cast Study of Religious and Political Convergence*, Paper Presented to British Sociological Association Conference on 'Sociology of Religion', London, 1979.

Taylor, D., *Militant Fundamentalism: Ulster's Debt to America*, Paper Presented to British Sociological Association Conference on 'Sociology of Religion', Birmingham, 1980.

Taylor, D., *'No Surrender': An Ethnographic View, of Ian Paisley's Ideological Rhetoric*, Paper presented to Conference of Irish Sociological Association, Limerick, 1981.

Taylor, L. and Nelson, S. (eds.), *Young People and Civil Conflict in Northern Ireland*, Belfast, 1977.

Taylor, P., *Beating the Terrorists? Interrogation in Omagh, Gough and Castlereagh*, Middlesex, Penguin, 1980.

Tomlinson, M., 'Housing, the State and the Politics of Segregation', in O'Dowd, L., Rolston, B. and Tomlinson, M., 1980a, 119–147.

Tomlinson, M., 'Reforming Repression', in O'Dowd, L., Rolston, B. and Tomlinson, M., 1980b, 178–202.

Tomlinson, M., 'Policing the Periphery—Ideologies of Repression in Northern Ireland', *Bulletin on Social Policy*, 5, 9–26, 1980c.

Treasury, H.M., *Needs Assessment Study*, London, H.M. Treasury, 1979.

Twining, W., *Emergency Powers: A Fresh Start*, Fabian Tract 416, London, Fabian Society, November 1972.

Ulster Unionist Party, *The Assembly Elections (1973) and the 1974 United Kingdom General Election*, Belfast, U.U.C., 1975.

Ulster Unionist Party, *The Convention Elections 1975*, Belfast, U.U.C., 1975.

Ulster Year Book, Belfast, HMSO, Annual.

Vogt, Hermann (Ed.), *Nordirland: Texte zu einen Konfessionellen, Politischen und Sozialen Konflikt*, Evang. Missionsverlag, 1972.

Walsh, B. M., *'Religion and Demographic Behaviour in Ireland*, Dublin, Economic and Social Research Institute, 1970.

Walsh, D., *The Diplock Court Process: Today and Tomorrow*, Paper presented to the Conference of the Administration of Justice, Belfast, 24th April, 1982.

Whyte, J., 'Intra-Unionist Disputes in the Northern Ireland House of Commons, 1921–72', *Economic and Social Review*, 5, 1, 1973, 99–104.

Whyte, J., 'Recent Writing on Northern Ireland', *American Political Science Review*, 70, 2, 1976, 592–596.

Whyte, J., 'Interpretations of the Northern Ireland Problem: An Appraisal', *Economic and Social Review*, 9, 4, July 1978, 257–282.

Whyte, J., 'How Much Discrimination Was There Under the Unionist Regime, 1921–68?', Unpublished Paper, Department of Political Science, Queen's University, Belfast, 1981.

Widgery Tribunal, *Report of the Tribunal Appointed to inquire into the Events on Sunday, 30th January 1972, which led to Loss of Life in Connection with the Procession in London on that day*, HC 220, London, HMSO, 1972.

Williams, T. (ed.), *Secret Societies in Ireland*, Dublin: Gill and Macmillan, 1974.

Wilson, T., *Economic Development in Northern Ireland*, Cmd. 479, Belfast, HMSO, 1965.

Winchester, S., *In Holy Terror: Reporting the Ulster Troubles*, London, Faber, 1974.

Workers Research Unit, *Repression*, Bulletin No. 2, Belfast, 1977.

Workers Research Unit, *The Law in Northern Ireland*, Bulletin No. 10, Belfast, 1982.

Wright, F., 'Protestant Ideology and Politics in Ulster', *European Journal of Sociology*, 14, 1973, 213–280.

Wright, S., 'New Police Technologies: An Exploration of the Social Implications and Unforseen Impacts of Some Recent Developments', *Journal of Peace Research*, XV, 4, 1978, 305–322.

Wright, S., 'Your Unfriendly Neighbourhood Bobby', *The Guardian*, 16th July, 1981.

Wright, S., 'An Assessment of the New Technologies of Repression', in Hoefnagels, M., (ed.), *Repression and Repressive Violence*, Amsterdam, Swets and Zeitlinger, 1977.

Index